COMPUTER
BOOK SERIES
FROM IDG

Approach 97
For Windows® For D...

MW00572425

The Approach 97 Screen

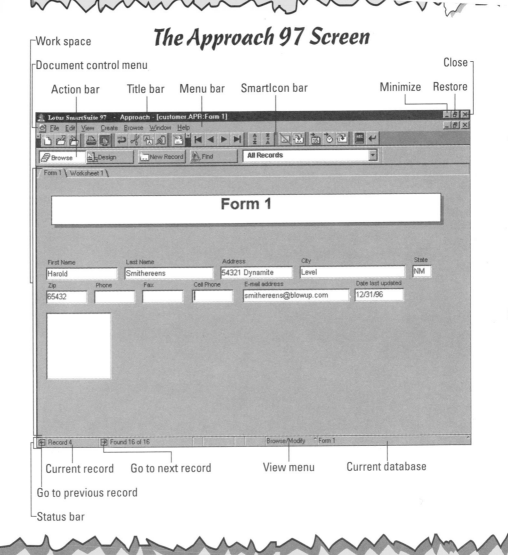

- Work space
- Document control menu
- Action bar
- Title bar
- Menu bar
- SmartIcon bar
- Close
- Minimize
- Restore

- Current record
- Go to next record
- View menu
- Current database
- Go to previous record
- Status bar

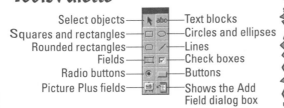

Tools Palette

- Select objects — Text blocks
- Squares and rectangles — Circles and ellipses
- Rounded rectangles — Lines
- Fields — Check boxes
- Radio buttons — Buttons
- Picture Plus fields — Shows the Add Field dialog box

Changing Modes

Mode	Keys
Design and Data Entry	Ctrl+D
Browse	Ctrl+B
Preview	Ctrl+Shift+B
Find	Ctrl+F
Find Assistant	Ctrl+I

...For Dummies: #1 Computer Book Series for Beginners

COMPUTER
BOOK SERIES
FROM IDG

Approach 97
For Windows® For Dummies®

Cheat Sheet

Browse SmartIcon Bar

New file   Preview   First record ┐ Next record   Duplicate current record

Save file   Cut   Paste   Sort ascending   Insert time ┌ Check spelling

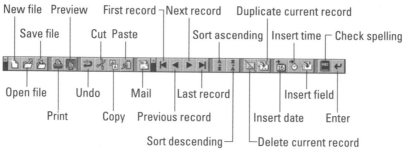

Open file   Undo   Mail   Last record   Insert field

Print   Copy   Previous record   Insert date   Enter

Sort descending ┘   └ Delete current record

Design SmartIcon Bar

New file   Preview   Properties   Group   Insert field

Save file   Cut   Paste   Bring forward   Insert date   Zoom in

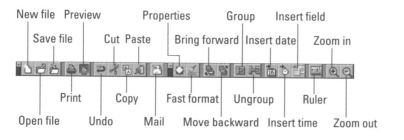

Print   Copy   Fast format   Ungroup   Ruler

Open file   Undo   Mail   Move backward   Insert time   Zoom out

Data Entry

Function	Keys
Go to the first record	Ctrl+Home
Go to the last record	Ctrl+End
Go to a specific record	Ctrl+W
Create a new record	Ctrl+N
Hide the record	Ctrl+H
Delete the record	Ctrl+Delete
Print the current view	Ctrl+P

Design Commands

Function	Keys
Properties dialog box	Ctrl+E or Alt+Enter
Tools palette	Ctrl+L
Fast format	Ctrl+M
Ruler	Ctrl+J
Snap to grid	Ctrl+Y
Group	Ctrl+G
Ungroup	Ctrl+U

IDG
BOOKS
WORLDWIDE

Copyright © 1997 IDG Books Worldwide, Inc.
All rights reserved.
Cheat Sheet $2.95 value. Item 0001-5.
For more information about IDG Books,
call 1-800-762-2974.

...For Dummies: #1 Computer Book Series for Beginners

APPROACH® 97
FOR WINDOWS®
FOR DUMMIES®

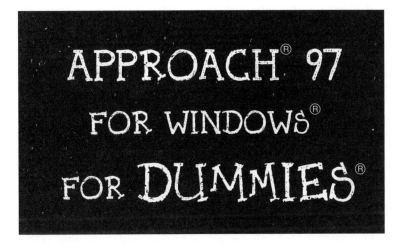

APPROACH® 97 FOR WINDOWS® FOR DUMMIES®

by Deborah S. Ray and Eric J. Ray

IDG Books Worldwide, Inc.
An International Data Group Company

Foster City, CA ♦ Chicago, IL ♦ Indianapolis, IN ♦ Southlake, TX

Approach® 97 For Windows® For Dummies®

Published by
IDG Books Worldwide, Inc.
An International Data Group Company
919 E. Hillsdale Blvd.
Suite 400
Foster City, CA 94404
http://www.idgbooks.com (IDG Books Worldwide Web site)
http://www.dummies.com (Dummies Press Web site)

Library of Congress Catalog Card No.: 96-76360

ISBN: 0-7645-0001-5

Printed in the United States of America

10 9 8 7 6 5 4 3 2 1

1O/RS/QT/ZX/IN

Distributed in the United States by IDG Books Worldwide, Inc.

Distributed by Macmillan Canada for Canada; by Transworld Publishers Limited in the United Kingdom and Europe; by WoodsLane Pty. Ltd. for Australia; by WoodsLane Enterprises Ltd. for New Zealand; by Longman Singapore Publishers Ltd. for Singapore, Malaysia, Thailand, and Indonesia; by Simron Pty. Ltd. for South Africa; by Toppan Company Ltd. for Japan; by Distribuidora Cuspide for Argentina; by Livraria Cultura for Brazil; by Ediciencia S.A. for Ecuador; by Addison-Wesley Publishing Company for Korea; by Ediciones ZETA S.C.R. Ltda. for Peru; by WS Computer Publishing Company, Inc., for the Philippines; by Unalis Corporation for Taiwan; by Contemporanea de Ediciones for Venezuela. Authorized Sales Agent: Anthony Rudkin Associates for the Middle East and North Africa.

For general information on IDG Books Worldwide's books in the U.S., please call our Consumer Customer Service department at 800-762-2974. For reseller information, including discounts and premium sales, please call our Reseller Customer Service department at 800-434-3422.

For information on where to purchase IDG Books Worldwide's books outside the U.S., please contact our International Sales department at 415-655-3023 or fax 415-655-3299.

For information on foreign language translations, please contact our Foreign & Subsidiary Rights department at 415-655-3021 or fax 415-655-3281.

For sales inquiries and special prices for bulk quantities, please contact our Sales department at 415-655-3200 or write to the address above.

For information on using IDG Books Worldwide's books in the classroom or for ordering examination copies, please contact our Educational Sales department at 800-434-2086 or fax 817-251-8174.

For press review copies, author interviews, or other publicity information, please contact our Public Relations department at 415-655-3000 or fax 415-655-3299.

For authorization to photocopy items for corporate, personal, or educational use, please contact Copyright Clearance Center, 222 Rosewood Drive, Danvers, MA 01923, or fax 508-750-4470.

is a trademark under exclusive license to IDG Books Worldwide, Inc., from International Data Group, Inc.

About the Authors

Deborah S. Ray and **Eric J. Ray,** co-authors of *HTML For Dummies Quick Reference* and *Dummies 101: HTML,* are co-owners of RayComm, Inc., a technical communications consulting firm. They spend a large part of their time on HTML-related development, training, and consulting, in addition to using and writing about other cool stuff.

Deborah, a technical communicator for the past three years, has been involved with the Internet for the past two. She has quite varied technical experience, including creating computer and engineering documents as well as teaching technical writing to college students. Her areas of emphasis include writing, designing, and illustrating documents to meet various audiences' information needs. Deborah is well-accomplished in technical communication, having received awards from the Society for Technical Communication as well as from previous employers for her achievements in the field.

Eric has been a hard-core techno-geek for years, including contributing thousands of hours of over-involvement to the Internet, developing database applications, and generally just putzing around with computers and calling it work. Eric has also made numerous presentations and published several papers about HTML and online information. His technical experience includes a wide range of technical support and Internet-related projects. As a technical communicator, Eric has received numerous awards from the Society for Technical Communication as well as from previous employers for his contributions to technical communication projects.

ABOUT IDG BOOKS WORLDWIDE

Welcome to the world of IDG Books Worldwide.

IDG Books Worldwide, Inc., is a subsidiary of International Data Group, the world's largest publisher of computer-related information and the leading global provider of information services on information technology. IDG was founded more than 25 years ago and now employs more than 8,500 people worldwide. IDG publishes more than 275 computer publications in over 75 countries (see listing below). More than 60 million people read one or more IDG publications each month.

Launched in 1990, IDG Books Worldwide is today the #1 publisher of best-selling computer books in the United States. We are proud to have received eight awards from the Computer Press Association in recognition of editorial excellence and three from *Computer Currents'* First Annual Readers' Choice Awards. Our best-selling *...For Dummies*® series has more than 30 million copies in print with translations in 30 languages. IDG Books Worldwide, through a joint venture with IDG's Hi-Tech Beijing, became the first U.S. publisher to publish a computer book in the People's Republic of China. In record time, IDG Books Worldwide has become the first choice for millions of readers around the world who want to learn how to better manage their businesses.

Our mission is simple: Every one of our books is designed to bring extra value and skill-building instructions to the reader. Our books are written by experts who understand and care about our readers. The knowledge base of our editorial staff comes from years of experience in publishing, education, and journalism — experience we use to produce books for the '90s. In short, we care about books, so we attract the best people. We devote special attention to details such as audience, interior design, use of icons, and illustrations. And because we use an efficient process of authoring, editing, and desktop publishing our books electronically, we can spend more time ensuring superior content and spend less time on the technicalities of making books.

You can count on our commitment to deliver high-quality books at competitive prices on topics you want to read about. At IDG Books Worldwide, we continue in the IDG tradition of delivering quality for more than 25 years. You'll find no better book on a subject than one from IDG Books Worldwide.

John Kilcullen
CEO
IDG Books Worldwide, Inc.

*Eighth Annual
Computer Press
Awards ≥1992*

*Ninth Annual
Computer Press
Awards ≥1993*

*Tenth Annual
Computer Press
Awards ≥1994*

*Eleventh Annual
Computer Press
Awards ≥1995*

IDG Books Worldwide, Inc., is a subsidiary of International Data Group, the world's largest publisher of computer-related information and the leading global provider of information services on information technology. International Data Group publishes over 275 computer publications in over 75 countries. Sixty million people read one or more International Data Group publications each month. International Data Group's publications include: ARGENTINA: Buyer's Guide, Computerworld Argentina, PC World Argentina; AUSTRALIA: Australian Macworld, Australian PC World, Australian Reseller News, Computerworld, IT Casebook, Network World, Publish, Webmaster; AUSTRIA: Computerwelt Osterreich, Networks Austria, PC Tip Austria; BANGLADESH: PC World Bangladesh; BELARUS: PC World Belarus; BELGIUM: Data News; BRAZIL: Annuario de Informatica, Computerworld, Connections, Macworld, PC Player, PC World, Publish, Reseller News, Supergamepower; BULGARIA: Computerworld Bulgaria, Network World Bulgaria, PC & MacWorld Bulgaria; CANADA: CIO Canada, Client/Server World, ComputerWorld Canada, InfoWorld Canada, NetworkWorld Canada, WebWorld; CHILE: Computerworld Chile, PC World Chile; COLOMBIA: Computerworld Colombia, PC World Colombia; COSTA RICA: PC World Centro America; THE CZECH AND SLOVAK REPUBLICS: Computerworld Czechoslovakia, Macworld Czech Republic, PC World Czechoslovakia; DENMARK: Communications World Danmark, Computerworld Danmark, Macworld Danmark, PC World Danmark, Techworld Denmark; DOMINICAN REPUBLIC: PC World Republica Dominicana; ECUADOR: PC World Ecuador; EGYPT: Computerworld Middle East, PC World Middle East; EL SALVADOR: PC World Centro America; FINLAND: MikroPC, Tietoverkko, Tietoviikko; FRANCE: Distributique, Hebdo, Info PC, Le Monde Informatique, Macworld, Reseaux & Telecoms, WebMaster France; GERMANY: Computer Partner, Computerwoche, Computerwoche Extra, Computerwoche FOCUS, Global Online, Macwelt, PC Welt; GREECE: Amiga Computing, GamePro Greece, Multimedia World; GUATEMALA: PC World Centro America; HONDURAS: PC World Centro America; HONG KONG: Computerworld Hong Kong, PC World Hong Kong, Publish in Asia; HUNGARY: ABCD CD-ROM, Computerworld Szamitastechnika, Internetto online Magazine, PC World Hungary, PC-X Magazin Hungary; ICELAND: Tolvuheimur PC World Island; INDIA: Information Communications World, Information Systems Computerworld, PC World India, Publish in Asia; INDONESIA: InfoKomputer PC World, Komputek Computerworld, Publish in Asia; IRELAND: ComputerScope, PC Live!; ISRAEL: Macworld Israel, People & Computers/Computerworld; ITALY: Computerworld Italia, Macworld Italia, Networking Italia, PC World Italia; JAPAN: DTP World, Macworld Japan, Nikkei Personal Computing, OS/2 World Japan, SunWorld Japan, Windows NT World, Windows World Japan; KENYA: PC World East African; KOREA: Hi-Tech Information, Macworld Korea, PC World Korea; MACEDONIA: PC World Macedonia; MALAYSIA: Computerworld Malaysia, PC World Malaysia, Publish in Asia; MALTA: PC World Malta; MEXICO: Computerworld Mexico, PC World Mexico; MYANMAR: PC World Myanmar; NETHERLANDS: Computer! Totaal, LAN Internetworking Magazine, LAN World Buyers Guide, Macworld Netherlands, Net, WebWereld; NEW ZEALAND: Absolute Beginners Guide and Plain & Simple Series, Computer Buyer, Computer Industry Directory, Computerworld New Zealand, MTB, Network World, PC World New Zealand; NICARAGUA: PC World Centro America; NORWAY: Computerworld Norge, CW Rapport, Datamagasinet, Financial Rapport, Kursguide Norge, Macworld Norge, Multimediaworld Norge, PC World Ekspress Norge, PC World Nettverk, PC World Norge, PC World ProduktGuide Norge; PAKISTAN: Computerworld Pakistan; PANAMA: PC World Panama; PEOPLE'S REPUBLIC OF CHINA: China Computer Users, China Computerworld, China InfoWorld, China Telecom World Weekly, Computer & Communication, Electronic Design China, Electronics Today, Electronics Weekly, Game Software, PC World China, Popular Computer Week, Software Weekly, Software World, Telecom World; PERU: Computerworld Peru, PC World Profesional Peru, PC World SoHo Peru; PHILIPPINES: Click!, Computerworld Philippines, PC World Philippines, Publish in Asia; POLAND: Computerworld Poland, Computerworld Special Report Poland, Cyber, Macworld Poland, Networld Poland, PC World Komputer; PORTUGAL: Cerebro/PC World, Computerworld/Correio Informático, Dealer World Portugal, Mac*In/PC*In Portugal, Multimedia World; PUERTO RICO: PC World Puerto Rico; ROMANIA: Computerworld Romania, PC World Romania, Telecom Romania; RUSSIA: Computerworld Russia, Mir PK, Publish, Seti; SINGAPORE: Computerworld Singapore, PC World Singapore, Publish in Asia; SLOVENIA: Monitor; SOUTH AFRICA: Computing SA, Network World SA, Software World SA; SPAIN: Communicaciones World España, Computerworld España, Dealer World España, Macworld España, PC World España; SRI LANKA: Infolink PC World; SWEDEN: CAP&Design, Computer Sweden, Corporate Computing Sweden, Internetworld Sweden, it.branschen, Macworld Sweden, MaxiData Sweden, MikroDatorn, Nätverk & Kommunikation, PC World Sweden, PCaktiv, Windows World Sweden; SWITZERLAND: Computerworld Schweiz, Macworld Schweiz, PCtip; TAIWAN: Computerworld Taiwan, Macworld Taiwan, NEW ViSiON/Publish, PC World Taiwan, Windows World Taiwan; THAILAND: Publish in Asia, Thai Computerworld; TURKEY: Computerworld Turkiye, Macworld Turkiye, Network World Turkiye, PC World Turkiye; UKRAINE: Computerworld Kiev, Multimedia World Ukraine, PC World Ukraine; UNITED KINGDOM: Acorn User UK, Amiga Action UK, Amiga Computing UK, Apple Talk UK, Computing, Macworld, Parents and Computers UK, PC Advisor, PC Home, PSX Pro, The WEB; UNITED STATES: Cable in the Classroom, CIO Magazine, Computerworld, DOS World, Federal Computer Week, GamePro Magazine, InfoWorld, I-Way, Macworld, Network World, PC Games, PC World, Publish, Video Event, THE WEB Magazine, and WebMaster; online webzines: JavaWorld, NetscapeWorld, and SunWorld Online; URUGUAY: InfoWorld Uruguay; VENEZUELA: Computerworld Venezuela, PC World Venezuela; and VIETNAM: PC World Vietnam.
2/14/97

Dedication

We'd like to dedicate this book to some of the people who helped show us how to *Approach* (ahem) and conquer seemingly impossible tasks. This list is in no particular order.

Deb wishes to thank:

Harold Born: You expected a lot from me, trusted me to complete new challenges, and gave me confidence to take the initiative to try new things. Thanks for your confidence.

Terry Zambon: You gave me direction when I needed it most. You showed me that I am capable. You let me go only when I was ready. Thank you. (I know you're still watching.)

Arlie Winemiller: You convinced me that I needed to broaden my horizons even beyond the challenging projects you offered me. Thanks. (I hope *you* enjoy *your* copy of this book.)

Eric would like to thank:

Washington University faculty members: Well, I didn't quite end up where I expected, but thanks for the challenges, the high expectations, and the constant pressure to excel. It couldn't have been better than Wash U.

Bob Graalman: You decided to take a chance on me. Since then, one open door has led to another, but they all started back when. Thanks.

Bill G.: I never quite got a chance to tell you how much I respect you and how very much you taught me. Thanks so much for everything.

Publisher's Acknowledgments

We're proud of this book; please send us your comments about it by using the Reader Response Card at the back of the book or by e-mailing us at feedback/dummies@idgbooks.com. Some of the people who helped bring this book to market include the following:

Acquisitions, Development, & Editorial

Project Editor: Mary Goodwin

Acquisitions Editor: Gareth Hancock

Copy Editor: Diane Smith

Technical Reviewer: Jim McCarter

Editorial Manager: Mary C. Corder

Editorial Assistants: Constance Carlisle, Chris H. Collins, and Steven Hayes

Production

Project Coordinators: E. Shawn Aylsworth, Debbie Stailey

Layout and Graphics: Dominique DeFelice, Maridee V. Ennis, Todd Klemme, Jane E. Martin, Mark C. Owens

Proofreaders: Melissa D. Buddendeck, Joel K. Draper, Nancy Price, Nancy Reinhardt, Robert Springer, Karen York

Indexer: Joan Griffits

General and Administrative

IDG Books Worldwide, Inc.: John Kilcullen, CEO; Steven Berkowitz, President and Publisher

IDG Books Technology Publishing: Brenda McLaughlin, Senior Vice President and Group Publisher

Dummies Technology Press and Dummies Editorial: Diane Graves Steele, Vice President and Associate Publisher; Judith A. Taylor, Brand Manager; Kristin A. Cocks, Editorial Director

Dummies Trade Press: Kathleen A. Welton, Vice President and Publisher; Stacy S. Collins, Brand Manager

IDG Books Production for Dummies Press: Beth Jenkins, Production Director; Cindy L. Phipps, Supervisor of Project Coordination, Production Proofreading, and Indexing; Kathie S. Schutte, Supervisor of Page Layout; Shelley Lea, Supervisor of Graphics and Design; Debbie J. Gates, Production Systems Specialist; Tony Augsburger, Supervisor of Reprints and Bluelines; Leslie Popplewell, Media Archive Coordinator

Dummies Packaging and Book Design: Patti Sandez, Packaging Specialist; Lance Kayser, Packaging Assistant; Kavish+Kavish, Cover Design

◆

The publisher would like to give special thanks to Patrick J. McGovern, without whom this book would not have been possible.

◆

Authors' Acknowledgments

We owe many people a big round of thanks for helping put this book together. First, many thanks go to Doug Lowe, author of *Approach 3 For Windows For Dummies*. The outstanding content, organization, and, of course, humor of *Approach 3 For Windows For Dummies* provided a solid foundation for this book, our first book in the . . .*For Dummies* series.

Thanks also to the very talented people at IDG Books Worldwide, Inc. In particular, we want to thank our fantastic project editor, Mary Goodwin, for providing guidance and insight for this book, as well as a steady reminder that deadlines approacheth. So to speak. Seriously, she helped take a big, hairy project and turn it into a well-groomed book that we hope will let a lot of people do nifty stuff. And a big thank-you goes to Gareth Hancock, Acquisitions Editor, for his continued confidence in us.

Finally, we'd like to thank the "behind the scenes" people who greatly contributed to this book. We are particularly grateful to our Technical Reviewer, Jim McCarter, and our Copy Editor, Diane Smith, who significantly improved the quality and usability of this book. Also, thank you to the entire production team for doing a great job of taking our submissions and turning them into a finished, polished product.

Contents at a Glance

Cartoons at a Glance

By Rich Tennant • Fax: 508-546-7747 • E-mail: the5wave@tiac.net

page 7

page 303

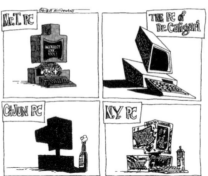

page 203

page 109

page 247

Table of Contents

Introduction

*W*elcome to *Approach 97 For Windows For Dummies,* the book written especially for those of you who are forced to use Approach 97 at gunpoint and want to learn just enough to get by or just enough to be able to talk like you know what's going on.

Has your boss just dumped a shoe box full of customer receipts on your desk and ordered you to organize them into a database by Tuesday or find a new job? You need Approach 97. Are you frustrated because your seven-year-old version of El-CheapoBase can't create the reports you need? You need Approach 97. Have you all but given up on figuring out how to send out 400 letters to the parents at your kid's school to beg for donations to the PTA? You *really* need Approach 97.

Or maybe you're one of those hapless people who bought Lotus SmartSuite 97 because it was such a bargain, and you needed a Windows word processor and a spreadsheet anyway, and, hey, you're not even sure what Approach 97 is, but it was practically free and you love things that are free. What now?

Good news! You've found the right book. Help is here, within these humble pages.

This book talks about Approach 97 in everyday — and often irreverent — terms. No lofty prose here; the whole thing checks in at about the fifth-grade reading level. We've no Pulitzer expectations for this book (maybe one of these days we'll write a novel). Our goal is to make an otherwise dull and lifeless subject at least tolerable, if not kind of fun.

About This Book

This book isn't the kind of book you pick up and read from start to finish, as if it were a cheap novel. If we ever see anyone reading this book at the beach, we'll laugh at you! This book is more like a reference, the kind of book you can pick up, turn to just about any page, and start reading. Each chapter in the book covers a specific aspect of using Approach 97, such as creating reports, using macros, or joining databases. Just turn to the chapter you're interested in (or have to brush up on) and start reading.

Each chapter is divided into self-contained chunks, all related to the major theme of the chapter.

For example, the chapter on drawing pictures on database forms contains nuggets such as these:

- ✔ Drawing simple lines and shapes
- ✔ Drawing text objects
- ✔ Creating drop shadows, embossed effects, and other fancy looks
- ✔ Understanding layers and groups
- ✔ Lining things up
- ✔ Stealing pictures from other programs

You don't have to memorize anything in this book. It's a "need-to-know" book: You pick it up when you need to know something. Need to know how to create a new form? Pick up the book. Need to know how to add a picture to your database? Pick up the book. Otherwise, put it down and get on with your life.

How to Use This Book

This book works like a reference. Start with the topic that you want to learn about and look for it in the table of contents or in the index to get going. The table of contents is detailed enough that you should be able to find most of the topics you need. If not, turn to the index, where you find even more detail.

After you find your topic in the table of contents or the index, turn to the area of interest and read as much or as little as you need or want. Then close the book and get to it.

On occasion, this book directs you to use specific keyboard shortcuts to get things done. When you see something like this

```
Ctrl+Z
```

it means to hold down the Ctrl key while you press the Z key and then release both keys at the same time. Don't type the plus sign.

Sometimes we tell you to use a menu command, such as this one:

    File➪Open

When you see a line like this, you know to use the keyboard or mouse to open the File menu and then select the Open command. (The underlined letters are the keyboard hot keys for the command. To use them, first press the Alt key. In the preceding example, you would press and release the Alt key, press and release the F key, and then press and release the O key. It's easier to do than to describe.)

Whenever we talk about a message or information that you see on the screen, it looks like this:

```
Are we having fun yet?
```

Anything you are instructed to type appears in boldface type, like so: Type **B:SETUP** in the Run dialog box. You type exactly what you see, with or without spaces.

Another little nicety about this book is that when we direct you to click on one of those little icons that appears on the Approach 97 screen, we show the appropriate icon in the margin of the book. These icons in the margin show you what the icon looks like so you can find it on the screen. It sure beats squinting and guessing.

This book rarely directs you elsewhere for information — just about everything you need to know about using Approach 97 is right here. On occasion, we suggest that you turn to *DOS For Dummies* (by Dan Gookin, published by IDG Books Worldwide, Inc.) or to *Windows 95 For Dummies* (by Andy Rathbone, also published by IDG Books) for more specific information about ancient Egypt and the etymology of certain Klingon words — oops — we mean DOS and Windows.

What You Don't Need to Read

Some stuff in this book is skippable. We carefully place extra-technical information in self-contained sidebars and clearly mark them so you can give them a wide berth. Don't read this stuff unless you just *have* to know and you feel really lucky. Don't worry; we won't be offended if you don't read every word.

Foolish Assumptions

We're making only three assumptions about you, no matter how foolish they may be:

- ✔ You use a computer.
- ✔ You use Windows.
- ✔ You use or are thinking about using Approach 97.

Nothing else. We don't assume that you're a computer guru who knows how to change a controller card or configure memory for optimal usage. Heck, you don't even have to admit to knowing what a controller card is, and if you think that memory is something that can be helped with mnemonics, that's fine. Many computer chores are best handled by people who *like* computers. We hope that you are on speaking terms with such a person. Do your best to keep it that way.

How This Book Is Organized

Inside this book, the chapters are arranged into five parts that each address a specific general theme. Each chapter within those parts is divided into sections that cover various aspects of the chapter's main subject. The chapters are in a logical sequence, so reading them in order makes sense if you want to read the book that way. But you don't have to read them in order. You can flip the book open to any page and start reading. Here's the lowdown on what's in each of the five parts:

Part I: Basic Approach 97 Stuff

In this part, you learn the basics of using Approach 97. This is a good place to start if you're clueless about what Approach 97 is, let alone about how to use it. Don't worry, by the end of this section, you won't be clueless.

Part II: Polishing Your Database

The six chapters in this part show you how to create top-quality Approach 97 databases that not only work but also look good. You learn how to make spiffy forms and reports that help you get all the right information into and out of your database, plus how to embellish databases with pictures, sounds, and other fancy stuff.

Part III: Getting Real Work Done

The chapters in this part show you how to create form letters, mailing labels, worksheets, crosstabs, and charts.

Part IV: Definitely Database Grad School Stuff

The four chapters in this part are for those adventurous souls who want to go a bit beyond the basics. These chapters show you how to create and use macros, how to run Approach 97 on a network and on the Internet, how to customize the Approach 97 preferences, and how to convert data to and from other file formats.

Part V: The Part of Tens

This wouldn't be a . . .*For Dummies* book without lists of interesting snippets: Ten Database Commandments, Ten Approach 97 Shortcuts, Ten Things That Often Go Wrong, Ten Great Things about Approach 97, and so on.

Icons Used in This Book

As you are reading all this wonderful prose, you occasionally see the following icons. They appear in the margins to draw your attention to important information.

Did we tell you about the memory course we took?

Watch out! Some technical drivel is just around the corner. Read only if you have your pocket protector firmly attached.

Pay special attention to this icon — it lets you know that some particularly useful tidbit is at hand, perhaps a shortcut or a way of using a command you may not have considered.

Danger! Danger! Danger! Stand back, Will Robinson!

How'd It Go?

Yes, you can get there from here. With this book in hand, you're ready to charge full speed ahead into the strange and wonderful world of Approach 97. Browse through the table of contents and decide where you want to start. Be bold! Be courageous! Be adventurous! Above all else, have fun!

Then, if you want, let us know how it went. You can contact us via e-mail at `debray@raycomm.com` and `ejray@raycomm.com`. We'd love to hear from you.

Part I

Basic Approach 97 Stuff

"THERE! THERE! I TELL YOU IT JUST MOVED AGAIN!"

In this part ...

*J*ust a few short years ago, database programs were so complicated that only true computer gurus, brandishing pocket protectors and taped-together glasses, would dare to use them. Now Approach 97 brings the power of relational database management (whatever that means) to the average user. Oh boy.

The chapters in this part comprise a bare-bones introduction to Approach 97. You figure out what the program is and how to use it to create simple databases. Specifically, we discuss ground-zero database topics like creating database fields, asking Approach 97 for help, entering data into a database, doing finds and sorts, checking your spelling, and joining databases. More advanced stuff, such as creating forms and incorporating graphics into your database, is covered in other parts of this book. Consider this part to be just the beginning. As a great king once advised, begin at the beginning and go on 'til you come to the end. Then stop.

Chapter 1

Database 101

•••

In This Chapter

▶ Introducing databases in general and Approach 97 in particular

▶ Looking at database data

▶ Starting Approach 97 and creating a new database

▶ Filling out a form

▶ Using a worksheet

▶ Printing a database

▶ Saving, retrieving, and closing a database

▶ Exiting Approach 97

•••

*T*his chapter is sort of the kindergarten of Approach 97. It takes your hand and walks you around, telling you what a database program is and what you can do with one, explaining why Approach 97 is such a great database program, and showing you how to start the program. If you get tired midway through this chapter, feel free to have some milk and graham crackers and maybe even take a nap.

What the Hex Is a Database?

It's time to put on your pointy cap, sharpen your Number 2 pencil, and prepare yourself for a definition. Here it is: A *database* is a collection of information. Here are some examples of databases from everyday life:

- ✔ Your personal address book
- ✔ The shoe box that contains your tax records for the year
- ✔ Your baseball card collection
- ✔ All those parking tickets conveniently stuffed into your car's glove compartment
- ✔ The phone book

✔ The pile of score cards that has been accumulating in the bottom of your golf bag for 15 years

✔ For you compulsive types, your Rolodex file and your Day Timer

You can think of each of these databases as a collection of records. In the database *lingua franca* (that's not a type of pasta), a *record* consists of all the useful information you can gather about a particular thing. In your address book (or that beat-up thing you keep phone numbers in), each record represents one of your friends or enemies. For your tax records database, each receipt in the shoe box is a record. Each baseball card in your card collection is a record, as is each parking ticket stuffed into the glove compartment.

Each little snippet of information that makes up a record is called a *field*. Using the address book as an example again, each person's record — that is, each entry in the address book — consists of several fields: name, street address, city, state, zip code, and phone number. The record may also include other information, such as the person's birthday, whether you received a Christmas card from that person last year, and how much money that person owes you.

An Approach 97 database is much like these noncomputerized databases. Like your address book or shoe box full of tax records, an Approach 97 database is a collection of records, and each record is a collection of fields. The biggest difference is that when you use Approach 97, your database is recorded on the computer's hard disk rather than on paper. Using the hard disk gives Approach 97 several distinct advantages over address books and shoe boxes. For example, searching an Approach 97 database for a particular receipt is much easier than riffling through an overstuffed shoe box.

Approach 97 automatically keeps records organized and enables you to conduct a search — based on any field — for particular records in the database. For example, if you kept your address book as an Approach 97 database, you could quickly print a list of all your friends who live in Iowa and owe you more than $10. Try that trick with your noncomputerized address book.

As the old saying goes, there's no such thing as a free lunch, and Approach 97 is no exception. Approach 97 does have some disadvantages if compared with an old-fashioned address book or a shoe box. For starters, Approach 97 (and any other computerized database program, for that matter) forces you to think ahead before you start saving data in a database. Before you can add information to an Approach 97 database, you must *design* the database. Yuck. Fortunately, Approach 97 comes with a slew of already-designed databases for such common uses as address books, business contacts, inventories, and even a wine list. But you still must look at the fields provided by these database templates, add missing, but needed fields, and remove unnecessary fields. Fortunately, you can easily add fields later if you forget some important detail. So, designing a database isn't something to lose sleep over.

An even bigger drawback of using Approach 97 is that it forces you to use your computer. Double-yuck. You must deal with such unpleasantries as Windows 95, the Windows Explorer, filenames, folders, mouse clicks and double-clicks, an occasional drag, backing up, and all of the other routine chores of using a computer. Not to mention the simple fact that dropping an address book into your handbag is much easier than dropping a typical desktop computer into it.

If you're uneasy with the basic aspects of using your computer, check out *PCs For Dummies* by Dan Gookin and Andy Rathbone. For more specific information about working with Windows 95, see *Windows 95 For Dummies* by Andy Rathbone. Both books are published by IDG Books Worldwide, Inc.

Relational nonsense you can skip

One of the most used and abused buzzwords in the computer business is *relational database*. The term relational database has a few common meanings:

✔ A type of database in which data is stored in tables made up of rows and columns, and relationships are established among the various tables. These relationships are based on information stored in fields common to multiple tables — for example, a customer table and an invoice table may both have a customer number field that enables you to establish a relationship between the tables. Hence the name, *relational database.*

This definition sounds kind of like a Tim Allen routine. "Say Al, do you think they call it a *relational database* because it's good at dealing with relationships?"

"I don't think so, Tim."

Actually, Al's response is correct. Relational databases do not get their name from the fact that you can create relationships among tables. See the second definition to find out why.

✔ A database model that is based upon a Conehead branch of mathematics called *Set Theory.*

In mathematics, a *relation* is an unordered set of *n-tuples*. Never mind what an n-tuple is, because we're not about to tell you and it doesn't matter anyway. We wouldn't even mention the term, except that we want to point out that the term *relational database* is derived from an esoteric mathematical concept that has nothing to do with the way normal people ordinarily use the word *relational*. The term *relation* refers to the way data is arranged into tables of rows and columns, not to relationships between tables.

(It is a little-known fact that relational database theory was invented at about the same time that the Coneheads from the planet Remulak first came to earth, back in the 1970s. We have always suspected that these two developments are — dare we say it? — *related.*)

✔ Any database system developed since 1980, with the exception of a few cutting-edge, *object-oriented* databases that have recently appeared.

Marketers quickly figured out that the way to sell database programs was to advertise them as relational. Relational zealots had fits when programs such as dBase claimed to be relational,

(continued)

(continued)

although they clearly violated basic tenets of relational databases. But the marketers prevailed, and just about every database program ever made claims to be relational.

It wasn't until recently, when the new *object-oriented* databases began to emerge, that database companies started to let go of the relational label. We'd love to explain what an *object-oriented* database is. But that's another book.

Where does Approach 97 fit into all of this? The program may not qualify as a truly relational database according to all the criteria of the relational creed, but it's pretty darn close. Approach 97 certainly is as relational as other popular database programs, including Access, FoxPro, dBase, and Paradox.

What's So Hot about Approach 97?

Approach 97 is different from most database programs. For years, full-fledged database programs have been considered too complicated for typical computer users. Only computer gurus were expected to do any reasonable work with programs such as dBase IV or Paradox. The less knowledgeable were expected to use watered-down database programs that were easier to use but too limited in function to be useful for anything more complicated than simple address lists. (These watered-down programs are often called *flat-file* databases by relational database snobs.)

Approach 97 is one of the first database programs that is as powerful as dBase IV or Paradox but is easy enough for mere mortals to use. You don't need a Ph.D. in computer science or seven years of programming experience to use Approach 97 to set up even a sophisticated database.

Here are a few of the nifty features that make Approach 97 one of the best database programs available:

- ✔ Approach 97 comes with a truckload of predefined database templates that you can use out of the box or modify to suit your needs. Many of these templates are designed to work together for complete business applications.

- ✔ A feature called SmartMasters enables you to create great-looking database entry forms and reports without the hassle of setting dozens of formatting options.

- ✔ Approach 97 can work with existing databases that were created with dBase III or dBase IV, Paradox 3.5 or 4.0 (including Paradox for Windows), FoxPro 2.1, Lotus Notes, and other file formats you've probably never heard of, such as Microsoft/Sybase SQL Server, Oracle SQL, or IBM's DB2. Approach 97 works directly with these file formats, sparing you the drudgery of a complicated conversion process.

Version diversion

Way back in March 1992, a small software company called Approach released Version 1.0 of Approach for Windows. In October 1992, the company released Version 2.0 of Approach. The following summer, a funny thing happened: The giant software company, Lotus, looking for a database program to add to its SmartSuite collection, purchased Approach. In September 1993, Lotus released Approach Version 2.1, which provided essentially the same features as Approach 2.0 but had new menus and buttons and whatnot to make it look more like a Lotus program. In fact, Lotus referred to this version as the *Lotus-ized* version of Approach.

At the same time, Lotus set the Approach programmers to work on a totally new version of Approach that would offer major improvements over the earlier versions. Thus was born Approach 3.0.

1995 was a big year for Approach. The giant software company Lotus was purchased by the even more giant computer company, IBM, so different people signed the checks, again. Additionally, Windows 95 was released in August 1995, enabling programmers to take advantage of all kinds of new capabilities and power. IBM/Lotus did just that, releasing Approach 96 at the end of 1995 (but it sure looked punctual).

Approach 96 provided additional features and power for database developers, in addition to having the same *interface* as Windows 95. (*Interface* is computerese for the look and feel of a program.)

Then in 1996, Lotus released Approach 97. Approach 97 offered some bright new features, including Internet-based support, changes to make the program easier to use, and tools to provide easier interactivity with other SmartSuite programs.

This book is written specifically for Approach 97. If you're still using an older version of Approach, strongly consider upgrading to Approach 97. The new features are well worth the upgrade cost.

✔ Approach 97 enables you to join data from two or more databases. For example, suppose that you own a video rental store and you have two databases: one containing customer information and the other containing information about the videotapes. By joining these databases, you can easily display a list of all the videotapes currently rented to a particular customer. The customer's name and address comes from the customer database, and the videotape information is obtained from the videotape database. (This important feature is standard fare for muscle-bound database programs such as dBase or Paradox, but it is a rarity in more down-to-earth database programs such as Approach 97.)

✔ Approach 97 is automatically set up to work on a network. No fancy network twiddling is required.

✔ Approach 97 looks and works like 1-2-3 for Windows and Word Pro. If you know how to use either of those programs, you already know how to use many of the Approach 97 basic features.

 ✔ One of the best things about Approach 97 is that you can get it practically free. Lotus bundles it with 1-2-3, Word Pro, Freelance Graphics, and Organizer for a ridiculously low price in a package called SmartSuite 97. The whole SmartSuite 97 package costs about what 1-2-3 and Word Pro would cost if purchased separately, so everything else is essentially free.

 ✔ *You* can use it. We promise.

Forms, Reports, and Other Database Portals

One of the most important features of Approach 97 is that it does not confine you to a single way of viewing the information in a database. For example, even though a database of customer information may contain detailed sales and credit information, you may not want to see all that information every time you look at the customer's record. Approach 97 enables you to extract just the currently desired fields and arrange them neatly on the screen however you want them. You can also embellish the screen layout with fancy text or drawings. This feature sometimes makes Approach 97 almost fun to use.

Here is the lowdown on the various types of views you can create to get information into and out of a database:

 ✔ **Form:** A layout showing how information from each database record is presented on the screen. You can design several forms for a database, thereby giving yourself several ways to peek at the data. Sometimes you may want to see every bit of detail on record for a customer, but other times you may want only the name and address. When you work in a form view, you work with database records one at a time, just like working with one person's information in your address list.

 When you create a new database, Approach 97 automatically creates a form view that includes all the fields in the database, lined up neatly. You can easily modify this default form to make it more attractive and functional.

 ✔ **Report:** A layout showing and summarizing information from a database. Reports are generally printed on the printer. As opposed, we suppose, to printed on the modem, printed on the refrigerator, or printed on the carpet. You can design as many reports for a particular database as you need. Reports can include information summarized from several database records (such as a total of all sales for a particular customer) or values that are calculated from fields in one record (such as a customer's total sales minus the customer's total returns).

 ✔ **Worksheet:** If you're familiar with spreadsheet programs such as Lotus 1-2-3, you can understand the worksheet view right away. It presents the data in a database in a worksheet format — arranged as a grid of rows and columns. Each row in the worksheet represents one record in the database, and each column represents one field. An advantage of using a worksheet view, rather than a form view, is that the worksheet view enables you to display more than one record at a time on the screen.

Approach 97 automatically creates a default worksheet view when you create a new database.

✔ **Crosstab:** A crosstab is like a worksheet, except that each row does not correspond to a single database record. Instead, each cell contains information that is summarized from several related database records. For example, if you have a sales database with one record for every invoice, you can create a crosstab that contains one row for each sales rep that summarizes the rep's total sales.

✔ **Chart:** This view would be Ross Perot's favorite part of Approach 97. If Ross had had an Approach 97 database listing all the poultry sales from Arkansas during the 1980s, he could have used this feature to quickly prepare a pie chart for one of his infomercials. It may have changed history.

✔ **Form letter:** You can use Approach 97 to create your own junk mail by creating a form letter view. The form letter can include fields extracted from database records, such as a name and address or a salutation. For sophisticated mail merge operations, you may want to use a full-fledged word-processing program, such as WordPro, WordPerfect for Windows, or Word for Windows. But simple merge letters are much easier to do correctly if you use the Approach 97 form letter view. Just don't send us one to prove you could do it.

✔ **Mailing label:** For a database that contains names and addresses, you can use a mailing label view to print labels quickly. Approach 97 automatically works with Avery label formats, but you can create your own custom formats if you prefer a different brand of labels.

Approach 97 lingo you can't escape

We hate to be the bearer of bad news, but if you expect to have a satisfying relationship with Approach 97, you must speak its language. Here are a few of the most important terms, de-technobabbleized for your reading enjoyment:

✔ **Database:** A collection of related information. For example, a customer database contains information about a company's valued customers; a parts database contains information about the various parts in stock at a shop; a wine list database contains information about favorite wines.

✔ **Record:** A database is a collection of records. Each record contains information about a particular customer, part, wine, or whatever.

✔ **Field:** A record is a collection of fields. Each field contains one snippet of information, such as the name of a customer, the number of a part, or the price of a wine.

(continued)

(continued)

✔ **Database file:** A disk file that contains the information for a database. Approach 97 can work with database files in any of several popular disk formats — dBase, Paradox, and FoxPro — and a few other esoteric file formats, such as IBM DB2, Oracle SQL, or SQL Server. In fact, Approach 97 has no database format to call its own. When you create a new database, Approach 97 uses the popular dBase IV format unless you tell it to use one of the other formats. (There's little reason to change formats unless you want to access the database using another database program such as Paradox or FoxPro.)

✔ **View:** A way of looking at the data in a database file. Suppose that a database file contains customer records with 50 different fields of information for each customer. You may not want to look at all 50 fields every time you display a customer record. By creating a view, you can select just the fields you're interested in — perhaps the customer's name, address, and credit status. Approach 97 enables you to create several different types of views: forms, reports, worksheets, crosstabs, charts, merge letters, and mailing labels.

✔ **Join:** A way of combining information from two or more database files. For example, if you have a customer database and a sales database, you can join the two databases to access information about the sales for a particular customer. The sales information comes from the sales database, but the customer's name and address information comes from the customer database.

✔ **Approach file:** A file that enables you to access a database file using Approach 97. The Approach file contains information about the layout of the data stored in the database file, plus all the views used to get at the data stored in the database file. If you joined several database files, information about the join is stored in the Approach file as well.

Starting Approach 97

Enough of the preliminaries; it's time to get to work. The first step in learning how to use Approach 97 is learning how to get it started. Here's the procedure:

1. Get ready.

Light some votive candles. Take two aspirin. Sit in the Lotus Position facing Redmond, Washington and recite the Windows creed three times:

Windows is my friend. Windows loves me, and I love Windows.
Windows is my friend. Windows loves me, and I love Windows.
Windows is my friend. Windows loves me, and I love Windows.

2. Start your engines.

Turn on your computer. You may need to flip only one switch, but if the computer, monitor, and printer are plugged in separately, you must turn on each one separately.

Because you're using Windows 95, Windows starts right up when you start your computer.

3. **Start Approach 97.**

Click on the Start menu (lower-left corner of the screen). Let the cursor hover over the word Programs until the next set of menus appears. Move the cursor to Lotus SmartSuite and do that hover thing again. Another menu pops out with the words Lotus Approach 97 in it. Click on the words Lotus Approach 97.

Stare at the screen for a few seconds while the hard disk whirs and gyrates. In a few moments, Approach 97 pops to life. (Approach 97 actually starts up pretty fast, especially compared with certain other database programs that shall not be named here for fear of litigation. If you're lucky enough to have the new Binford 800MHz Ultra-Octium Deluxe with 256MB of RAM and alloy trim, Approach 97 sometimes appears 2 to 3 seconds before you click on the menu item.)

4. **Take off your shoes and sit a spell.**

Other than the bright yellow logo screen, which displays for a few moments while Approach 97 starts up, the first thing you notice about Approach 97 is the welcome screen shown in Figure 1-1. (This welcome screen is more formally known as the Welcome to Lotus Approach dialog box, but we like to call it the *welcome mat.*) The welcome mat cordially invites you to pick whether you want to create a new database using a SmartMaster (template) or work with an existing database. It also lists the five Approach files you worked with most recently (hidden under the Open an Existing Approach File tab) so you can quickly get back to work.

You can skip the welcome mat for now by clicking on Cancel, but don't worry: It's covered in the next chapter, where you find out how to create database files. We just wanted you to see it here so you get an idea of how friendly Approach 97 is, for a database program.

Figure 1-1:
The
Approach 97
welcome
mat,
otherwise
known
as the
Welcome
to Lotus
Approach
dialog box.

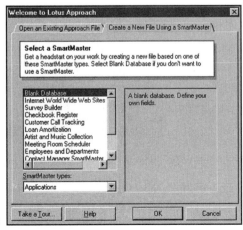

The mouse is your friend

Remember that scene in *Star Trek IV* when Scotty, having been zapped back into the 1980s and forced to use a primitive computer (it was a Macintosh), picked up the mouse and talked into it as if it were a microphone? "Computer! Hello computer! Humph. How quaint."

You don't get very far with Approach 97 (or any other Windows program) until you learn how to use the mouse. You can try picking it up and talking to it if you want, but you won't get any better results than Scotty did.

Most mice have two or three buttons on top and a ball underneath. When you move the mouse, the ball rolls. The rolling motion is detected by little wheels inside the mouse and sent to the computer, which responds to the mouse movements by moving the mouse pointer on-screen. What will they think of next?

Some people, usually notebook computer users, have a mouse-substitute called a trackball. This device is just like an upside-down mouse. You have to roll the little ball around instead of letting the desk do it for you. And some notebook computer users have to use a little pad, which takes a steady hand.

A mouse works best if you use it with a *mouse pad*, a small (7-x-9-inch or so) rubbery pad that gives better traction for the rolling ball on the mouse's rump. You can use the mouse directly on a desk surface, but it doesn't roll as smoothly.

Here's a list of the various acts of mouse dexterity that you are asked to perform while using Approach 97:

✔ To *move* or *point* the mouse means to move it, without pressing any mouse buttons, so that the mouse pointer moves to a desired screen location. Remember to leave the mouse on the mouse pad as you move it; if you pick it up, the ball doesn't roll, and your movement doesn't register.

✔ To *click* means to press and release the left mouse button. Usually, you are asked to click on something, which means to point to the something and then click the left button.

✔ To *double-click* means to press and release the left mouse button twice, as quickly as you can.

✔ To *triple-click* means to press and release the left mouse button three times, as quickly as you can.

✔ To *right-click* means to click the right mouse button rather than the left one.

✔ To *drag* something with the mouse means to point at it, press the left button (or right button, depending on the task), and move the mouse while holding down the button. After you arrive at your destination, you release the mouse button.

✔ To *hover* means to just let the mouse pointer sit over something on the screen, without clicking or doing anything. This usually causes something to happen on-screen, because the little people in the computer notice when your mouse hovers over their heads, just as you notice a helicopter hovering over yours.

✔ To *stay* the mouse means to let go of the mouse and give it the command "Stay!" You do not need to raise your voice. Speak in a normal but confident and firm voice. If the mouse obeys, give it a treat. (They are especially fond of cheese curls.) But if the mouse starts to walk away, say, "No," put it back in its original position, and repeat the command "Stay!" Under no circumstances should you strike the mouse. Remember, there are no bad mice.

What Is All This Stuff?

After you get past the superficial simplicity of the welcome mat, Approach 97 greets you with a screen that's so cluttered you'll soon be considering a shoe box as a reasonable alternative to computerizing your database. Just about every nook and cranny is filled with a menu, button, field, status indicator, or some other barely recognizable gizmo or doohickey. What is all this stuff?

Well, if you're already a user of other Lotus SmartSuite 97 applications, much of this may look mighty familiar to you. Lotus has been working on getting all its applications to look and act the same, so if you know one, you know them all. However, if you're just now diving in, here's a quick start.

Figure 1-2 provides a road map to the Approach 97 screen. Look over this map briefly to get your bearings. North is up.

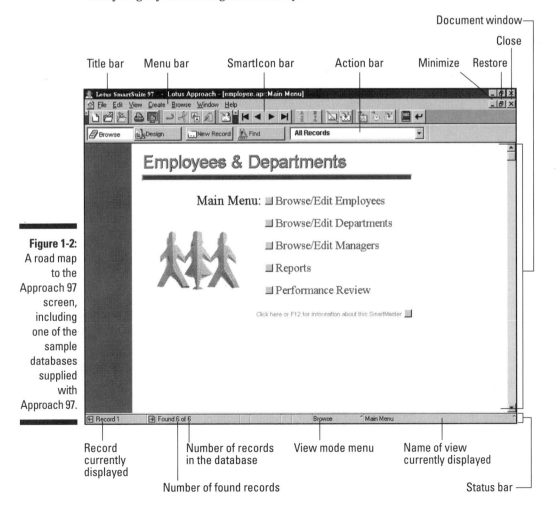

Figure 1-2: A road map to the Approach 97 screen, including one of the sample databases supplied with Approach 97.

Many items on the Approach 97 screen are worthy of attention:

✔ Across the top of the screen, just below the Lotus Approach title, is the *menu bar.* The program's deepest and darkest secrets are hidden within the menu bar. Wear eye protection when exploring it.

✔ Just below the menu bar is the *SmartIcon bar,* which contains a useful collection of little buttons that Lotus calls *SmartIcons.* Each of the SmartIcons executes a commonly used command that you would ordinarily have to rummage through the menu bar to find. As you work with Approach 97, you'll notice that the SmartIcons appearing on the SmartIcon bar change according to the task at hand.

✔ Next on the agenda is the Action bar, complete with buttons to switch into Browse or Design mode, to create a new record, to find a set of records, or (the drop-down list that isn't a button at all) to select which set of found records to see. The buttons don't have much in common except that they get you where you need to be to take Action. Oh, well. Logical grouping or not, they're handy.

✔ Right smack in the middle of the screen is the *document window,* where you see the file that you're working on. The appearance of the document window depends on the view in which you're working. In Figure 1-2, the view is the default menu (from the Employees & Departments database, which is one of the templates that comes with Approach 97), which contains the fields for a single database record. If you switch to other views, such as a worksheet, report, or form letter view, the document window changes accordingly.

✔ At the bottom of the screen is the *status bar,* which tells you the view that is currently displayed, what record is displayed, the number of records in the database, and other useful information. The status bar contains helpful pop-up menus for carrying out common tasks, such as changing modes or views. Also, the status bar occasionally morphs itself to reveal information that's pertinent to the task at hand.

Here are a few points to ponder as you meditate on the complexity of the Approach 97 screen:

✔ You'll never get anything done if you feel that you have to understand every pixel of the Approach 97 screen before you can do anything. Don't worry about the stuff you don't understand; just concentrate on what you need to know to get the job done.

✔ A great deal of stuff is crammed into the Approach 97 screen — enough stuff that the program works best if you run it in *full-screen* mode. If Approach 97 doesn't cover the entire screen, click on the Restore button located next to the X in the upper-right corner of the Approach 97 window. This action *maximizes* the window, and Approach 97 takes over the entire screen. (When the window is maximized, the Maximize button changes to the Restore button visible in Figure 1-2.)

✔ The status bar contains a most useful pop-up menu called the *View menu*. This menu enables you to switch among the Approach 97 working environments, which we call *modes*. Click on the View menu to reveal a list of the mode choices; then click on the mode that you want to switch to. Table 1-1 summarizes the various Approach 97 modes.

Table 1-1	Approach 97 Modes
Mode	*What It Does*
Browse	Displays information from the database and enables you to add or update individual records. This mode is the one you work in most.
Design	Enables you to design the layout of views, such as forms, reports, form letters, and so on.
Find	Enables you to search for records that match a search criteria that you set up. For example, you work in Find mode to search for all friends who live in Iowa and owe you more than $10.
Preview	Shows what the current view looks like when printed, thus helping to save the forests.

✔ If you're not sure about the function of any of the SmartIcons on the SmartIcon bar, point to the SmartIcon with the mouse, let the mouse hover over the SmartIcon for a moment, and a brightly colored cartoon balloon appears, containing a brief description of the SmartIcon's function. Pretty cool, isn't it?

Creating a New Database

If you want to set up a brand-new database file, follow these steps:

1. **Start Approach 97 by clicking on its icon in the Lotus SmartSuite group from the Start menu.**

   Approach 97 starts up and displays the Welcome to Lotus Approach dialog box (refer to Figure 1-1).

2. **Click once on the Create a New File Using a SmartMaster tab to make sure that it is selected.**

3. **Pick a database from the list box to use as a model for your new database.**

SmartMasters come in two flavors: the complete application flavor (extremely little work required) or the template flavor (not much work required). By default, Approach 97 shows you the list of complete applications. If one of the applications is close to what you want, select it.

If none of the applications seem quite right, click on the down arrow in the drop-down box by SmartMaster types and select Templates, and then see if something in the list box looks more appropriate. Choices, choices, choices.

The list in the box contains 52 different database templates, which should probably cover anything you want to do. Select the one that most closely resembles the type of database you want to create.

4. **Click on the OK button.**

If you chose a template in Step 3, Approach 97 displays a New dialog box similar to the one shown in Figure 1-3.

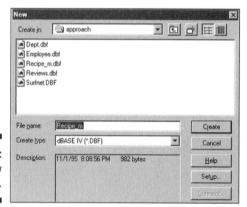

Figure 1-3:
The New
dialog box.

Approach 97 suggests a filename for the new database file. You can use the filename proposed by Approach 97 or supply your own filename.

If you chose an application in Step 3, skip to Step 6.

5. **If the filename proposed by Approach 97 is acceptable, click on the Create button; otherwise, type a filename in the File name box that you like better and then click on the Create button.**

Make sure that you don't use the name of an existing database.

6. **Approach 97 creates the file.**

Approach 97 displays either a blank form that you can use to add records to the new database or the welcome screen if you choose an application. Glance back at Figure 1-2 to see what a welcome screen may look like.

Here are some things to consider when you create a new database file:

✔ The new database file created by Approach 97 is empty. Add records to it by typing in the data for each record. See the following section, "Filling Out a Form," for the procedure.

✔ If a SmartMaster Application is very close to what you want, go ahead and select it — the less work for you, the better. However, in all likelihood, you'll need to select a SmartMaster template, rather than an application, that gets reasonably close to your needs and then work from there to finish the project. Don't worry about it. This book gets you all fixed up and the templates take most of the drudgery and confusion out of the process.

✔ If you're *interested* in — God forbid — finding out about building your own databases, the applications provide a good sample of a complete and polished database you can use as a model.

✔ Unfortunately, Approach 97 does not provide a way to preview the database template before you create a database. As a result, you can easily make all kinds of silly mistakes, such as using the Wine List template when you want to compile a database of your favorite complaints. If you select the wrong template, close the database and then use Windows Explorer to delete the files you inadvertently created.

✔ Turn to Chapter 2 for more information about creating databases, especially for adding or removing database fields and changing the layout of the database form.

✔ If you try to create a database that uses a filename you have already used for a database in the same directory, Approach 97 displays a dialog box with the message, "This file already exists. Replace existing file?" Be careful! If you click on the Yes button, the existing file, along with all of its records, is irretrievably lost. If you see this message, click on the No button and type a different filename to avoid destroying an existing database.

✔ If the Welcome to Lotus Approach dialog box disappears, you can get it back by opening a database (any database will do) and then closing it. In the absence of the Welcome dialog box, you can create a new database by choosing File⇨New Database. However, because this procedure is more complicated (trust us), we won't describe it in detail until Chapter 2.

Filling Out a Form

After you create a database, you must type in the information for each database record. The details of entering and editing this data are in Chapter 4. Figure 1-4 shows a sample form so that you can see what we're talking about.

![Screenshot of Lotus SmartSuite 97 Approach showing a "Recipes - Main" form with fields for Recipe Name, Recipe Description, Recipe ID, Time to Prepare, Number of Servings, Calories/Servings, Instructions, Source, and Note.]

Figure 1-4:
A sample
Approach 97
form.

Here are enough basics to get you going:

✔ An *insertion point* marks the spot where text you type will be inserted on the screen. The insertion point is a special type of cursor that appears on-screen as a flashing vertical line. You can move the insertion point from field to field by pressing the Tab key, or you can click the mouse on any field to move the insertion point directly to the field.

✔ If you have typed in all of the information for one record and you want to start a new record, click on the New Record button, press Ctrl+N, or choose Browse⇨New Record. Approach 97 records the information you just typed and then presents you with a new, blank record.

✔ If Approach 97 just beeps at you when you try to type into a field, you're probably trying to type some illegal characters or you typed more characters than will fit in the field. For example, you can type only numbers into a date field. If you try to type anything other than numbers, Approach 97 just beeps. Be thankful that the penalty for illegal typing is a mere beep. Some less-civilized programs cart you off and flog you with a cane for typing illegal characters or too many characters.

✔ No rule exists that says that you necessarily have to type something into every field on the form. If you don't have anything to type into a field, press Tab to skip the field. If your boss told you to complete every blank no matter what, we're sorry. (Actually, some people set up Approach 97 databases so you can't complete a record without completing certain fields, but don't worry about that now. We talk more about that in Chapter 2.)

✔ New database records are automatically inserted at the end of the database, but you can tell Approach 97 to store database records in a sorting sequence (for example, alphabetical). In that case, new records are inserted into their proper location so that the sorting sequence is preserved. You can find all the information that's worth knowing about sorting database records in Chapter 6.

✔ If you want to review the records you entered into a database, you can click on the left and right arrows that appear on the status bar at the bottom of the screen and on the SmartIcon bar. The left arrow moves back through the database one record at a time; the right arrow moves forward one record at a time. The left arrow pointing to a line moves back to the first record, and the right arrow pointing to a line moves up to the last record.

Looking at the Worksheet

A worksheet view enables you to access the fields and records in an Approach 97 database in an arrangement similar to a spreadsheet in a program such as Lotus 1-2-3. A row in the worksheet represents each database record, and a column represents each field.

When you create an Approach 97 database, a default worksheet view named Worksheet 1 is automatically created for you. To switch to this worksheet view, click on the tab labeled Worksheet 1 at the top of the file window. Figure 1-5 shows a worksheet view of a database.

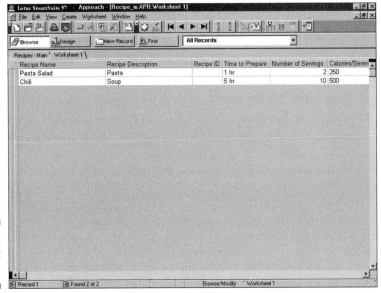

Figure 1-5:
Worksheet
view.

Unlike forms, which show one database record at a time, worksheets show as many database records as Approach 97 can fit on the screen, and each record is in a separate worksheet row.

Chapter 17 covers the details of using worksheet views. For now, here are some basics to get you going:

- ✔ Your Lotus 1-2-3 instincts, if you have any, should serve you well in worksheet view. The basics of navigating around the worksheet — such as using the arrow keys to move from cell to cell — are the same and fairly intuitive. (By intuitive, we mean that keys with arrows generally move you in that direction, the cursor follows the mouse, and so forth.)

- ✔ Inserting a new record in worksheet view is the same as inserting a new record in a form. You click on the New Record button, press Ctrl+N, or choose Browse⇨New Record.

- ✔ If a worksheet column is not wide enough to display all the data it contains, you can increase the column's width by positioning the mouse pointer at the right edge of the column's header and dragging the header to the right.

- ✔ You can freely rearrange the order of columns in the worksheet, and you can even remove entire columns to hide fields that you're not interested in. For details, see Chapter 17.

Printing a Database

After you have gone to the trouble of entering thousands of database records into your computer, you will probably want to print them, even though forests everywhere will hate you for it. For high-class and spiffy printouts, you can create a custom report, following the procedures outlined in Chapter 10. For quick-and-dirty printouts, follow these steps:

1. **Make sure that the printer is turned on and is ready to print.**

   Make sure that the select or online light is turned on. If it isn't, press the select or online button to turn on the light. Check the paper while you're at it.

2. **Switch to the view that you want to print.**

   To print only a single record, switch to a form view (such as Form 1) and call up the record you want to print. To print all the records in a database, switch to a worksheet view (such as Worksheet 1).

3. **Click on the Print SmartIcon.**

Or if you prefer, choose File⇨Print or press Ctrl+P. However you do it, the Print dialog box appears. This box offers myriad options that you can fiddle with to print your database just so, but you can also just leave them alone (that is, accept the default values) to print the current view.

4. **Click on the Print button or press Enter.**

Make sure that you say, "Engage," in a knowing manner and point at your printer as you do so. The main idea is to fool your printer into thinking that you're the boss.

Printed pages should soon appear on the printer. In all likelihood, you won't be completely satisfied with the layout of the printed output. To print a proper database listing, you need to design a custom report. Fortunately, the procedure is simple, and you can find everything you need to know in Chapter 10.

Saving Your Work

Any good Windows user knows about the importance of choosing File⇨Save to save work. Approach 97 works a little differently from most other Windows programs, though. Whenever you make a change to a database by adding a new record or deleting or changing an existing record, the change is immediately recorded in the database file. As a result, you don't have to bother with saving the file after making database changes.

But wait . . . Approach 97 offers a File⇨Save Approach File command, and a Save SmartIcon appears on the icon bar. What gives?

Here's the story: Approach 97 automatically saves any changes you make to the *data* in a database, but it does not save any changes you make to database views, such as forms, worksheets, or reports. When you create a database, you have to save any new views that you have created for it. And any time you change the design of a view or create a new view, you have to save the views again.

At least two files are stored on disk for each Approach 97 database. The *database file* contains the actual records of the database. Database files usually have a .DBF or .DB filename extension, depending on the database file format you select; the default is .DBF. The Approach 97 file contains the views that are used to access the data in the database file. Approach 97 files have .APR as their filename extension. Whenever you change the contents of a database, the changes are automatically recorded in the database file. However, you must manually save changes to the Approach file.

You can save an Approach file in any of the following four ways:

✔ Choose File➪Save Approach File.

✔ Click on the Save Approach File SmartIcon on the icon bar.

✔ Press Ctrl+S.

✔ Close the file by choosing File➪Close or exit Approach 97 by choosing File➪Exit Approach. If you have made changes to any views, Approach 97 asks whether you want to save the Approach file.

Whenever you save your Approach file, Approach 97 automatically uses the same filename and folder you selected when you created the file. No problem. Subsequent saves update the Approach file with any changes that you made to the database views since the last time you saved it.

If you want to save your Approach 97 database under a different name or in different folder, you can do so. Just choose File➪Save As and fill in a name in the dialog box that appears.

Here are some points to keep in mind when you save Approach files:

✔ If you opt for a name other than the name proposed by Approach 97, use your noggin. You will use the filename to recognize the file later on, so pick a meaningful name that suggests the file's contents.

✔ Database changes are automatically recorded in the database file. Choose File➪Save Approach File only to save changes you make to database views.

✔ If you're not sure about how to make up a filename, just type in something descriptive with up to 255 characters, including spaces. You can't use these characters: \ / : * ? " < > |, but anything else is fine.

Retrieving a Database from Disk

Having entered thousands upon thousands of records into a database, you'll probably long for some method of retrieving those records later, either to print a report, to change records that are out of date, or just to gloat (for example, I can't believe I typed the whole thing!).

You can open a database in any of three ways:

✔ Choose File➪Open.

✔ Click on the Open a File SmartIcon on the icon bar.

✔ Press Ctrl+O.

All three methods pop up the Open dialog box, which gives you a list of files to select from. Click on the name of the file you want to open and then click on the Open button or press Enter.

Here are a few points to ruminate on when you are opening files:

- ✔ The Open dialog box has controls that enable you to rummage through the various directories on the hard disk to search for files. If you know how to open a file in any Windows 95 application, you know how to do it in Approach 97, because the Open dialog box is pretty much the same as the Open dialog boxes you encounter in other Windows programs.

- ✔ You can quickly open a file from the Open dialog box by double-clicking on the file that you want to open. This method spares you from clicking on the file and then clicking on the Open button. It also exercises the fast-twitch muscles in your index finger.

- ✔ Approach 97 keeps track of the last five files you opened and displays them on the File menu. To open a file that you recently opened, click on the File menu and inspect the list at the bottom of the menu. If the file you want is on the list, click on it to open it.

- ✔ You can also open a file from the Welcome to Lotus Approach dialog box. Click on the Open an Existing Approach File tab that's displayed when you start Approach 97 or when you close a database. Refer to Figure 1-1 if you've forgotten what the dialog box looks like.

Closing a Database

After you finish working on a database, you will want to close it. Closing a database is kind of like stuffing your important papers back into the shoe box and shoving the shoe box back onto the top shelf in the closet. Out of sight, out of mind. The database disappears from the computer screen, but don't worry. It's tucked safely away on the hard disk where you can get to it later if you need to. To close a file, choose File⇨Close.

Here are some closing arguments to consider:

- ✔ Closing a file closes both the database file and the Approach file that contains the views used to access the database. You cannot close one of these files without simultaneously closing the other.

- ✔ Yet another way to close a file is to double-click on the control box that appears on the far-left edge of the menu bar.

- ✔ You don't have to close a file before you exit Approach 97. If you exit Approach 97 without closing a file, the program graciously closes the file for you. The only time you may want to close a file is when you want to work on a different file, and you don't want to keep both files open at the same time.

✔ If you made changes to the views in the Approach file, Approach 97 offers to save the file before closing it. Click on the <u>Y</u>es button to save the file or click on the <u>N</u>o button to abandon the changes.

✔ After you close a file, Approach 97 politely offers up the Welcome to Lotus Approach dialog box so that you can easily create a new database or open an existing database. Presenting the dialog box is a deliberate attempt to discourage you from playing solitaire rather than continuing with your work. Boo-hiss!

Exiting Approach 97

Had enough excitement for one day? Use any of the following techniques to shut down Approach 97:

✔ Choose <u>F</u>ile⇨E<u>x</u>it Approach.

✔ Double-click on the control box in the upper-left corner of the Approach 97 window.

✔ Press Alt+F4.

Bammo! Approach 97 is outta here.

You should know a few things about exiting Approach 97:

✔ Approach 97 doesn't let you exit without first considering whether you want to save changes you made to a view stored in an Approach file. If you made any design changes, Approach 97 offers to save the changes for you. Accept its generous offer with gratitude.

✔ Never, never, never ever, never, no never turn off the computer while Approach 97 or any other Windows program is running. You may as well pour acid into the keyboard or drop the system unit from the top of the Chrysler building. Always exit Approach 97 and any other program that's running before you turn off your computer.

✔ In fact, you'd best get clean out of Windows before you shut down the computer. Exit all the programs the same way you exited Approach 97. Then, after Windows is the only thing left, go to the Start menu and choose Shut Down. Select Shut Down Computer from the dialog box and don't turn off the computer until it tells you to do so.

Chapter 2
Creating Database Fields

*T*his chapter is a good news/bad news chapter. The bad news is that you have to design and create a database before you can get any useful work done with Approach 97. This task involves figuring out what fields (or snippets of information) to include in each database record, what to name the fields, how to format each field, and so on. If you're incredibly lucky, someone else has done this work for you — or will if you bribe them sufficiently. If not, you're on your own. You can find more information about fields — what they are and what you use them for — throughout this chapter.

The good news is that Approach 97 is very flexible when it comes to designing and creating databases. When you use Approach 97, you can create a database by copying fields from one of the templates that comes with Approach 97, or you can start with a blank template and add your own fields. The important thing to remember is that the database layout is never fixed in stone. You can easily revisit your design at any time to add fields that you forgot, delete fields that you no longer need, and change fields that you originally defined as too small or too large.

Finding Out about Fields

A field is a field is a field, right? Wrong. Approach 97 enables you to create nine different types of database fields. Table 2-1 summarizes the nine field types and gives quickie examples. The following sections describe each type of field in excruciating detail.

Table 2-1	**Approach 97 Field Types**	
Field Types	*Characteristics*	*Examples*
Text	Holds text such as names, addresses, titles, and so on; can be up to 255 characters in length	Roseanne, Domestic Goddess
Numeric	Holds numbers such as sales amounts, prices, quantities, and so on.	Holds only numbers, not text describing the numbers 27 (pounds) $27 (dollars), 1 (gaggle of geese)
Memo	Holds extra-long text information	Ninety-nine bottles of beer on the wall, ninety-nine bottles of beer — take one down, pass it around, ninety-eight bottles of beer on the wall. (Let us know when you're done. We'll wait.)
Boolean	Holds a yes or no answer to a question	Has the customer paid in full? Yes. Are the bananas on sale this week? No.
Date	Holds a date	December 31, 1998 (Don't confuse this with having a date or holding hands.)
Time	Holds a time	2:09 PM (Don't confuse this with making a reservation at your favorite restaurant.)
PicturePlus	Holds a graphic or an OLE object. (OLE is pronounced *oh-lay*, as in what the bullfighters say. OLE lets you insert a document created by one application into another document.)	Inserting part of a Lotus 1-2-3 spreadsheet into a WordPro document or inserting a picture into your database.
Calculated	Holds the result of a calculation derived from other fields	87.3359 (which is the average number of rude jokes the average sitcom makes per episode).
Variable	Used by Approach 97 gurus to hold temporary results in macros	Gurus put all kinds of stuff here. Just nod and look impressed when they tell you how they used the variable field.

Text fields

A *text field* is a database field that holds text information. Text can be any combination of characters that you can type on the keyboard, including letters, numerals, and special symbols. Text fields are used for names, addresses, titles, descriptions, and other similar information.

Here are a few points to ponder concerning text fields:

✔ You have to specify a maximum length for the field when you define a text field. (When we say *define* a text field, we mean to create a text field; define is the common quasi-technical term that we use throughout the book.) Approach 97 doesn't let you type more characters than the maximum number into the field — kind of like those irritating IRS forms that don't provide enough spaces to write in your really long last name. If more characters exist than spaces, the extra characters won't be entered into the field and your user's futile attempts will be greeted with obnoxious beeps.

✔ In most database file types, including the Approach 97 defaults, you get up to 255 characters (including blank spaces) per text field. If you need to store more text than that, use a memo field instead. Of course, if you need more than 255 characters for a text field, you may want to hire a relief typist.

✔ You may think that a text field sometimes looks like a numeric field. For example, a zip code or phone number field may look like a number, although they are text fields. You can't use such a text field in a numeric calculation, even though it contains numbers.

✔ You can search a database for records that contain specific text in a text field. See Chapter 5 for more information about searching text fields.

✔ You can sort a database into sequence by basing the sort on a text field. Say what? For example, you can sort a customer database into alphabetical order by basing the sort on each customer's last name. Chapter 6 covers sorting.

Numeric fields

Numeric fields contain — you guessed it — numeric values. Use numeric fields to store information such as sales amounts, prices, quantities, and so on.

Keep the following in mind when you are using numeric fields:

✔ You can type certain non-numeric characters into a numeric field. For example, if you type $123.45, Approach 97 ignores the dollar sign and treats the number as 123.45.

✔ You can specify the size of the numeric data that can be stored in a numeric field by telling Approach 97 how many digits to allow on the left and the right of the decimal point. For example, if you specify 10.2,

Approach 97 allows ten digits to the left of the decimal point and two to the right. The largest value that you can store in a number field of that size is 9,999,999,999.99 (ten digits before the decimal and two after), which still isn't large enough to store Bill Gates' net worth.

✔ You can use numeric fields in calculations. In an invoicing database, for example, you can use a subtotal field to calculate a sales tax field and then add both fields together to calculate a total field. In this case, the sales tax field is numeric, and the subtotal and total fields are calculated. For more information on including calculations in your database, see Chapter 13.

✔ You can search database records for the value stored in numeric fields. For example, in an invoice database, you can search for all invoices whose Invoice Total field is $100 or more. Chapter 5 explains how to conduct such a search.

✔ You can sort a database into sequence by numeric fields. For example, you can base a sort on a Year-To-Date Sales field to sort a customer database into sequence. Chapter 6 covers sorting.

Memo fields

Memo fields are used for text information that doesn't fit into a normal text field — fields that are more than 255 characters long. Memo fields are usually used as a place to store extra information or notes about a database record. For example, you can use a memo field in a client database to jot down notes about the client's product preferences, family, or pets' names (or pet names, for that matter). Then you can review these notes before you meet with the client, and the client thinks that you have a remarkable memory.

Here are some thoughts to mull over when you use memo fields:

✔ The maximum length of a memo field is 64K (64,000 characters or so) in the default database file types used by Approach 97, but it may be less for certain less-common database file types. Unless you're extremely prolific, you can think of memo fields as providing practically unlimited text storage.

✔ Memo fields are stored in a separate memo file rather than in the main database file. The memo file extension depends on the database file type used. The file extensions for these pesky memo fields are as follows:

- dBase is .DBT.

- FoxPro is .FPT.

- Paradox is .DBQ.

✔ You can search for text in a memo field, but you can't sort a database in a sequence based on a memo field. See Chapter 5 for instructions on searching memo fields.

Boolean fields

Boolean fields hold a yes/no answer to a question. Or, if you prefer, a true/false answer. A Boolean field is usually shown on forms as a check box. Use Boolean fields to record information, such as "Did I send this customer a mailing last month?" or "Did I call this customer regarding her order?"

Here are some thoughts to consider when using Boolean fields:

- ✔ Boolean fields have only two values: yes or no. To enter a yes response into a field, you can type **Yes**, **Y**, **yes**, **y**, or **1** into the field. To enter a no response, you can type **No**, **N**, **no**, **n**, or **0**. Or, if you've set up a check box, you choose Yes or No by clicking your mouse on the appropriate box.

- ✔ The easiest way to work with Boolean fields is to set them up in your forms as check boxes. Then the user clicks on the check box to choose a yes or no value for the field. Chapter 9 offers instructions for setting up check box form fields.

- ✔ Boolean fields are very useful when you set up *conditional calculations*. An example of a conditional calculation at work is a customer database that includes a Boolean field to indicate whether a customer is tax exempt. This field can be used in a conditional sales tax calculation to make sure that tax-exempt customers are not charged sales tax.

Date fields

Date fields store dates, for example: Invoice Date, Last Order Date, Due Date, Birth Date, Date Joined, and so on. You get the idea.

- ✔ You can display dates in several formats, such as the following:

```
09/30/94
Feb 12, 1994
Monday, May 16, 1994
```

You can enter two or four digits for the year. If you enter two digits, the twentieth century is assumed. If you omit the year altogether, the current year is assumed.

Chapter 14 explains how to set the appropriate date format when you design a form, report, or other view. Approach 97 provides many date formats for you to select from, or you can even modify existing formats and create your own.

✔ Date fields are usually set up so that you enter the date into a field that's preformatted with separator characters, like this:

_ _ / _ _ / _ _

Then you type numbers for the month, day, and year. After you move out of the field by pressing the Tab key, Approach 97 redisplays the date according to the date format you selected for the field. Again, see Chapter 14 for details.

✔ You can press Ctrl+Shift+D to enter the current date into a date field (or into any field your cursor is in, for that matter).

✔ You can use dates in calculations. For example, to calculate the number of days between two date fields, just subtract one date field from the other. Chapter 14 explains this type of calculation.

Time fields

Time fields store times, as in 8:00 PM or 3:42:23 AM. Time fields are fairly easy to understand, as long as you keep the following points in mind:

✔ You can enter a time value that uses 12-hour or 24-hour notation. For example, 13:35 and 1:35 PM represent the same time. If you enter an hour that's less than 12, Approach 97 assumes the time is AM unless you type PM following the time. Obviously, Approach 97 wasn't designed by night owls.

✔ Most of the time, you enter just the hours and minutes; for example, 5:56 PM. For more precise times, you can enter the seconds as well; for example, 5:56:32 PM. You can even enter hundredths of seconds, as in 5:56:32.58 PM, but by the time you finish typing, the time you enter is inaccurate anyway.

✔ To enter the current time, press Ctrl+Shift+T. This command pastes the current time as text into the field you have selected.

PicturePlus fields

PicturePlus fields store a picture or an embedded object created by another Windows program. You can, for example, store a sound file, a chart, or a range of cells from a spreadsheet program such as 1-2-3 in a PicturePlus field. PicturePlus fields most often store pictures of customers or products in a customer or inventory database.

PicturePlus fields are complicated enough that we devote an entire chapter to them (see Chapter 12). Until you get to that chapter, the following snippets of information should satisfy your curiosity:

✔ You can place a picture into a PicturePlus field by opening the picture in a drawing program (such as Paintbrush), copying the picture to the Clipboard, switching to Approach 97, and pasting the picture from the Clipboard into the PicturePlus field. Or you can choose Edit⇨Paste Special to copy a picture directly from a file into a PicturePlus field.

✔ If you want to, you can create an OLE link to a graphic or any other type of OLE object, such as a sound, chart, or spreadsheet range. Then, when you double-click on the object in the PicturePlus field, the program that created the object opens so that you can edit the object.

✔ OLE stands for *Object Linking and Embedding,* but that doesn't matter now. In fact, the whole subject of OLE and PicturePlus fields is too far out for an introductory chapter like this one. If you really have to know about these things, jump ahead to Chapter 12.

Calculated fields

A *calculated field* is a field with a value that Approach 97 calculates automatically, basing the calculations on other fields in the record. For example, an Invoice database can represent sales tax by using a calculated field. Then Approach 97 can calculate the sales tax by basing it on the invoice subtotal.

If you think of a calculated field as being like a formula in a spreadsheet cell, you have the right idea; the concept is the same. The advantage of using calculated fields is that they eliminate the possibility that a lowly human will make a dumb mistake, such as charging $70 sales tax on a $10 order.

✔ When you define a calculated field, you type a formula that calculates the field's value. Here are some typical formulas for calculated fields:

```
Subtotal * 0.0725
Subtotal + Tax
IF(Taxable,Subtotal*0.0725,0)
PMT(Prin,Rate,48)
```

✔ We devote an entire chapter of this book, Chapter 13, to devising these types of formulas. See that chapter for more information.

✔ You cannot type a value directly into a calculated field. Instead, Approach 97 calculates the field's value each time you display a record. The calculated field's value is recalculated whenever you change a field that is mentioned in the calculated field's formula. For example, if a Sales Tax field multiplies a Subtotal field by a fixed tax rate, the Sales Tax field automatically updates whenever you change the value of the Subtotal field.

✔ The value of a calculated field is not stored in the database file. Instead, the value is recalculated each time a record is retrieved from the database file. This method saves space in the database file and assures that calculated fields always have up-to-date values.

Variable fields

A *variable field* is not really a database field, at least not in the same sense that the other types of fields are. Variable fields are used in macros (mini-programs that automate database functions) to temporarily store calculated results. Variable fields are best used by computer gurus who don't realize that life consists of more than writing macros. Because you do have a life outside of macros, we'll stop here with the description.

Adding Fields to a Database

After you create a blank database, you must add fields before you can store data in the database. To add fields to a new database, follow these steps:

1. **In the Welcome to Lotus Approach dialog box, click on the gray tab called Create a New File Using a SmartMaster.**

   Or, if the Welcome to Lotus Approach dialog box isn't visible, choose File⇨New Database. A dialog box appears with a list of templates to select from.

2. **Select Blank Database as the template and click on the OK button.**

3. **After the New dialog box appears, type a filename for the new database and click on the Create button.**

   The Creating New Database dialog box appears, as shown in Figure 2-1.

Figure 2-1:
The Creating
New
Database
dialog box.

4. **In the Field Name column, type the name of the first field you want to create.**

   The number of characters you can use in the field name depends on the type of database file you created. For the default dBase file format and for FoxPro files, you can use up to 32 characters for each field name. For Paradox files, the limit is 25 characters. Either way, the name can include spaces, so names such as Customer Number and Risk Factor are perfectly valid field names.

5. **Press Tab.**

   When you press Tab, the insertion point jumps to the Data Type column.

6. **Select the field's data type from the drop-down list that appears in the Data Type column for the field.**

   When the insertion point moves into the Data Type column, a drop-down list appears. Click on the down arrow to read the contents of the drop-down list, as shown in Figure 2-2. Scroll through this list to find the data type that you want to use and click on the data type to select it.

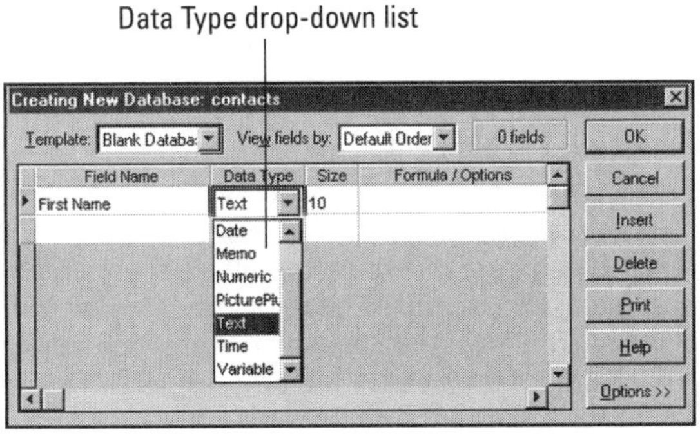

Data Type drop-down list

Figure 2-2: The Data Type drop-down list.

7. **Press Tab to move to the Size field.**

8. **For text or numeric fields, type the field length for the field in the Size column.**

   For text fields, type the maximum number of characters that you want to allow for the field. The default size, 10, is adequate for short fields, but not for longer fields such as names and addresses.

   For numeric fields, type the number of digits to allow to the left of the decimal point, type a decimal point, and then type the number of digits to allow on the right of the decimal point. For example, type **7.2** to allow numbers ranging up to 9,999,999.99.

9. **Repeat Steps 3 through 5 for other fields you want to add to the database.**

10. **After you add all your new fields, click on the OK button to dismiss the Creating New Database dialog box.**

After you're finished, all the fields of the database are lined up neatly, as shown in Figure 2-3. If the database contains more fields than can be displayed at once in the Creating New Database dialog box, you can see additional fields by using the scroll bar to scroll through the list of fields. (You can work the scroll bar by dragging the slider box that starts out at the top of the scroll bar or by clicking on either of the arrow buttons that appear at the top and bottom of the scroll bar.)

List of newly created fields   Scroll bar

Figure 2-3:
The list of
newly
created
fields in the
Creating
New
Database
dialog box.

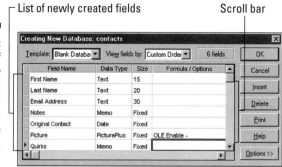

Here are some field-definition tidbits that are worthy of your consideration:

✔ If you want to copy fields from one of the database templates supplied with Approach 97, select the template that you want to use from the Template drop-down list. Be warned, however, that if you apply a template to a database, any fields that you have already defined for the database will be lost.

✔ You can use the drop-down list in the View fields by box to change the order in which database fields are displayed in the dialog box. The sort options for a brand-spanking new database are Default Order, Field Name, and Data Type. If you add more than one field, the sort options change to Field Name, Data Type, and Custom Order. Essentially, when you start adding fields, you're sorting a Custom Order, so that option appears in the window. The sort option affects how fields are displayed in the Creating New Database dialog box; it doesn't affect how fields are displayed in forms or how records are sorted in the database.

✔ New fields are normally added to the end of the list of database fields. If you want to insert a field in the middle of the list, click on the field immediately after the location where you want the new field inserted and then click on the Insert button. Approach 97 inserts a new row so that you can define a new field.

- ✔ Notice that just to the left of the OK button Approach 97 displays the total number of fields you have defined for the database. See? Computers *can* count, and they don't even need fingers.

- ✔ You can print a listing of the fields in your database by clicking on the Print button and then clicking on the Print button in the Print dialog box that appears.

- ✔ After you create a database, you can return to the Creating New Database dialog box at any time by choosing Create⇨Field Definition. Then you can add new fields, delete fields you don't need, or change the format of database fields. After you choose Create⇨Field Definition, the dialog box title changes from Creating New Database to Field Definition. Otherwise, the dialog box is the same. For more information, see the next section, "Adding, Changing, or Deleting Fields."

- ✔ As with many other neato Windows applications, you can click on the Help button in the Creating New Database dialog box for information specifically on — well — creating a new database.

- ✔ Err on the side of creating too many fields rather than not enough. The Ray Corollary to Murphy's Law of Databases says that if you put two different kinds of data into a single field, you'll be sorry. For example, don't combine city, state, and zip code into a single field even if you're only going to be using the database for mass mailings. If you do that, you won't be able to sort by zip code (because it isn't a separate field), and you won't get cheap(er) rates from the post office.

Adding, Changing, or Deleting Fields

After you create a database and use it for a while, you may decide that you want to modify it to better suit your needs. Or, possibly, you goofed up and need to do some major reconstruction. In either case, Approach 97 allows you to add more fields to a database, remove a database field that you don't need, or change a field's name, data type, size, and options. Just follow this painless procedure to edit your fields, or check out Chapter 9 if you want more information on working with fields.

1. **Open the database by clicking on the Open an Existing Approach File tab on the Welcome to Lotus Approach dialog box, choosing File⇨Open, or pressing Ctrl+O.**

2. **Select the database you want to open from the dialog box and click on the OK button.**

   You may have to look around on the disk for the file.

Your database should open. Heck, we'll go out on a limb and say that it will open, barring acts of God or the like.

3. **Choose Create⇨Field Definition.**

The Field Definition dialog box appears and enables you to use the following options to edit your fields:

- **To add a field,** scroll to the end of the field list, type the field name in the first available Field Name cell, and then select the data type and size for the field.

  If you prefer to insert the field somewhere in the middle of the list, click on the field immediately after the location where you want the new field inserted and click on the Insert button. Then type the name, field type, and length for the new field.

- **To delete a field,** select the field you want to delete by clicking on it, click on the Delete button, and after Approach 97 asks whether you're sure that you want to delete the field, click on the OK button.

  The field is deleted. Any data stored in the field in any records in the database is lost.

- **To change a field,** select the Field Name, Data Type, or Size settings for the field by clicking on them and then enter new values.

  The field is adjusted according to the new specifications.

- **To change a field's options,** select the field by clicking on it, click on the Options button, and change the options.

  A tabbed dialog box appears and provides you with options (specifically, Default Value and Validation options, discussed in the next two sections). After you select options, they appear in the Formula/Options column of the database, and the field is adjusted according to your new specifications.

Be sure to consider the following points before changing or deleting database fields:

- ✔ Any data contained in a field is lost when you delete the field. Make sure that you don't need the data in a field before you delete the field. (Approach 97 asks for confirmation with a message that goes something like, "Are you out of your mind?")

- ✔ If the field is used in a *join,* you have to unjoin the field before you can delete it. See Chapter 8 for more information about joins, which are simply two or more databases combined so they act as one.

- ✔ Think twice before deleting a field that is part of a calculated field. If you do, you'll probably have to change the calculated field's formula. For example, if a Sales Tax field is calculated with a formula such as Subtotal * 0.0725, you'll get bogus results in the Sales Tax field if you delete the Subtotal field.

> ✔ If you reduce a field's size, Approach 97 may be forced to whack off data that won't fit in the reduced field. The program warns you first, but be careful!

Creating Fields That Fill Themselves In

Approach 97 offers two nifty options that enable you to create fields that fill themselves in:

- ✔ **Default value option:** A *default value* is applied to a field unless the user manually changes the value. Default values are useful for fields with values that are predictable. For example, in a personal address book database, you can use the name of your hometown as the default value for the City field. Then you only have to type the city for friends who don't live in your hometown.

- ✔ **Validation option:** The validation option helps prevent bad data from getting into the database — it checks to make sure that the data you're entering meets specific criteria. Validation options can't eliminate all bad data, but they can eliminate many common data entry mistakes. For example, a validated field for a phone number would check to make sure that the entry only contains numbers, in a set of three (area code), three, and four. It would reject an entry with too many or too few digits as well as something with letters, but the field wouldn't know if you just mistyped the number.

These options are discussed in the following sections.

Default value options

Approach 97 provides several different kinds of default value options for database fields. You can select *only one* of these per field:

- ✔ **Nothing:** This default is used for most fields, probably partially because it is the Approach 97 default for default value. (Say that three times fast!). A field whose default option is set to Nothing is only given a value when you (or whoever is doing the data entry) type a value for the field.

- ✔ **Previous record:** A field takes on the same value as the database record that was most recently added or modified. This type of default setting is useful for fields with values that usually run in spurts. For example, in an Orders database, you can set the Salesperson field's default to Previous record to make entering a batch of orders for a particular salesperson easier.

- ✔ **Creation date:** A field's value is set to the current date when the record is created. Use this option only for date or text fields.

✔ **Modification date:** A field's value is set to the current date when the record is created and is updated whenever the record is modified. Use this option only for date or text fields.

✔ **Creation time:** A field's value is set to the current time when the record is created. Use this option only for time or text fields.

✔ **Modification time:** A field's value is set to the current time when the record is created and is updated whenever the record is modified. Use this value only for time or text fields.

✔ **Data:** A specific value is used as the default for a field. For example, for a Payroll Check database, you can set the default for the Pay To field to one lucky recipient, such as Ashleigh Ray (our daughter), who would then be in line to receive all the checks from your payroll. Likewise, you could set a default value of, say, $16.40 for the Hourly Rate in the same payroll database.

✔ **Serial number starting at:** A sequence number is used to uniquely identify each record in a database. Approach 97 automatically assigns the correct value to serial number fields whenever you create a record that contains one. Unless you specify otherwise in the Incremented by field, Approach 97 increments the serial numbers by one.

✔ **Creation formula:** This formula is used to calculate a value for a field. The calculation is made when the record is created. Using this option is different from making a field a calculated field. The user cannot change the value of a calculated field. But the user can type a new value to replace the value calculated by a default formula.

✔ **Modification formula:** This formula is used to calculate a value for a field. The calculation is made when the record is created; the calculation is updated whenever the record is modified.

✔ **Formula:** The Formula button takes you to a separate dialog box in which you can define a formula.

Setting a default value

Here is the procedure for setting a field's default value:

1. **In the Field Definition or Creating New Database dialog box, select the field for which you want to provide a default.**

   If the Field Definition or Creating New Database dialog box isn't visible, make sure that the database is open and then choose Create➪Field Definition to summon the Field Definition dialog box.

2. **Click on the Options button.**

   The dialog box expands to reveal the options settings, as shown in Figure 2-4. Notice that the bottom portion of the dialog box contains two tabbed sections — Default Value and Validation. If the Validation options are shown, click on the Default Value tab to switch to the Default Value options.

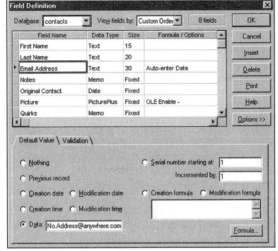

Figure 2-4:
Setting a
default
value for a
field.

3. **Select the Default Value option that you want for the field by clicking on the option.**

Remember, only one of the options listed on the Default Value tab can be in effect for a field. Note that for some field types, inappropriate option settings are disabled. If you're setting a default value for a date field, for example, the Creation time, Modification time, and Serial number starting at options are disabled because you can't use those default options for a date field.

4. **If you select the Data default option, you type the default value in the text box that is adjacent to the Data check box.**

For example, type **Deb and Eric Ray** to set our names as the default value.

5. **Select another database field to set its default value or click on the OK button to dismiss the Field Definition dialog box.**

Now every time a new record is created in this database, the default options appear in the appropriate fields.

Validation options

In Approach 97, you can set any of the following validation options for database fields. You can select *as many* of these options per field as you want:

✔ **Unique:** A field must have a different value for every record in the database. Be careful how you use this option. For example, if you specify Unique for a Last Name field, a database doesn't allow two records to have the same last name. Use Unique only for fields that must have unique values, such as Customer Number or Social Security Number.

✔ **From/to:** A field must have a value that falls within a range of values. This option is most useful for numeric fields or date fields. For example, you can specify that a Quantity Ordered field must be from 0 to 99,999. This setting eliminates unreasonably large orders (of course, exactly what constitutes an unreasonably large order depends on the kind of business you're in) and rejects negative numbers.

✔ **Filled in:** A field must be given a value by the user. Use this option for fields that are not optional, such as a customer's Last Name, an employee's Social Security Number, or a videotape's Title field. Approach 97 rebels and beeps wildly and displays an accusing dialog box until you click on the OK button (to get out of the dialog box) and complete the field.

✔ **One of:** This option is our personal favorite because you can use it to restrict a field to certain preset values. For example, suppose that you have a Territory field in a customer database, and you have four territories: North, South, East, and West. By using the One of validation option, you can prevent the user from entering anything other than North, South, East, or West for the field. If the user tries to enter only W, rather than West, Approach 97 slaps the user's hands (with a beep and a dialog box demanding the appropriate entry). (When you use One of validation, the best thing to do is to create a drop-down list for the field on the form. Chapter 9 explains how to create this type of list.)

✔ **Formula is true:** This option specifies a condition that must be true for the value of the field to be accepted. For example, you can use the formula >0 to ensure that only positive numbers are entered into the field. You can also use the Formula button to set up the formula, instead of just typing it.

✔ **In field:** This option is the trickiest validation option. It says that the value typed into a field must match a value stored in a different database field. The field can be in the same database, but it is more likely to be in a different database. For example, an Invoice database can contain a Customer Number field that always has to correspond to a Customer Number in a Customers database. To use this type of validation, the two databases must be joined. See Chapter 8 for information about joining databases.

Setting validation options

Here is the procedure for setting a field's validation options:

1. **In the Field Definition (or Creating New Database) dialog box, select the field for which you want to set the validation options.**

   If the Field Definition or Creating New Database dialog box isn't visible, make sure that the database is open and then choose Create➪Field Definition to summon the Field Definition dialog box.

2. **Click on the Options button if you haven't already done so to reveal the field options. Then click on the Validation tab to reveal the validation options.**

Figure 2-5 shows the Field Definition dialog box with the validation options visible.

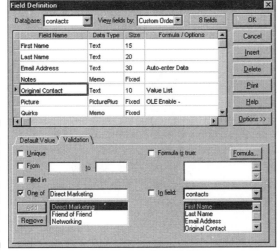

Figure 2-5:
Using the
validation
options in
the Field
Definition
dialog box.

3. **Select the validation options that you want to use by clicking on the appropriate check boxes.**

   Remember, unlike the default value options, you can check more than one validation option, such as Unique and within the From/to range.

4. **If you select the One of option, add all of the allowable field values to the list by typing each value in the text box immediately to the right of the One of caption and then clicking on the Add button.**

   In Figure 2-5, we created three allowable values for the Original Contact field: Friend of Friend, Networking, and Direct Marketing. If you make a mistake, trash the incorrect value by clicking on it and then click on the Remove button. Retype the value and click on the Add button to add the corrected value.

5. **Select another database field to set its validation options or click on the OK button to dismiss the Field Definition dialog box.**

Setting the Formula for a Calculated Field

When you create a calculated field, you must supply the formula that you want Approach 97 to use to calculate the field's value. When you set a field's Data Type to Calculated, Approach 97 expands the Creating New Database (or Field Definition) dialog box to show the formula options, as shown in Figure 2-6.

You can use two methods to construct the formula: Either type the formula in the Formula box or construct the formula piece by piece by clicking on fields, operators, and functions that you want to include in the formula. For example, to construct the formula shown in Figure 2-6, we first double-clicked on the Subtotal field in the Fields list, and then we double-clicked on the plus sign, and then we double-clicked the Sales Tax field. Each time you double-click on an element, Approach 97 adds it to the Formula box.

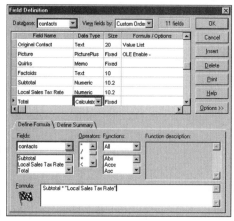

Figure 2-6:
Defining a
formula.

When you set the formula for a calculated field keep a few things in mind:

✔ Approach 97 formulas are similar to the formulas used in 1-2-3 or other spreadsheet programs. For all the gory details on creating formulas, see Chapter 13.

✔ If a field name consists of two or more words, such as Sales Tax, it must be enclosed in quotation marks in a formula. If you copy the field name into the formula by clicking on it in the Fields list, Approach 97 supplies the quotes for you. If you type the formula yourself, don't forget the quotes.

✔ The checkered flag next to the formula indicates whether the formula is acceptable. If the checkered flag has a red X through it, the formula isn't acceptable. Usually, a red X just means that you're in the process of building an acceptable formula and haven't finished adding all the pieces. After you complete the formula, the red X disappears, indicating that the formula is finished.

✔ See the Define Summary tab? Try to ignore it for now. Resist the temptation to click on it until you have read Chapter 13.

✔ Remember that the user cannot type a value into a calculated field. If you want to use a formula to provide a default field value that the user can override, use a default formula instead. See the section "Creating Fields That Fill Themselves In" in this chapter for details.

Chapter 3

Self-Help for Lonely Approach 97 Users

*T*he ideal way to use Approach 97 would be to have an Approach 97 expert sitting patiently at your side, answering your every question with a straightforward answer, gently correcting you when you make silly mistakes, and otherwise minding his or her own business. All you'd have to do is occasionally toss the expert a Twinkie and let him or her outside once a day.

Short of that, the next best thing is to learn how to use the Approach 97 built-in Help system. No matter how deeply you're lost in the Approach 97 jungle, help is never more than a few keystrokes or mouse clicks away.

The Approach 97 Help system is similar to the Help system found in other Windows 95 programs, so if you know how to use another program's Help, you'll have no trouble figuring out what Approach 97 has to offer.

Getting Help in Several Ways

As with everything else in Windows, more than one method is available for calling up help when you need it. The easiest thing to do would be to simply yell, "Skipper!!!!!!" in your best Gilligan voice. Otherwise, you have the following options:

✔ Press F1 at any time and help is on its way. If you press F1 when you're in the middle of something, odds are Approach 97 will come through with help on doing just the task you are trying to accomplish. This slick little bit of wizardry is called *context-sensitive help*.

- If you click on <u>H</u>elp on the menu bar, you get a short menu of help stuff, most of which is only moderately helpful. Choosing <u>H</u>elp⇨<u>H</u>elp Topics takes you to the Help dialog box (discussed later in this chapter). The Help dialog box is useful when you're not sure what you're looking for. Choosing <u>H</u>elp⇨<u>L</u>otus Internet Support and then choosing one of the three sub-choices that appears fires up your Web browser and Internet connection (assuming you have one) to get information direct from Lotus Internet sites. Details on finding your way around the <u>H</u>elp commands are found in later sections in this chapter.

- In most dialog boxes, you can click on the <u>H</u>elp button to call up specific help for that dialog box.

- If you're baffled by a SmartIcon, try pointing at it and letting your mouse hover there. After a second or so, a cartoon balloon appears, explaining the function of the SmartIcon. This balloon Help works the same as in other Lotus programs.

- If you are looking at a dialog box and it has a little ? icon in the upper-right corner, you can click on the ? icon to get a cursor with a question mark. You'll get a description of the next item you click on with that question mark cursor.

- With a sound card, a microphone, and the right voice recognition software, you probably could teach your computer to call up Help when you yell "Skipper!" That would be kind of silly, though, don't you think?

Finding Your Way Around in Help

If you choose <u>H</u>elp⇨<u>H</u>elp Topics, you see the dialog box shown in Figure 3-1. The Help Topics dialog box is similar to the Help found in most other Windows programs. If you know how to use Help in any other Windows program, you already have a head start, but we cover the basics in this section, just in case.

When you first call up the Help Topics dialog box, the Contents tab greets you, including a list of "books" on topics ranging from Getting Started to Troubleshooting.

To display help on one of these subjects, just double-click on the appropriate item or click once on the item and then click on the <u>O</u>pen button. A detailed contents list for the subject appears. For example, Figure 3-2 shows the Contents list that appears when you open the Getting Started book. (Double-click on items with book icons next to them to display another array of choices.)

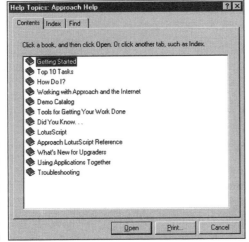

Figure 3-1:
The
Approach 97
Help Topics
dialog box.

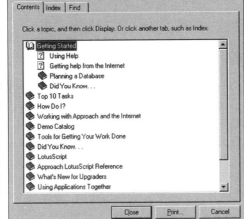

Figure 3-2:
The
Approach
Help dialog
box with the
Getting
Started
book open.

To display a particular Help topic, double-click on the topic title. For example, Figure 3-3 shows the Help topic that appears when you double-click on Getting help from the Internet.

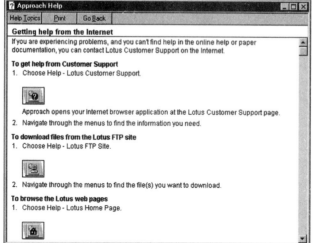

Figure 3-3:
Approach 97
Help for
Getting help
from the
Internet.

After you get yourself this deep into the Help system, you need to heed the following advice to find your way around and get out when you find out what you want to know:

- ✔ Click on the Help Topics button to return directly to the Help Topics dialog box.

- ✔ You can retrace your steps by clicking on the Help window's Go Back button. You can use Go Back over and over again, retracing all your steps if necessary.

- ✔ If you find a Help topic that you consider uncommonly useful, click on the Print button to print a copy of it.

- ✔ If you see a word or phrase underlined with a dotted line, click on the item to pop up a definition or explanation.

- ✔ If you see a word or phrase underlined with a solid line, you can click on the item to zip to a Help page that describes that word or phrase. By following these underlined words, you can bounce your way around from Help page to Help page until you eventually find the help you need or get hopelessly lost. At that point, close Help and start over. It happens to all of us sometimes.

- ✔ Help operates as a separate program in its own window, and you can resize the Help window to your taste. As you resize it, Windows automatically adjusts the text displayed in the window to fit the margins dictated by the new window size. You can press Alt+Tab to switch back and forth between Approach 97 and Help.

- ✔ When you have enough of Help, you can dismiss it by pressing the Esc key or by clicking on Help's Close button in the upper-right corner of the Help window.

Using Stay-on-Top Help Procedures

Approach 97 lets you display step-by-step procedures in Help topics while you work. For example, if you're not sure how to join databases, you can call up the procedure for joining databases and keep it on the screen while you follow the steps. This method is considerably more convenient than pasting little notes all over the computer screen. We call these *stay-on-top Help* procedures.

To call up a stay-on-top Help procedure, follow these steps:

1. **Choose Help⇨Help Topics and then click on the Contents tab.**

   You can find the stay-on-top Help procedures elsewhere in Help, but the easiest way to find them is through the Contents list.

2. **Double-click on the How Do I? item in the Contents list.**

   A list of topics appears.

3. **Double-click on the How Do I? item that relates most closely to your desired topic.**

   The topic's submenu appears.

4. **Double-click on the submenu item that describes the procedure you want to display.**

5. **If another submenu appears, find the specific procedure you want and double-click on it.**

6. **Approach 97 displays the stay-on-top procedure.**

   The procedure appears in its own Help window, which stays on top of the screen while you work. See Figure 3-4.

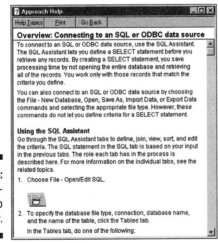

Figure 3-4:
A stay-on-top Help window.

7. **Follow the steps listed in the stay-on-top Help window.**

   The Help window stays visible, even while you work in Approach 97. That way, you can easily follow the steps listed in the procedure.

8. **If the Help window gets in the way, move it by dragging its title bar or minimize it by clicking on the Minimize button in the upper-right of the Help window.**

   Click on the Approach 97 Help button on the Taskbar to restore the Help window.

9. **When you're done using Help, click on the Help window and then press Esc.**

   The Help window quietly disappears.

Here are a few ponderables concerning stay-on-top windows:

✔ Some of the topics have a See related topics button at the bottom. Click on the button and you'll see a small dialog box called Topics Found with a list of related topics. Double-click on any of the topics to get information about that topic. To return to the Help Topics dialog box, click on the Help Topics button.

✔ To display additional details about a procedure, click on the Details icon, if it's visible.

✔ To print the procedure detailed in the stay-on-top window, click on the Print button.

Searching for Elusive Help Topics

If you can't find help for a nasty problem by browsing through the Contents tab, try using the Index tab, or, as a last resort, Find. The Index tab lets you whittle your way through an alphabetical listing of all of the Help topics that Approach 97 offers. With luck, you can quickly find the help you're looking for.

Discovering the Index tab

When you choose Help⇨Help Topics and click on the Index tab, Approach 97 produces the dialog box shown in Figure 3-5. In the Type the first few letters of the word you're looking for field, start typing a keyword, and Approach 97 quickly zips through the list to the words you want to find. If you see a match that looks as if it may be helpful, double-click on the item or click on the item and then click on the Display button.

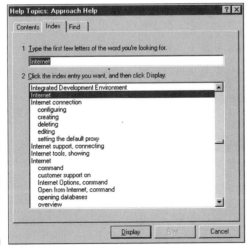

Figure 3-5:
The Index
tab of the
Help Topics
dialog box.

Instead of typing a word, you can just scroll through the entire list of Help topics. This method, although time consuming, is sometimes the only way to find the help you need.

Putting the Find tab to work

If you're really desperate, try the Find tab. It works very much like the Index tab, but with a much broader scope and a couple of other minor differences.

Choose Help➪Help Topics and click on the Find tab to display the dialog box shown in Figure 3-6. (The first time you choose this option, the Find Setup Wizard appears and asks you about your preferences for database size. You can choose Minimize database size (recommended), Maximize database size, or Customize search capabilities. Select Minimize database size (recommended) and then click on the Next button. In the next dialog box that appears, click on the Finish button. Approach 97 mulls over your selection and then presents you with the dialog box shown in Figure 3-6.)

Type the text that you want to search for in the Type the word(s) you want to find field. If you want, click on the Select some matching words text box to narrow the search. A list of all related topics appears in the bottom part of the window. If you see a match in the bottom text box that looks helpful, double-click on the item or click on the item and then click on the Display button.

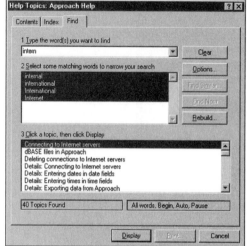

Figure 3-6:
The Find tab
of the Help
Topics
dialog box.

Getting Help from the Internet

If you're connected to the Internet and have a Web browser (like Netscape Navigator or Microsoft Internet Explorer) installed, you can pluck Approach 97 Help directly from the Internet, either from Lotus, the manufacturer of Approach 97, or directly from other Approach 97 users. Internet support should probably be a more-or-less last resort for those seemingly insurmountable problems that you suspect stem from bugs rather than user error. This book, Approach 97 documentation, and the online help system are your best sources for basic questions.

Asking Lotus for help

Lotus provides all kinds of goodies on the Internet to help its loyal users. Unfortunately, sites on the Internet change very quickly, so we can't tell you exactly what you may see at the time you access these help sites; therefore, we only provide the instructions to get you there. You'll have to read the text on the site and select likely looking choices to finish finding the information you need.

Here's the procedure:

1. **Choose Help⇨Lotus Internet Support⇨Lotus Customer Support.**

   Assuming that an Internet browser is installed and your Internet connection works, your Web browser starts up and brings up the Lotus Customer Support page.

You could also select the Lotus <u>H</u>ome Page or the Lotus <u>F</u>TP Site, but if you're looking for help on a specific issue, the Lotus Customer Support option is the most likely place to start. The Lotus <u>H</u>ome Page option offers more general information, including marketing and PR stuff, plus a link to the Customer Support page. Clicking on the the Lotus <u>F</u>TP Site option takes you to a place that is seriously user-friendliness-impaired, so steer clear of it. If you know the information you need is on the FTP site, the Customer Support page can link directly to the information you need. No sweat.

2. **Browse around and look for anything remotely relevant. Keep looking.**

3. **After you find the information you need, choose <u>F</u>ile⇨<u>P</u>rint or click on your browser's Print button to print anything that looks vaguely useful.**

   Print frequently because you never know if you'll be able to find the good stuff again. Murphy's Laws all apply to information on the Internet.

4. **Close your Web browser with a sigh of satisfaction and the information you need on paper in your hand.**

   Enjoy!

Asking others for help

Many unofficial resources exist for help with Approach 97. After you exhaust the possibilities of this book, the online help, and the (horrors!) documentation, you can always check out some of these online resources.

Approach 97 FAQ (Frequently Asked Questions)

To get these frequently asked questions, complete with answers, fire up your Web browser and connect to either of these sites.

✔ `ftp://rtfm.mit.edu/pub/usenet/comp.databases/`
  (Look for the Approach Users Mailing List FAQ.)

✔ `http://www.cis.ohio-state.edu/hypertext/faq/usenet/data-bases/approach-mailing-list-faq/faq.html`

Approach 97 Internet mailing list

A mailing list is an open discussion group in which the discussions take place through e-mail. If you send a question to the group, everyone on the discussion list can read your question and respond to it. Likewise, you get e-mailed copies of all the messages sent by anyone to the list.

To subscribe to the mailing list, send an e-mail message to `maiser@rmgate.pop.indiana.edu` and write `sub approach` in the body of the message. To unsubscribe, send an e-mail message to `maiser@rmgate.pop.indiana.edu` and write `unsub approach` in the body of the message.

To send a message to the list for everyone to see, send an e-mail message to `approach@rmgate.pop.indiana.edu`. Put your question or comment in the body of the message.

If you have questions about the discussion group, send them to the owner, John Brown, at `approach-owner@rmgate.pop.indiana.edu`.

Approach 97 CompuServe forums

If you're a member of CompuServe, you can access specific forums to discuss Approach 97 and ask questions. Try Go Approach 97 to access the Approach 97 Forum, or Go LotusA or Go LotusB to access forums about Lotus products in general.

Chapter 4
Entering and Updating Data

*T*he fun part of working with Approach 97 is designing databases, forms, reports, and other glitzy stuff. The not-so-fun part is doing real work: typing the names of 600 customers and prospects, updating records when people have the gall to move without first considering how much work the address changes cause you, and deleting records for customers you haven't heard from in umpteen years.

The best way to deal with this chapter is to delegate the responsibility of entering and updating data to someone else. Then you can hand this book to the person who is doing data entry and say, "Read Chapter 4! You'll love it!" If you haven't been able to find someone gullible enough to take the work off your hands, all we can say is, "Read Chapter 4! You'll love it!"

Working in Browse Mode

As we pointed out in Chapter 1, Approach 97 has four different modes in which you can work: Browse, Design, Find, and Preview. This chapter explains how to work in Browse mode to add new database records, update existing records, and delete records that you no longer need.

Keep these things about Browse mode in mind:

- ✔ When you open an existing database, you are automatically in Browse mode so that you can begin entering data.

- ✔ When you create a new database, you are automatically in Design mode so that you can lay out the database. You have to switch to Browse mode before you can enter data.

You can switch from any other mode to Browse mode by using any of the following techniques:

- ✔ Press Ctrl+B.

- ✔ Click on the Browse button.

- ✔ Choose View⇨Browse & Data Entry.

- ✔ Choose Browse mode from the View pop-up menu on the status bar.

When you work in Browse mode, you do not need to choose File⇨Save to save changes to the database file. You only need to choose File⇨Save Approach File to save changes that you make to the *design* of the database while you are working in *Design* mode.

Adding a New Record

To add a new record to a database, use one of the following techniques:

- ✔ Press Ctrl+N.

- ✔ Click on the New Record button on the Action bar.

- ✔ Choose Browse⇨New Record.

A new record is added at the end of the database. The new record is blank, except for fields that are given a default value. If you assigned a sort order for the database, the record is relocated to its proper location in the database only after you have entered the record's data.

Duplicating a Database Record

You may often find yourself entering a sequence of records that are similar, with data that varies in only a few of each record's fields. In this case, duplicating an existing record and changing a few of the fields is easier than entering the entire record from scratch.

To duplicate a database record, follow this procedure:

1. **Go to the record you want to duplicate.**

   For information about moving to a specific record, see the section, "Moving Around in a Database," in this chapter.

2. **Click on the Duplicate Record SmartIcon, press Ctrl+Alt+D, or choose Browse➪Duplicate Record.**

   Approach 97 inserts a new record containing data copied from the record that you were viewing.

3. **Make whatever changes you want to make to the duplicate record, if any, and then press Enter.**

Here are some points to ponder when you are duplicating database records:

✔ Database purists who need to get a life throw their arms up in disgust and emit vile sounds when told that Approach 97 enables you to create duplicate database records. According to their religious beliefs (that is, according to Relational Database Theory), duplicate records in a relational database are strictly anathema. They'll see the light after they re-enter hundreds of records that differ only in one or two fields.

✔ If a default value is specified for a field, and that default value was changed in the record from which you're copying, the default value appears in the copy rather than the value in the record that you copied. If the City field is set to default to Santa Clara, and the record you're copying has the City set to Seattle, the duplicate record will show Santa Clara for the City.

✔ To duplicate the value of a single field rather than an entire record, see "Duplicating a field's value" in this chapter.

Deleting a Record

Sometimes you need to delete a record. Suppose, for example, that the putz who owed you $100 finally paid up, and you want to take him off your collection database. To delete a database record, follow this procedure:

1. **Go to the record that you want to delete.**

   For information about moving to a specific record, see "Moving Around in a Database" in this chapter.

2. **To delete the record, click on the Delete SmartIcon, choose Browse➪Delete Record, or press Ctrl+Delete.**

   Approach 97 displays a gentle reminder that what you are about to do could be foolish.

3. Click on the Yes button if you're sure.

The record is deleted. Bye-bye.

Don't you dare forget the following important safety tips:

✔ Double-check that you selected the correct record before you delete it. You cannot recover a deleted record; you can only create a new record and retype the deleted record's information, if you remember it.

✔ You can quickly delete all the records that match a search criteria by first finding all of the records that you want to delete and then choosing Browse➪Delete Found Set. For more information about the Find command, see Chapter 5.

Moving Around in a Database

When you work with data in Browse mode, you work with one record at a time. To get any work done, you need to know how to move forward and backward through the database to work with different records, unless you're content to work with the same record every time you use Approach 97!

Moving forward one record

To move forward to the next record in the database, do any of the following:

✔ Click on the Next Record SmartIcon in the icon bar at the top of the screen.

✔ Click on the Next Record button on the status bar at the bottom of the screen.

✔ If you're viewing a form, press PgDn. (In a worksheet view, PgDn takes you to the last record.)

Moving backward one record

To move backward to the previous record in the database, do any of the following:

✔ Click on the Previous Record SmartIcon in the icon bar at the top of the screen.

✔ Click on the Previous Record button in the status bar at the bottom of the screen.

✔ If you're viewing a form, press PgUp. (In a worksheet view, pressing PgUp takes you to the first database record.)

Moving to the first record

To move directly to the first record in the database, do any of the following:

 ✔ Click on the First Record SmartIcon in the icon bar at the top of the screen.

✔ Press Ctrl+Home.

✔ In a *worksheet* view, press PgUp.

Moving to the last record

To move directly to the last record in the database, do any of the following:

 ✔ Click on the Last Record SmartIcon in the icon bar at the top of the screen.

✔ Press Ctrl+End.

✔ In a *worksheet* view, press PgDn.

Moving to a specific record

To move directly to a specific record in the database, follow this procedure:

1. Click on the record number in the status bar or press Ctrl+W.

The Go to Record dialog box shown in Figure 4-1 appears.

Figure 4-1:
The Go to
Record
dialog box.

2. Type the number of the record that you want to view.

3. Click on the OK button or press Enter.

Entering and Editing Data

To enter data into a form field, all you have to do is move the insertion point to the field and start typing. You need to know several techniques, such as how to move from field to field, how to select text, and so on. Although most of these techniques are similar to the techniques that you use to perform the same functions in other Windows programs, you need to be aware of a few variations.

Moving from field to field

You can move the insertion point from field to field in several ways:

- ✔ Click on the field to which you want to move the insertion point.

- ✔ Press the Tab key to move forward from field to field until the insertion point moves to the field you want.

- ✔ Press Shift+Tab to move backward from field to field until you arrive at the field you want.

  You can change the tabbing order for form fields if you choose. See Chapter 9 for details.

- ✔ If the Preferences are set up properly, you can also press Enter to move forward from field to field or press Shift+Enter to move backward. See Chapter 21 for information about setting the Preferences to work this way.

The normal way to enter values for a database record is to type the value for the first field and then press Tab (or Enter, if the Preferences are set to enable you to do so) to move to the next field. Type the value for the next field and then press Tab or Enter again until you have entered all of the field values.

To skip a field, press Tab twice so the insertion point jumps over that field to the next field in sequence. If the field you want to skip is defined with the Filled In validation option, you cannot use this method. In that case, after the insertion point enters the field, Approach 97 doesn't let it escape until you enter a value for the field.

You also may notice that some fields are given default values. You can change the default values if you want, or you can tab over the field to let the default value stand.

If you cannot select a field by clicking on it or by tabbing to it, the field is probably a calculated field. Approach 97 doesn't let you type anything into calculated fields because Approach 97 automatically computes the value of a calculated field by using a formula.

Moving the insertion point

As in other Windows programs, you can use the arrow keys alone or in combination with other keys to move the insertion point around and to select text. To move the insertion point around, use the keyboard keys listed in Table 4-1.

Table 4-1	Keyboard Tricks for Moving the Insertion Point
Keystroke	*What It Does*
→	Moves the insertion point one character to the right
←	Moves the insertion point one character to the left
↑	Moves the insertion point up one line (memo fields only)
↓	Moves the insertion point down one line (memo fields only)
End	Moves the insertion point to the end of the field value
Home	Moves the insertion point to the first character of the field
Ctrl+→	Moves the insertion point one word to the right
Ctrl+←	Moves the insertion point one word to the left
Tab	Moves the insertion point to the next field on the form
Shift+Tab	Moves the insertion point to the preceding field on the form

You also can move the insertion point to any location by moving the mouse pointer to the new location and clicking on the left mouse button.

To select text so that you can delete it or copy it, hold down the Shift key while you move the insertion point by using the appropriate keys. Or drag the mouse over the text you want to select. Two text-selecting shortcuts require a modest bit of mouse dexterity:

- ✔ To select an entire word, double-click anywhere on the word.
- ✔ To select all the text in a field, hold down Ctrl and click anywhere on the field.

Two commonly used keyboard combinations do unexpected things when you use them in Approach 97:

- ✔ **Ctrl+Delete:** This key combination deletes the current record. In most other Windows programs, Ctrl+Delete deletes the current word. Fortunately, Approach 97 asks for confirmation before it deletes the record.
- ✔ **Ctrl+Backspace:** This key combination doesn't delete the preceding word as it does in most other Windows programs. Actually, it doesn't do anything worthwhile, so don't use it.

Approach 97 always operates in Insert mode, in which characters you type at the keyboard are inserted at the location of the insertion point. In many other Windows programs, the Insert key switches between Insert mode and Overtype mode, in which characters you type at the keyboard replace existing text in the field. Not in Approach 97, however. Tough.

Cutting, copying, and pasting

You can use the standard Windows commands to cut, copy, and paste text from one field to another. When you cut a block of text, the text is removed from the field and placed on the Clipboard, where you can retrieve it later if you want. Copying text stores the text in the Clipboard but doesn't remove it from the field.

To cut text, first mark the block of text that you want to cut by using the keyboard or the mouse. Then conjure up the Cut command by using either of these methods:

- ✔ Click on the Cut SmartIcon.
- ✔ Choose Edit➪Cut.
- ✔ Press Ctrl+X.

The text vanishes from the screen, but don't worry. The text is safely nestled away in the Clipboard until you cut or copy something else on top of it.

To copy text, mark the block and invoke the Copy command by using one of these methods:

- ✔ Click on the Copy SmartIcon.
- ✔ Choose Edit➪Copy.
- ✔ Press Ctrl+C.

The text is copied to the Clipboard, but this time it doesn't vanish from the screen.

To paste text from the Clipboard, move the insertion point to the field where you want the text pasted. Then invoke the Paste command by using one of these techniques:

- ✔ Click on the Paste SmartIcon.
- ✔ Choose Edit➪Paste.
- ✔ Press Ctrl+V.

You can paste text into a different field within the same record, or you can paste text into a different record or even into a different database.

Duplicating a field's value

You can quickly duplicate a field value from another record by moving the insertion point to the field and using one of the following techniques:

✔ Click on the Previous Value SmartIcon.

✔ Press Ctrl+Shift+P.

✔ Choose Browse⟹Insert⟹Previous Value.

The value from the corresponding field in the most recently modified database record is copied into the field. Copying a value is useful when you're entering sequential records that have the same value for certain fields.

Setting a field to the same value throughout the database

Approach 97 provides a simple way to enter the same value into a field in every record in a database or in a set of records that match some criteria you specify. This feature is best used in conjunction with Find, which enables you to select a set of records to be modified based on any criteria you want.

Follow these steps to set a field to the same value for every record in a database:

1. **Use Find to select the records that you want to modify.**

   Skip this step if you want to set the field value for every record in the database. For details on using the Find command, see Chapter 5.

2. **Choose Browse⟹Fill Field.**

   The Fill Field dialog box appears, as shown in Figure 4-2.

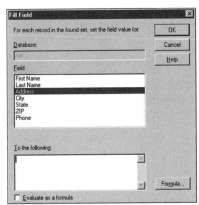

Figure 4-2:
The Fill Field dialog box.

3. **Select the field you want to modify in the top of the dialog box and type the value that you want to enter into every record in the dialog box.**

4. **After you're done, click on the OK button.**

   The fill value is copied into the selected field in every record.

The Fill Field command replaces any values that are currently in the selected field. You are *not* prompted before such replacements are made, so be sure to carefully read the message in the Fill Field dialog box to make sure that you have selected the correct field.

Entering Field Values

Entering a value into a field is as simple as selecting the field and typing the value. Well, almost. You need to be aware of a few details for certain field types.

Text fields

You can type any value that you want into a text field. The only restriction is that you cannot type more characters than you specified as the field length when you defined the field. In other words, if the field length is 30, you cannot type more than 30 characters into the field. If you try, Approach 97 will slap your typing fingers silly with a dialog box telling you that the field is limited to 30 characters.

Note that you can't always judge the maximum length of a field by its size on a form. When you lay out a form, you can make the form field as large or as small as you want. If the form field is not large enough to display the entire text of the field, the text automatically scrolls within the field.

Also, some text fields allow only certain values to be entered into the field. If you're lucky, such fields are set up in the entry form as a drop-down list that includes the allowable values. To select a value, you click on the down-arrow next to the field to reveal the list and then click on the value that you want to use for the field. If such a validated field doesn't use a drop-down list, you must guess, and Approach 97, again, tells you that the information isn't valid. You can repeat until you get it right, or you can call whoever designed the database and complain.

Numeric fields

Approach 97 ignores any non-numeric characters that you type into a numeric field. Thus, if you type $49.95, Approach 97 throws away the dollar sign and treats the number as 49.95.

If a numeric form field has the Use as Data Entry Format option setting, under-lines appear in the field to show how many digits you can enter.

Memo fields

You can type an almost unlimited amount of text into a memo field. If you type more text than will fit in the form field, a scroll bar appears so that you can scroll the text.

Boolean fields

To enter data into a Boolean field, type **Yes**, **Y**, **yes**, **y**, or **1** for a yes value or **No**, **N**, **no**, **n**, or **0** for a no value. If the Boolean field is a check box field, just click on the check box to switch between Yes and No values.

Date fields

To enter a date field, type the month, day, and year using numbers separated by non-numeric characters, such as 05/16/97 or 12/31/96.

To enter the current date in a date field, use one of the following techniques:

　　✔ Click on the Insert Today's Date SmartIcon.

　　✔ Press Ctrl+Shift+D.

　　✔ Choose Browse⇨Insert⇨Today's Date.

If date fields are set up with the Use as Data Entry Format option, separator characters and underlines appear in the fields to indicate how to type the date. In this case, you don't have to type the separator characters yourself; just type the month, day, and year values, and Approach 97 formats the date accordingly.

Time fields

When entering a time value, you can use a 12-hour clock or a 24-hour clock. Type the hour and minutes as numbers separated by colons, as in **11:30** or **7:15**. If you use a 12-hour clock, you must type **PM** to indicate a PM time; otherwise, Approach 97 assumes that you mean AM. If you want to, you can type seconds and even hundredths of seconds. For example, you can type 11:30:45 or 11:30:45.99.

To enter the current time in a time field, use one of the following techniques:

- Click on the Insert Current Time SmartIcon.
- Press Ctrl+Shift+T.
- Choose Browse➪Insert➪Current Time.

As with date fields, you can use the Use as Data Entry Format option when you set up time fields. Separator characters and underlines appear in the fields to indicate how to type the time. Then you just type the hours and minutes (and seconds if indicated), and Approach 97 formats the time accordingly.

PicturePlus fields

PicturePlus fields can hold graphics or embedded OLE objects such as sound files, charts, spreadsheet ranges, or Lord knows what. It's like a miscellaneous junk drawer for your database. For details on entering values into PicturePlus fields, turn to Chapter 12.

Chapter 5
Finders Keepers

· ·

In This Chapter

▶ Working in Find mode

▶ Using the all-powerful Find

▶ Using advanced search criteria

▶ Using multiple find requests

▶ Dealing with duplicates

· ·

*T*he Find feature has many uses. For example, it can help you find that elusive record that you know is in the database somewhere when you're too busy to examine 5,000 records, one at a time, to locate it. Or it can enable you to restrict reports to records that meet certain criteria, such as everyone who owes you more than $20 or all left-handed bald customers. Or it can enable you to get the answers to silly questions, such as, "I wonder how many of my customers live in California?" or, better yet, "I wonder how many of my customers live in California, are left-handed, bald, and owe me more than $20?"

It can't, however, find lost car keys, stuff that falls out of your pockets, or that huge dustball that you swept under the carpet before your mother came to visit — so don't get too carried away with it.

Archimedes (287 – 212 B.C.), the ancient mathematician of Syracuse on whom you can blame much of high school geometry, would have loved Find. You can almost hear him shouting, "Eureka! I found it!" as the Find command completes a painstaking search of a database.

Understanding Find Mode

In Chapter 1, we pointed out that Approach 97 has several modes — four to be exact: Browse, Design, Find, and Preview. In this chapter, we cover the Find mode, which enables you to search the database for specific information — or, okay, to *find* stuff in your database (duh!).

To search a database for certain records, you first need to enter Find mode. Entering Find mode brings up the views (forms, reports, worksheets, and so on) that you have created for the database so that you can type search values into database fields. For example, to find all of your customers who have the pleasure of living in Los Angeles, type **Los Angeles** in the City field and press Enter.

You'll find (pardon) it easiest to use Find from a Form, rather than from a Worksheet, view. If you're really into worksheets, though, it's fine to use that view as well.

You can switch to Find mode by using any of the following techniques:

- ✔ Clicking on the Find button
- ✔ Choosing Find from the View menu on the status bar at the bottom of the screen
- ✔ Choosing Browse➪Find➪Find using Form
- ✔ Pressing Ctrl+F

Each of these methods displays the current database form so that you can type the search values for which you want to look.

After you finish typing the search criteria and click on the OK button, Approach 97 searches the database and selects the records that match the search criteria. Approach 97 then automatically puts you back in Browse mode, but this time it displays only the records found in the search. Approach 97 calls these records the *found set.*

The status bar at the bottom of the screen indicates how many records are included in the found set. For example, if Find selects 75 records from a database that contains a total of 300 records, the status bar displays the message Found 75 of 300. (The only way to tell that you are working with the entire database, rather than with a found set, is that both numbers in the status bar are the same — for example, Found 300 of 300.)

Here are some important facts to keep in mind when you are using Find:

- ✔ The values you type into database fields for a Find are called *search criteria.* Each form you fill in with search criteria is called a *find request.* You combine find criteria to narrow your searches. For example, you could type Los Angeles in the City field and Jones in the Last Name field to find the Los Angeles Joneses.

✔ Although you usually work with forms when you are setting up a find request, you can also work with worksheets or reports. The database view that is active when you choose the Find command is the one that's used to create the find request.

✔ You can search for a specific value in a field by typing the value in the field, or you can use special symbols to search for a range of values. For example, type **>100** in a numeric field to find all records that have a value greater than 100 in the field.

✔ You can search for values in more than one database field at a time. For example, you may want to find all customers who live in Los Angeles *and* owe you more than $100. To perform that task, type **Los Angeles** in the City field and **>100** in the Amount Owed field.

✔ To cancel a Find and redisplay all the records in the database, choose Browse➪Find➪Find All or press Ctrl+A.

Using Find

The simplest way to use Find is to look for records with specific values in one or more database fields. Follow this procedure:

1. Open the database you want to search if it is not already open.

Choose File➪Open, click on the Open SmartIcon, press Ctrl+O, or open the database file from the Welcome to Lotus Approach dialog box.

2. Click on the tab of a Form.

Blank Database will do if you haven't created any other forms.

3. Click on the Find button to switch to Find mode.

Or choose Find from the View pop-up menu in the status bar at the bottom of the screen and choose Browse➪Find➪Find using Form, or press Ctrl+F. Any way you do it, the form is displayed in Find Mode, shown in Figure 5-1.

4. Type the search criteria into each field on which you want to search.

You can use the Tab key to hop from field to field, or you can just click your cursor on each field you want to work with.

In Figure 5-1, we typed Palo Alto into the City field but left all the other fields blank. The Find will select all records with Palo Alto in the City field.

5. Click on the OK button.

Alternatively, press the Enter key or click on the Enter SmartIcon.

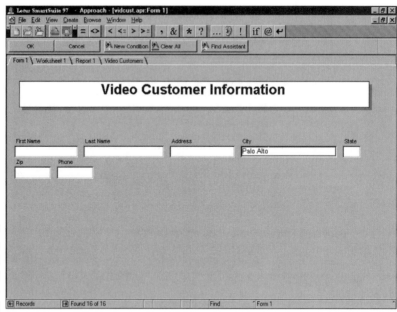

Figure 5-1:
Entering
search
criteria.

6. Marvel at the results.

Approach 97 puts you back into Browse mode, displaying just the records that match the search criteria, as Figure 5-2 shows. Notice how the status bar indicates how many records are in the found set — in this case, by displaying the message `Found 3 of 16`.

Here are a few deep thoughts concerning Find:

- ✔ If the database has a large number of records and you realize midway through a Find that you made a boo-boo, you can halt Approach 97 in the middle of the Find by pressing Esc.

- ✔ To "unfind" records and redisplay all of the records in the database, choose Browse➪Find➪Find All or press Ctrl+A.

- ✔ To delete all records that match a criteria, first use Find to find the records you want to delete. Then choose Browse➪Delete Found Set to delete the duplicate records that Approach 97 finds.

- ✔ Each time you use Find, the previous found set is discarded, and the entire database is searched again. For example, if you first use Find to display all Los Angeles customers and then use Find again to display all customers who owe you more than $100, every customer who owes you more than $100 is displayed, regardless of where they live. If you want to display all Los Angeles customers who owe you more than $100, you must do a single Find by entering the search criteria for both fields at once.

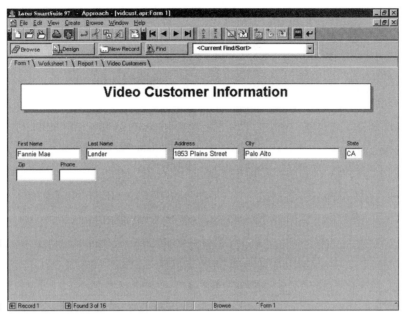

Figure 5-2:
Sample Find
results.

Discovering Fiendishly Advanced Finds

If you could search only for records that contained specific values in specific fields, Find would be useful only in limited situations. For example, you could find customers who live in Los Angeles, but what if you wanted to find customers who live in Los Angeles or in San Francisco? Or what if you wanted to find customers who live in California but not in Los Angeles?

Fortunately, Approach 97 enables you to search for just about every oddball combination of field values by using special *operators* in the search criteria. Table 5-1 summarizes these operators, and the following sections describe them in detail. Note that you can type the operators directly into a field, or you can click on the specific operator SmartIcon to insert it into a field.

Table 5-1	Search Operators	
Operator	*SmartIcon*	*What It Means*
=	=	Equal to
<>	<>	Not equal to
<	<	Less than

(continued)

Table 5-1 *(continued)*

Operator	SmartIcon	What It Means
<=	<=	Less than or equal to
>	>	Greater than
>=	>=	Greater than or equal to
,	,	Or (within a field)
&	&	And (within a field)
*	*	Wild card for zero or more characters
?	?	Wild card for a single character
...	...	Range of values (for example, 500 through 1000)
~		Sounds like
!	!	Case sensitive
if	if	Advanced comparisons for database geeks
@	@	Formula

The > (greater than), < (less than), and other comparative operators

The comparison operators are used mostly with numbers to search for field values that are greater than or less than a particular value. Here are some examples:

- ✔ **>0:** Any value greater than zero
- ✔ **>=0:** Any value greater than or equal to zero

🖝 **<1000:** Any value less than 1,000

🖝 **<=10:** Any value less than or equal to 10

These operators can also be used with dates and times:

🖝 **>=1/1/94:** January 1, 1994, or later

🖝 **<12:00:** Before 12:00 noon

You can also use the equal sign as an operator, but doing so is not usually necessary. For example, to match the number 100, you can type **100** or **=100**. The result is the same, but one requires more typing than the other. We voted for the less-typing option, too.

The = (equal to) and <> (not equal to) operators

To find all records in which a particular field is blank, type = (an equal sign) by itself as the search criteria for the field.

To find all records in which a particular field is not blank, but has a value typed into it, type <> (the less-than and greater-than signs) as the search criteria for the field.

You can also use the <> operator to find all records in which a particular field's value is anything but the value you specify. For example, to find all customers who do not live in Los Angeles, type **<>Los Angeles** as the search criteria for the City field.

The . . . (ellipsis) operator

To search for a range of values in a field, use the . . . (ellipsis) operator. For example, type **0 . . . 100** as a search criteria to search for all values from 0 to 100.

You can use . . . ranges in text fields, too. For example, typing **A . . . M** finds all strings that begin with A through M. This operator is perfect for assigning main dishes or desserts for a potluck — search for the names of dishes that begin with the letters from A through M and give them to the first victims, and then search for dishes that start with N to Z and give those to the next victims.

This operator can also help out with searches for ranges of dates. For example, to find any date in the 1960s, type **1/1/60 . . . 12/31/69**.

The & (and) and , (or) operators

The & (and) and , (or) operators enable you to set up more complex tests. Use the or operator to test for any of several values in a field. For example, to find all customers who live in Los Angeles or in San Francisco, type **Los Angeles, San Francisco** as the search criteria.

The operator & (and) is a bit confusing. You use it when you want to find all records in which a field's value meets two distinct conditions. For example, to find customers who owe you $100 or more, but not more than $1,000, type **>=100 & <=1000.** (However, you can more easily express this condition as a range by typing **100 . . . 1000.**)

You have to be careful how you use &; you can all too easily concoct conditions that can never be met. For example, if you type **Los Angeles & San Francisco,** no records are selected, except for those few customers who have figured out how to make some sort of cross-dimensional leap so that they are able to be in two places at the same time.

One way to use & is in conjunction with wild card characters, which we describe in the next section. For example, suppose that a database contains a text field named Hobbies. To find anyone who enjoys both hiking and fishing, you type ***hiking*&*fishing*** as the search criteria.

The * (wild card) operator

Approach 97 enables you to use *wild cards* when you search text fields. These wild cards stand for unknown characters in the field's value.

You can use two types of wild cards, * (asterisk) and ? (question mark) . The * wild card searches for any combination of characters, including no characters at all. For example:

- ✔ The search John* finds John, Johnson, Johnny, and John Smith.
- ✔ The search *son finds Johnson, Olson, Carlson, and Son.
- ✔ The search *s*on finds Johnson, Olson, Carlson, Son, Johnston, and Stallion.
- ✔ The search *son* finds Johnson, Olson, Carlson, Son, Sonny, and Arsonist.

The question mark (?) stands in for a single character in your search, like these:

- ✔ The search jo?n finds John and Join.
- ✔ The search ??join finds Enjoin or Rejoin.
- ✔ The search ???? finds all four-letter words.

The @ operator

 You can incorporate a formula or function into a search criteria by using the @ operator. This operator is most often used in conjunction with the Today function, which provides the current date. For example:

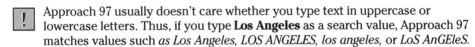

- ✔ @today() finds all date values that match today's date.
- ✔ <@today() finds all date values that precede today's date.
- ✔ >=@today() + 30 finds all date values that are 30 or more days from today's date.

The ! operator

 Approach 97 usually doesn't care whether you type text in uppercase or lowercase letters. Thus, if you type **Los Angeles** as a search value, Approach 97 matches values such *as Los Angeles, LOS ANGELES, los angeles,* or *LoS AnGEleS.*

You can limit your search to specific capitalization by using the ! operator. For example, if you specify **!Los Angeles** as the search value, Approach 97 matches only fields in which both the L and the A are capitalized and all the other letters are lowercase.

The ~ (sounds like) operator

The sounds like operator (~) lets you fudge a bit on the spelling. For example, if you search for *~Jeff,* Approach 97 finds *Jeff, Jeph, Jaf,* and even *Geoff.* Sounds like is great for catching simple misspellings, but it's also good for words that may have several alternative spellings. Pretty clever, isn't it?

The sounds like operator freely substitutes vowels, ignores doubled letters, and accounts for consonants that sometimes sound similar, such as *G* and *J* or *C* and *S.* It is also aware of like-sounding letter combinations such as *ck* and *k* and can properly ignore the silent *e* that frequently shows up at the end of words.

Sounds like doesn't catch every possible phonetic misspelling. I tried it on George Bernard Shaw's famous alternative spelling of the word *fish: ghoti.* (That's *gh* as in *enough, o* as in *women,* and *ti* as in *fictitious.*) It didn't work, so be careful how you spell *fish.*

Find It Again, Sam

One way to search fields for several values is to use the or operator (,) to separate the values in the search criteria. For example, typing **Los Angeles, San Francisco** in the City field finds everyone who lives in Los Angeles or Frisco. But what if you want to find everyone who lives in Los Angeles *or* owes you more than $100? Your first instinct would be to type **Los Angeles** in the City field and **>100** in the Amount Owed field, but that method doesn't work. It finds only those people in Los Angeles who owe you more than $100.

To find everyone who either lives in Los Angeles or owes you more than $100, you must set up two separate find requests: one that specifies Los Angeles in the City field and another that specifies >100 in the Amount Owed field. Then, when Approach 97 searches the database, it selects all records that match either of the find requests.

It's a good thing that Approach 97 designers planned on this need and set it up so that you can do just these types of separate find requests all at once.

Here is the procedure for setting up multiple find requests:

1. **Switch to a form in your database by clicking on the tab.**

   Blank database will do if you haven't set up any other forms.

2. **Call up Find mode by clicking on the Find button.**

   Or choose Browse⇨Find⇨Find using Form, choose Find from the View pop-up menu in the status bar, or press Ctrl+F.

3. **Fill in the search criteria for the first find request.**

   For the example, type **Los Angeles** in the City field.

4. **Click on the New Condition button.**

   You see a blank form into which you can type additional search criteria.

5. **Fill in the search criteria for the second find request.**

   Again using the example, type **>100** in the Amount Owed field.

6. **If you want to create even more find requests, repeat Steps 3 and 4.**

7. **After you have completed all the find requests you can tolerate, click on the OK button to initiate the search.**

   Approach 97 searches the database, selecting all records that match any of the find requests you create.

Here are a few titillating details regarding multiple finds:

- ✔ If you realize that you made a mistake in one of the find requests, you can cycle through the various find requests by clicking on the arrows that appear in the status bar at the bottom of the screen or pressing PgUp or PgDn.

- ✔ You can think of each find request as being connected by one giant or operator. In other words, Approach 97 searches for all records that meet the search criteria on the first find request, or the second find request, or the third find request, and so on.

- ✔ To search for records with one of several values in a single field, type the values in a single find request, separated by commas. The only time you need to use multiple find requests is when the or operation involves two or more fields.

- ✔ Don't press Enter or click on the OK button until you create all of the find requests.

Skip this iffy stuff about if statements

Real database geeks don't mess around with fill-in-the-blanks search criteria. Instead, they grab a handful of potato chips and get straight to work typing if statements. If statements do the same thing as regular search criteria, but they look more like stuff Scotty would type when recalibrating the warp core or inventing transparent aluminum.

An If statement enables you to lay out the search criteria as a conditional expression, such as the following:

```
if(City = 'Los Angeles')
```

This if statement has the same effect as simply typing Los Angeles in the City field. A more useful way to use the if statement is to compare two different fields on the form. For example, if you type the following, the record is included in the found set if the OnHand field is less than the Usage field:

```
if(OnHand < Usage)
```

You can gang conditions up on one another, too:

```
if(OnHand < Usage) And (Usage >
   10)
```

In this case, the record is selected if the OnHand field is less than the Usage field, and the Usage field is greater than 10.

The weird thing about if statements is that you can type them into any field you want; you don't have to type them into the field they test. If we were to use if statements (we don't if we can avoid it, but just in case we did), we would type them into the first available text field on the form.

Another weird thing about if statements is the way that you use quotation marks and apostrophes. Quotation marks are required whenever you use a field name that includes a space or a special character that Approach 97 may otherwise think is a math symbol, such as +, -, /, and so on (for example, "State/province" and "Customer Name"). Apostrophes are used to mark text field values.

Using the Find/Sort Assistant

Approach 97 provides a special Find command to help you set up all kinds of interesting finds. The Find/Sort Assistant does a great deal of the busy work for you on complex or frequently used finds. In particular, you can use it for finding duplicate records, unique records, or the highest or lowest records in a range.

Technically, you can use the Find/Sort Assistant for all types of finds, but that tends to be more work than it's worth. It's like hiring an assistant to file ten pieces of paper each week. In theory, it's a good idea, but by the time you get all the training and stuff out of the way, it would have been easier to just do it yourself.

We present an example of using the Find/Sort Assistant to weed out duplicate records in a database. You can use the same procedure for anything else the Find/Sort Assistant does. You can use it in two ways:

✔ You can search for all records that have duplicate values for certain fields. The found set includes all the duplicate records.

✔ You can search for all records with duplicate values for certain fields but then exclude the first occurrence of each set of duplicates. This option is most useful if you plan on deleting the duplicates; it leaves one copy of each duplicated record intact.

Here is the procedure for finding duplicate records:

1. Switch to a form in your database by clicking on the tab.

Blank database will do if you haven't set up any other forms.

2. Choose <u>B</u>rowse⇨<u>F</u>ind⇨Find As<u>s</u>istant or Ctrl+I.

Or click on the Find Assistant button if you're already in Find mode.

The Find/Sort Assistant dialog box appears, as shown in Figure 5-3.

3. Select the Type of <u>f</u>ind you want to use and click on the <u>N</u>ext button.

- To do a basic find (similar to the examples in this chapter), select the Basic Find option.

- To find all duplicate values, select the Find duplicate records option.

- To find specific records, say, about one particular customer, select the Find distinct or unique records option.

- To find the top or lowest values, such as the top five sales people in your group, select the Find the top or lowest values option.

- To find more sophisticated conditions that require operators and similarly techie stuff, select Find using Query by Box.

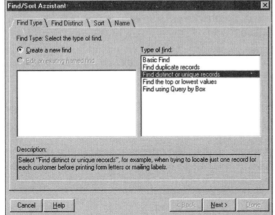

Figure 5-3:
The Find/
Sort
Assistant
dialog box.

4. Click on Next to move to the next tab in the Find/Sort Assistant.

The Basic find takes you to the Condition 1 tab. However, if you choose to find duplicates, you'll be at the Find Duplicates tab, and if you're letting the Find/Sort Assistant help you with other finds, your dialog box looks slightly different. But never fear, the Find/Sort Assistant helps you through the whole process.

5. Select the fields you want Approach 97 to use for comparing records.

To select a field, click on it in the Fields list and then click on the Add button.

6. Repeat Step 5 until you've selected all the fields you want to search on.

7. If you want to sort your found set, click on the Next button to move to the Sort tab.

Select the Field you want to sort on and then click on the Add button. You can select multiple fields if you want.

8. Click on the Done button.

Approach 97 searches the entire database and finds records according to the type of Find you picked in Step 3.

9. You're done!

Some other details about the Find/Sort Assistant that you may find (so to speak) useful:

If you set up a Find that you plan to use repeatedly, you can use the Find/Sort Assistant to name it so that you can call on it at a later date, such as "Yo! Giovanni! Do that find thing again, will you?" All you've got to do is set up the find you want, and then — before you click on the Done button — click on the

Name tab in the Find/Sort Assistant. Check the Named Find/Sort check box and type in a name. Giovanni isn't bad, but something like "Find Top Ten Salespeople from Los Angeles" may be more useful in the long run.

If you're one of those people who has to be doing two things at once (walking and chewing gum, reading and driving, talking on the phone and watching TV), you'll be pleased to learn that you can sort at the same time that you find. Just click on the Sort tab after you set up your Find and specify the fields on which you want to sort.

And with that, you find yourself at the end of your journey through the perils of Find. We hope the road at your feet (leading to the next chapter) finds you well and that you can find the time to go find yourself a snack so you'll be able to find the energy to keep going.

Chapter 6

Putting Your Affairs in Order (Or Sorting Database Records)

··

In This Chapter

▶ Sorting a database the easy way

▶ Sorting a database the hard way

▶ Creating a default sort sequence

··

*O*rdinarily, Approach 97 stores database records in the order you enter them. For some databases, that sequence is the most practical one in which to store records. More often than not, however, another sequence is more helpful. For example, you may want to list customers by last name, inventory parts by item description, or employees by Social Security number.

Never fear, Sort is here! By using the Sort command, you can change the order in which database records are displayed. This change affects the order in which records are retrieved when you are using a form, viewing a worksheet, printing a report, or using any other database view.

The Easy Way to Sort a Database

You can sort the records in a database the easy way or the hard way. This section focuses on the easy way, named so because all you have to do is pick the field you want to sort by and click on a button. The downside is that it limits you to sorting records by only one field.

Here's how to sort the easy way:

1. **Open the database you want to sort.**

    Choose File➪Open, click on the Open SmartIcon, press Ctrl+O, or select Open an Existing File from the Welcome to Lotus Approach dialog box.

2. **Click on the field you are going to use to sort the database.**

3. **Select the type of sort you wish to perform and click on the button that represents it.**

For example, to sort customer records into alphabetical last name sequence, click on the Last Name field and then click on the Ascending Sort SmartIcon.

You can also choose Browse⇨Sort⇨Ascending. Either way, the database is sorted into *ascending* sequence according to the values in the field (in other words, A, B, C, D, and so on).

If you want to sort records into *descending* sequence (Z, Y, X, and so on), click on the Sort field in descending order SmartIcon or choose Browse⇨Sort⇨Descending.

4. **Wait while Approach 97 sorts the database.**

The sort may take only a few seconds unless the database is really huge, such as a list of all the observable stars in the galaxy or, even worse, a list of all the line items in the federal budget.

5. **Gasp in amazement when Approach 97 displays the record in the new, hopefully more useful, sequence.**

An utterance such as "Isn't that amazing?" is appropriate here. However, your irrational sense of euphoria over what is really nothing more than a mundane computer task soon passes. Computers have been good at sorting since about 1950, so it's really nothing to get excited about.

Here are a few sorting pointers, in no particular order:

✔ If you find yourself growing accustomed to those cool Approach 97 Assistants and wonder why in the world the program doesn't provide an Assistant to help with sorting as well, never fear! Get thee to Chapter 5, read up on the Find/Sort Assistant, and pay close attention to that Sort tab. If you don't want to find — you just want sorted records — use a generic find for a required field that is not blank and then proceed full speed ahead.

✔ If you sort a database by clicking on one of the Sort SmartIcons, and then you select a different field and click on a Sort SmartIcon again, Approach 97 re-sorts the file according to the new sort field. The only way to create a two-level sort with primary and secondary sort fields is to use the Sort command described in the next section.

✔ If you sort the database into ascending sequence, numerals come before the letters of the alphabet. If you sort it into descending sequence, numerals come after letters.

✔ If you choose to sort by a calculated field, the resulting order is based on the results of the formula calculation.

✔ If the database is under the influence of a Find command, only the records in the found set are sorted.

Sorting terminology you can't avoid

Sorting is fairly straightforward as far as computer chores go, but a few special words have been coined by computer propellerheads in an effort to make sorting sound more complicated than it really is. Here are the more important terms demystified.

Sort field: These database fields are used to sort the database records. If you sort a database into alphabetical order by using a field called Last Name, Last Name is the sort field.

Primary sort field: This main field is used to sort the database records, just like a generic sort field. Most sorts use only a primary sort field. However, if more than one record in the database is likely to have the same value in the primary sort field, you can specify additional sort fields, called *secondary sort fields,* to further refine the sort.

Secondary sort field: This additional sort field is used to sort records with the same value for the primary sort field. For example, if you use Last Name as the field by which to sort a database, you probably want to specify First Name as the

secondary sort field. Then any records that have the same last name are further sorted by first name.

Ascending sequence: This sequence starts at the beginning and moves to the end — 0123456789ABCDEFGHIJKLMNOPQRSTUVWXYZ, not counting special characters such as #$%^& and *).

Descending sequence: This sequence starts at the end and moves to the beginning — ZYXWVUTSRQPONMLKJIHGFEDCBA 9876543210, not counting special characters such as *&^%$ and #.

Default sequence: Records are stored in the database and generally displayed in this sequence. This sequence is usually the order in which you added records to the database, but you can change the default sort sequence for a database by choosing File⇨User Setup⇨Approach Preferences and clicking on the Order tab. See "The Way to Create a Default Sort Sequence" in this chapter.

The Hard Way to Sort a Database

Sorting databases the hard way — by using the Sort command — enables you to draw several sort fields into the fray instead of sorting by just one field. If you want to sort by more than one field, you have no alternative but to use the somewhat intimidating Sort command.

Follow this step-by-step procedure:

1. Choose Browse⇨Sort⇨Define.

Or use the handy keyboard shortcut Ctrl+T. Either way, the Sort dialog box appears, as shown in Figure 6-1.

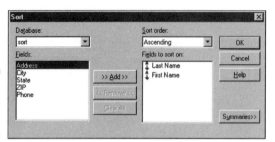

Figure 6-1:
The Sort
dialog box.

2. **Scroll through the Fields list until you find the field you want to use as the primary sort field, click on the desired field, and then click on the Add button.**

   The field name is copied to the Fields to sort on list.

3. **Select Ascending or Descending from the Sort order box to specify whether you want the records sorted on the field in ascending or descending sequence.**

4. **Repeat Steps 2 and 3 for any additional sort fields you want to use.**

   In Figure 6-1, we selected two sort fields: Last Name and First Name.

5. **Click on the OK button to sort the database.**

6. **Wait.**

   You probably won't have to wait more than a few seconds unless the database contains a huge amount of data, such as a detailed listing of your favorite politician's broken campaign promises.

7. **Behold your data, sorted!**

Here are a few consoling thoughts concerning the Sort dialog box:

✔ If you make a mistake and want to remove a field from the Fields to sort on list, click on the field you want to remove in the Fields to sort on list and then click on the Remove button.

✔ To remove all sort fields from the Fields to sort on list, select a field in the list and click on the Clear All button.

✔ Wouldn't it be great if you could attach a sort sequence to a form, report, or other view? You can, but only by using a macro. See Chapter 19 if you're brave and have nothing better to do.

✔ Don't include sort fields that you don't really need. For example, we could have included City as a third sort field in Figure 6-1. That way, any friends who have the same first and last name would be further sorted by City. But is it really necessary to make sure that Joseph McGillicudy in Detroit comes before Joseph McGillicudy in Sioux City? Really?

The Way to Create a Default Sort Sequence

Approach 97 usually keeps records sorted in the order in which you enter them. That is, whenever you add a record to a database, that record is stored at the end of the database. If you find that you're frequently sorting the database into some other sequence, consider changing the default sort sequence for the field. Here's the procedure:

1. **Open the database you want to sort.**

   Choose File⇨Open, click on the Open SmartIcon, press Ctrl+O, or select Open an Existing File from the Welcome to Lotus Approach dialog box.

2. **Choose File⇨User Setup⇨Approach Preferences.**

   The Preferences dialog box appears, as shown in Figure 6-2.

Figure 6-2:
Changing
the default
sort order
for the
database.

3. **Click on the Order tab if the sort order options are not shown.**

4. **Scroll through the Fields list until you find the field that you want to use as the primary sort field, click on it, and then click on the Add button.**

   The field name is copied to the Fields to sort on list.

5. **Select Ascending or Descending from the Sort order box to specify whether the records should be sorted on the field in ascending or descending sequence.**

6. **Repeat Steps 4 and 5 for any additional sort fields that you want to use.**

7. **Click on the OK button.**

   You're done!

The Order options in the Preferences dialog box are similar to the Sort dialog box options, so you won't have any trouble using one if you know how to use the other.

Chapter 7

Checking Your Speling

. . . .

In This Chapter

▶ Checking your spelling

▶ Editing the user dictionary

▶ Changing spelling options

. . . .

We're both lousy spellers. Many days we can't even spell well enough to look up the words in the dictionary. As a matter of fact, we should probably consider giving our spell checkers co-author credit on our books — they certainly do a lot of the work.

Once was the day that only word processors had spell checkers. Now, just about every program imaginable has a spell checker. Not wanting to be left out, Lotus vested Approach 97 with an excellent spell checker. The same spell checker, in fact, is used by other Lotus programs such as WordPro and 1-2-3.

Checking Your Spelling

Mrs. Thistlecorn from the third grade didn't have anything on the Approach 97 spell checker. It works its way through your database, looking up every word in its massive list of correctly spelled words and bringing any misspelled words to your attention. It performs this task without giggling or snickering. It gives you the opportunity, in fact, to tell it that you are right and it is wrong and that it should learn how to spell words the way you do. That's fun.

Approach 97 lets you check the spelling in a single field of a single database record, all fields in the current record, all records in the database or in a found set, or the same field in every database record.

The following steps detail the procedure for checking spelling in an Approach 97 database:

1. **Open a database to spell check.**

   Choose File➪Open, click on the Open SmartIcon, or select Open an Existing File from the Welcome to Lotus Approach dialog box.

   You can spell check from any view in Approach 97 — a form, worksheet, report, or other view.

2. **Select the field or record you wish to spell check.**

   If you want to check the spelling in only one record, go to that record.

   If you plan to spell check an entire database, you can start in any record.

   If you want to check the spelling in only one field, click on that field to select it.

   To spell check all of the fields in the view, make sure that no field is selected. Click anywhere on the view's background to unselect any fields.

   If you want to spell check a range of text in a text or memo, drag the mouse over the text to highlight it.

3. **Fire up the spell checker.**

   Click on the Check Spelling SmartIcon, choose Edit➪Check Spelling, or press Ctrl+F2. Whichever way you choose, the Spell Check dialog box appears, as shown in Figure 7-1.

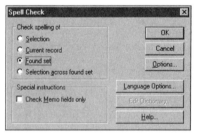

Figure 7-1:
The Spell
Check
dialog box.

4. **Tell spell check what data you want it to check.**

   Click on one of these four radio buttons in the Spell Check dialog box to clue in Approach 97:

   Selection: Spell checks a single field or a range of text that is highlighted. If nothing's selected, this button is grayed out and unavailable.

   Current record: Spell checks all fields in the current record.

   Found set: Spell checks all fields in all records in the current found set. If you haven't used the Find command, Found set checks all records in the database.

Selection across found set: Spell checks a single field in all records in the current found set or in the entire database if you haven't used the Find command.

5. Click on the OK button.

6. Tap your fingers.

Approach 97 is searching your database for misspelled words. Be patient.

7. Don't be startled if Approach 97 finds a spelling error.

If Approach 97 finds a spelling error, it displays the dialog box shown in Figure 7-2 to show you misspelled words along with suggested alternatives.

Figure 7-2:
Oops!
Approach 97
lets you
know about
your
spelling
errors.

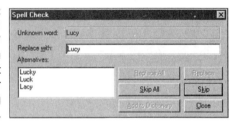

8. Choose the correct spelling or laugh in Approach's face.

If you agree that the word is misspelled, scan the list of alternatives that Approach 97 offers and click on the one you like. Then click on the Replace button. If you like the way you spelled the word in the first place (maybe it's an unusual word that isn't in the Approach 97 dictionary, or maybe you like to spell the way that Chaucer did), click on the Skip button. Enjoy knowing that you really *do* know more than the computer. . . .

9. Repeat Steps 7 and 8 until Approach 97 gives up.

When you see the dialog box shown in Figure 7-3, you know that you've won.

10. Click on the OK button to thank Approach 97 for checking your spelling.

You are now free to go about your business.

The remainder of this section presents some random thoughts to ponder as you spell check a database.

✔ The Approach 97 dictionary is surprisingly complete when it comes to names. It doesn't find everything, such as Lucy in Figure 7-2, but it does find common names such as Richard, Janet, Cindy, and Brian.

Figure 7-3:
Done!

▶ If Approach 97 can't come up with a suggestion or if none of its alternatives is correct, you can type your own correction in the Replace with field and click on the Replace button. If the word you type isn't in the dictionary, Approach 97 flags that word too as an error. Click on the Skip button again to tell Approach you really mean it.

▶ If you want Approach 97 to ignore all occurrences of a particular misspelling, click on the Skip All button. Likewise, if you want Approach 97 to correct all occurrences of a particular misspelling, click on the Replace All button.

▶ If you become bored with having Approach 97 always complain about a word that's not in its dictionary, click on the Add to Dictionary button to add the word to the user dictionary. If you can't sleep at night until you know more about the user dictionary, read the following section, "Using the User Dictionary."

Using the User Dictionary

The Approach 97 spell checker uses two spelling dictionaries: a *standard dictionary,* which contains untold thousands of words all reviewed for correctness by George Bernard Shaw himself (just kidding!), and a *user dictionary,* which contains words you add to the Approach 97 dictionary by clicking on the Add to Dictionary button when the spell checker finds a spelling "error."

You can edit the user dictionary directly by calling up the spell checker and clicking on the Edit Dictionary button. Doing so brings up the Edit Dictionary dialog box that is shown in Figure 7-4.

To add a new word to the dictionary, type the word in the New word field and click on the Add button. Words are automatically added in alphabetical order.

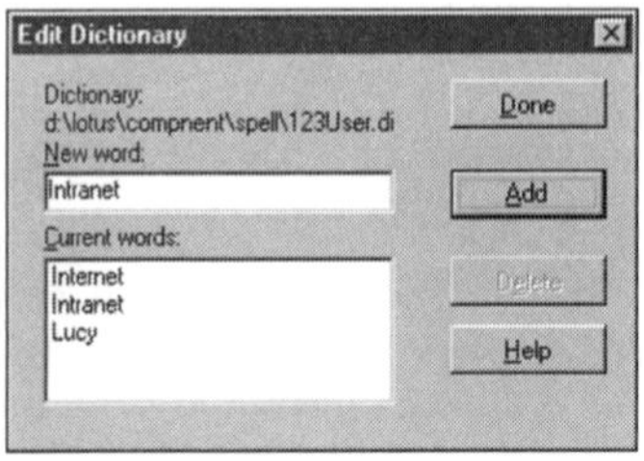

Figure 7-4:
The Edit
Dictionary
dialog box.

To delete a word from the user dictionary, scroll through the list of words in the Current words list until you find the word. Then select the word and click on the Delete button.

Here are a couple of things to note when you are tinkering with the user dictionary:

✔ You usually use the user dictionary for proper nouns and specialized jargon that aren't in the main dictionary. When you first begin to use the spell checker, you can expect to spend a bit of time adding entries to the user dictionary. This task requires less time, however, as the user dictionary becomes saturated with the oddball words you use most often.

✔ Approach 97 shares the user dictionary with other Lotus applications. Thus, words that you add in Word Pro or 1-2-3 are included when you spell check Approach 97 databases.

Setting the Spelling Options

If you call up the spell checker and click on the Options button, the Speller Options dialog box shown in Figure 7-5 appears. This dialog box enables you to control four speller options:

Figure 7-5:
The Speller
Options
dialog box.

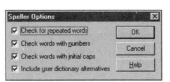

✔ **Check for repeated words:** Tells Approach 97 to to check for for repeated words in your your database. Make sure to enable this option.

✔ **Check words with numbers:** Tells Approach 97 to check words that include numerals, such as T1000. If the databases include values that often mix letters and numerals (for example, B10 or I24 — Bingo!), you may want to disable this option.

✔ **Check words with initial caps:** Tells Approach 97 to check words that begin with capital letters. If you deactivate this option, Approach 97 skips most proper nouns, so you won't have to worry about adding them to a user dictionary.

✔ **Include user dictionary alternatives:** Tells Approach 97 to use the user dictionary as well as the main dictionary when it suggests words as alternatives to a misspelled word.

To change the speller options, call up the spell checker, click on the Options button, check the options you want to use, and click on the OK button.

Changing the Language Options

The Approach 97 default spell-check language depends on the country in which you purchase the program. The default for the United States is American English. However, if your database is full of correctly spelled words in another language, you're not locked into American English. If you call up the spell checker and click on the Language Options button, the Language Options dialog box shown in Figure 7-6 appears. This dialog box lets you set the preferred language dictionary (from the ones installed when you installed Approach 97). For example, if many of the words in your database favour British spellings, in your defence, you can select the British dictionary from the Language drop-down list and then click on the OK button. Dismiss the Spell Check dialog box by clicking on the Close (X) button in the top-right corner of the dialog box.

Figure 7-6:
The
Language
Options
dialog box.

Chapter 8
Joining Databases

• •

• •

*M*etaphor alert! The following paragraphs contain a sincere yet futile attempt on our part to draw an analogy between the dry and lifeless database concept of *joins* and the real-life concept of human relationships. We computer book authors often lie awake at night, pondering the eternal significance of our writing and feeling guilty about the fact that, while we spend our lives hammering out meaningless computer books and actually make a decent living at it, our old college buddies who are actually far better writers are happy to sell their beautifully crafted short stories to obscure literary journals for $100. Well, we don't feel *too* guilty.

Relationships add spice to database life. Without relationships, databases would be empty and unsatisfied, without substance or meaning. For just as no man is an island, no database is an island; all datakind is linked in an ever-expanding web of relationships, a vast computerized tapestry of databases joined to databases joined to databases in the never-ending circle of data.

And so it came to pass that the customer database knew the sales database, and the sales database knew the products database, and thus did they beget more databases, all related, each after its kind. And they all lived happily ever after — or something like that. That's the literature quotient for this book.

This chapter is a gentle introduction to *joins,* the amazing Approach 97 feature that enables you to connect one database to another. If you manage to stay awake through this entire chapter, you'll discover that joins are one of the most useful features in Approach 97, useful enough that they are worth the mental and emotional struggle necessary to figure out how they work.

Understanding Joins

Suppose that you own a small video rental store and you decide to use Approach 97 to computerize your business. You immediately create a database of all your videotapes because the excitement of your new software overpowered the attraction of the living room recliner. The records in the Videos database contain information about each of the videotapes, as well as information about the customers who rent them:

- ✔ Video number (an otherwise meaningless number assigned to each tape so that you can keep track of it)
- ✔ Title
- ✔ Status (in or out of stock)
- ✔ Due date
- ✔ Customer ID number (usually the customer's phone number)
- ✔ Customer's last and first names
- ✔ Customer's street address, city, state, and zip code
- ✔ Customer's credit card number (in case the customer skips town)

Before long, you realize that every time a customer rents a videotape, you must type in the customer's name, address, and credit card number. To make matters worse, if the customer rents all available *Star Trek* movies on the same day, you must type this information numerous times. (Odds are that a customer who wants all available *Star Trek* movies will immediately point out how illogical such a database design is.)

Being the wise database user that you are, you divide the video database into two smaller databases, one for videotapes and the other for customers. The Videos database includes the following information:

- ✔ Video number (an otherwise meaningless number assigned to each tape so that you can keep track of it)
- ✔ Title
- ✔ Status (in or out of stock)
- ✔ Due date
- ✔ Customer ID number

The Vidcust database includes:

- ✔ Customer ID number
- ✔ Customer's last and first names

✔ Customer's street address, city, state, and zip code

✔ Customer's credit card number (in case the customer skips town)

Now, whenever a customer rents a videotape, all you have to do is call up the Video record for the tape and type in the customer ID number and due date. You have to type in the customer's name, address, and credit card information only one time, in the Vidcust database. Plus, your database design no longer wastes disk space by needlessly duplicating this information.

That's all well and good, but what a bother to have to look up information in both databases constantly. Wouldn't it be great if you could combine these two databases onto the same form so that they appear to be a single database? We thought you'd never ask. That capability is exactly what joins accomplish.

Join types

Just as there are different types of relationships in real life — for example, husbands and wives, parents and children, aunts and uncles, nieces and nephews, and, of course, in-laws — there are different types of database relationships that you can create with joins — four to be exact. These four types of relationships are illustrated in Figure 8-1.

One-to-one relationships: In a one-to-one relationship, each record in one database is related to one and only one record in another database. Think of each record in a database as having a monogamous relationship with another record. One-to-one joins aren't used too often because you may as well combine the two databases into a single database.

Note that one-to-one relationships are useful if the databases weren't planned very well from the start. For example, perhaps the credit department sets up a customer database to track each customer's credit history, and the marketing department sets up a customer database to track each customer's sales history. A one-to-one join enables you to combine these databases as if they were a single database, which they probably should have been in the first place.

One-to-many relationships: In a one-to-many relationship, each record in one database can be related to several records in another database. This sounds illegal and, well — er — unethical, we know, but it's actually very legal and also very useful.

The relationship of the Vidcust database to the Videos database is an example: Each customer can have more than one videotape rented out. The following are other examples of one-to-many relationships:

✔ A customer database and an invoice database: Each customer can have more than one invoice.

One-to-one relationship

One-to-many relationship

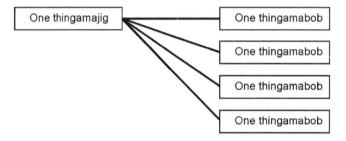

Many-to-one relationship

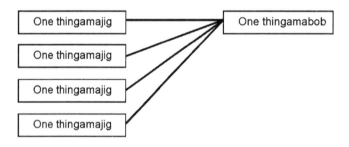

Many-to-many relationship

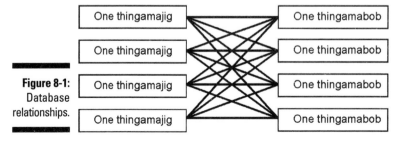

Figure 8-1:
Database
relationships.

✔ An invoice database and a line item (entry on an invoice) database: Each invoice can have more than one line item.

✔ A class database and a student database: Each class can have more than one student.

✔ An instructor database and a class database: Each instructor can have more than one class.

✔ A team database and a player database: Each team can have more than one player.

✔ A department database and an employee database: Each department can have more than one employee.

Notice that in a one-to-many relationship, *many* can mean zero, one, or more than one. Thus, a customer may not have any invoices. Likewise, a student may not have any classes, if he or she can figure out a way to make that happen. (Hint: Play football at certain state universities.)

Many-to-one relationships: A many-to-one relationship is the opposite of a one-to-many relationship. It occurs when more than one record in a database can be related to a particular record in another database. For example, more than one invoice record can be related to the same customer record, and more than one employee record relates to the same department record.

Note that any two databases joined in a one-to-many relationship can also be joined in the opposite many-to-one relationship. For example, if you join customers to invoices in a one-to-many relationship, you can also join invoices to customers in a many-to-one relationship.

Many-to-many relationships: A many-to-many relationship exists if records in one database can be related to many records in another database, and vice versa. For example, consider a suppliers and parts database in which each supplier can supply many different parts, and each part can be obtained from several different suppliers. The relationship between the parts database and the suppliers database is many-to-many.

Unfortunately, Approach 97 cannot directly support this type of many-to-many relationship. To implement this kind of relationship, you need to create a third database that contains one record for each part/supplier combination. The Parts/Suppliers database has a one-to-many relationship with the Parts database and the Suppliers database (see Figure 8-2).

In Figure 8-2, a Parts/Suppliers database links the Parts and Suppliers databases in a many-to-many relationship. You can use this database to determine which suppliers provide Framis Valves (Western Supply and Metalworks) and which parts are supplied by Infinity Supplies (Transtators and Infindibulators).

Figure 8-2:
Many-to-
many
relationships
require an
intermediate
database.

Parts	
Part	**Description**
1000	Framis valve
1001	Transtator
1002	Infindibulator

Parts/Suppliers	
Part	**Supplier**
1000	100
1000	101
1001	100
1001	101
1001	102
1002	102

Suppliers	
Supplier	**Name**
100	Western Supply
101	Metalworks
102	Infinity Supplies

Join fields

Creating a join establishes a relationship between two databases. This relationship is based on a *join field,* which is simply a field that the two databases have in common. In the video store example, the join field is Customer ID Number, which appears in both the Videos database and the Vidcust database. Whenever you call up a videotape record in the Videos database, Approach 97 automatically looks up the correct Vidcust customer record by using the join field as a search key.

Here are several things to be aware of concerning join fields:

✔ The join field must have unique values in at least one of the databases. The easiest way to ensure that the values are unique is to set up the join field as a serial number in one of the databases. Or the field can be some other unique value that identifies records. For example, video stores routinely use phone numbers to uniquely identify each customer. (Of course, you need to make sure that the number you use is unique for each record. For example, what if two members of the same household want to open separate accounts?)

✔ The join fields do not need to have the same name in both databases. For example, the field may be named Customer ID Number in the Videos database and Cust Phone in the Vidcust database. Regardless of whether the fields have the same name, however, they should be of the same data type, and they should represent the same thing. You'll make your life easier if you use the same name.

✔ If you want to join databases, but the databases don't have a field in common, just create a field with which to join them. Make the field a serial number in one of the databases to ensure uniqueness.

✔ In official Relational Database jargon, the join field is called a *key.* In the database in which the key is unique, the join field is called the *primary key.* In the other database (in which the key does not have to be unique), the join field is simply called a *foreign key.*

Joining Databases

The procedure for joining databases is kind of like a wedding ceremony. You have to do the whole formal procedure. No shortcuts are possible, so don't even think about eloping. Here is the liturgy:

1. **Create the two databases that you want to join, paying special attention to the join field in both databases.**

   This step is the courtship phase of the relationship, in which the two databases get to know one another's likes and dislikes in an effort to find out whether they are compatible. If you cannot find common ground for a join (that is, a join field that is unique in at least one of the databases), the best thing to do is call the whole thing off right now, before anyone gets hurt. By the way, no moving-in-together phase exists in the world of database joins.

2. **Open the Approach file in which you want to record the join.**

   This step is kind of like picking a church or other location for the wedding. The join doesn't actually reside in either of the database files but in the Approach file, along with the forms, reports, and other views that you use to access database data. Open the Approach file for the database that you want to be the *main* database for the view. For example, if you want to view customers' records to see which videos are currently rented to a particular customer, open the Approach file for the Vidcust database. On the other hand, if you want to look up a specific videotape to see who has checked it out, open the Approach file for the Videos database.

3. **Choose Create⇨Join.**

   The Join dialog box appears, as shown in Figure 8-3. Initially, only one database is shown in the Join dialog box, similar to the way the groom nervously stands alone at the front of the church, waiting for the processional to begin.

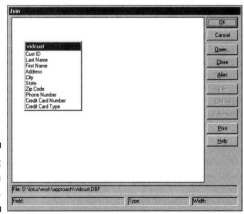

Figure 8-3:
The Join
dialog box.

 4. **Click on the Open button, select the name of the database you want to join to the main database, and click on the Open button.**

 After you click on the Open button, you see an Open dialog box identical to the one that appears when you choose File⇨Open. Select the database you want to include in the join and click on the Open button to open it. After you perform this action, the name of the second database is added to the Join dialog box. It is customary to stand as the bride-to-be enters the dialog box.

 5. **Click on the field you want to use as the join field in both databases and then click on the Join button.**

 Approach 97 draws a line to indicate that the databases are joined on the field you selected, as shown in Figure 8-4. You may want to say something such as, "Do you, Cust ID in the Vidcust database, take Cust ID in the Videos database to be your lawfully wedded foreign key? If so, click on the OK button."

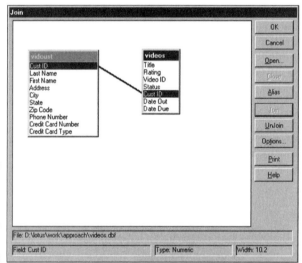

Figure 8-4:
Approach 97
draws lines
to show
joins.

 6. **Click on the OK button.**

 The wedding is complete, so the Join dialog box vanishes, off on the honeymoon. The process didn't take long and wasn't even painful, was it?

Here are a few additional thoughts to consider when you join databases:

 ✔ Instead of selecting the join field in both databases and clicking on the Join button, you can use the more mousy technique of pointing at the join field in either one of the databases, pressing the left mouse button, and dragging the mouse to the join field in the other database. After you release the mouse button, Approach 97 joins the databases on this field with a line.

✔ You can create joins that involve three or more databases by opening the additional databases, selecting the join fields, and clicking on the Join button or dragging the mouse as described in the preceding bullet. See the section "Considering Database Polygamy" in this chapter.

✔ Unfortunately, the results of a successful join are not immediately visible. Database forms and reports are not automatically updated to reflect the joined database. Instead, you need to modify forms and reports to show fields from the joined databases. For more information about making those changes, turn to Chapters 9 and 10.

✔ To cancel a join, choose Create⇨Join, select the line that marks the join, and click on the Unjoin command. (Having lawyers draw up papers first is best.)

✔ Don't forget that information about database joins is stored in the Approach files, not in the database files themselves. If you create a join between two databases and then close the Approach file and open a different Approach file (any file ending with the extension .APR) that includes one of the databases, the join is not shown.

✔ Every database opened in the Join dialog box has to be joined to another database. If you open a database and then decide not to join it, select it by clicking on one of its fields and then close it by clicking on the Close button. This action is the database equivalent of calling off the wedding.

✔ You can print a graphic representation of a join by calling up the Join dialog box and clicking on the Print button. The printed output resembles the join diagram shown in Figure 8-4.

Considering Database Polygamy

Unlike the real world (at least in our home state), Approach 97 permits joins between more than two databases. You can join three, four, or however many databases you want as long as all the databases involved are consenting adults.

Figure 8-5 shows an example of a four-way join. In this example, the Customer database (Cust) is joined to the Invoice database (Invoice) by using Cust ID as the join field. As a result, each customer can have one or more invoices. The Invoice database is in turn joined to the Line Item database (lineitem) so that each invoice can have one or more line items. The line item database is in turn joined to the Item inventory database (items) in a many-to-one relationship; that is, each item can appear in more than one line item.

The joins shown in Figure 8-5 enable you to print invoices that show the customer's name and address, which are obtained from the Cust database, line item details, which are obtained from the Line Item database, and an item description for each line item, which is obtained from the Item database.

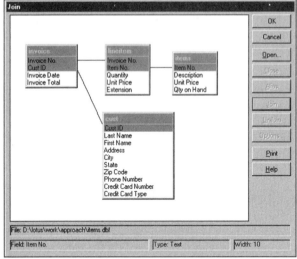

Figure 8-5:
Approach 97
permits
multiple
joins
(polygamy, if
you will).

Certain nonsensical types of polygamous joins are not allowed. In particular, you cannot create circular joins, in which database A is joined to database B, which is joined back to database A. Odds are you wouldn't want to attempt such a thing, but if you do, Approach 97 will call a foul. (Well, Approach 97 does provide a way to do circular joins. The technique is called an *Alias,* but it's an advanced process that only licensed database wonks should attempt.)

Discovering Join Options

Approach 97 enables you to set several strange but useful options for database joins. These options are designed to help prevent weird situations from occurring within joined databases. For example, what happens if you delete the record for a customer who has invoices . . . should the customer's invoice records be deleted as well?

In the language of professional database gurus, such to-delete-or-not-to-delete-associated-records issues are referred to as *referential integrity.* Even if you don't understand what referential integrity is, you're bound to impress your friends by telling them that you've "taken every precaution to ensure referential integrity" in your database system.

To set join options, follow this procedure:

1. **In the Join dialog box, select the join whose options you want to set by clicking on the line that marks the join.**

   You can set options independently for each join.

2. **Click on the Options button.**

   The Relational Options dialog box appears, as shown in Figure 8-6. Notice how this dialog box names the databases that are involved. Aren't computers amazing?

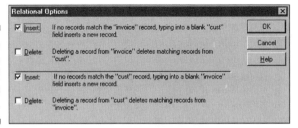

Figure 8-6:
The
Relational
Options
dialog box.

3. **Check the options you want Approach 97 to enforce and then click on the OK button.**

   You're done!

The Relational options enable you to tell Approach 97 what to do when it inserts and deletes records on both sides of the join. If you check either of the Insert options, Approach 97 automatically creates records in the joined databases when you type a value in the join field. For example, if you type a customer number in the Cust ID field of the Invoice database, Approach 97 automatically creates a new customer record, if necessary.

The Delete options tell Approach 97 whether to automatically delete related records when you delete joined records. For example, if you delete a customer record, should the program delete corresponding invoice records? Or, if you delete an invoice record, should Approach 97 delete corresponding customer records? (We would say no.)

✔ The default settings for these options are to enable both Insert options and disable both Delete options (refer to Figure 8-6). Usually, leaving the Insert options on is best. As for the Delete options, you should think carefully before enabling either of them. In the join shown back in Figure 8-6, enabling the second Delete option probably makes sense. After all, if you delete a customer record, you should probably delete the customer's invoices as well. But deleting a customer record when you delete an invoice record makes no sense — what would happen if the customer had other outstanding invoices?

✔ If you disable the Insert options, you may want to set the validation options of the join fields so that the user cannot enter incorrect data. For example, if an Invoice database is joined to a Customer database by using the Cust ID fields in both databases, set the validation options of the Invoice database's Cust ID field so that it will only accept values that exist in the Cust ID field of the Customer database. (In Propellerhead Database Lingo, you're *ensuring the validity of a foreign key*.)

To set this option, choose Create➪Field Definition. Select the database from the Database drop-down list and then select whatever field you used for the join field from the Field Name list. Click on the Options button to reveal the field options and then click on the Validation tab. Finally, check the In field check box and select the field you used for the join from the joined database in the field list that's next to the In field check box. Catch all that? Click on the OK button, and you're done. Whew! Check Figure 8-7 for a sample of how this may look in our example.

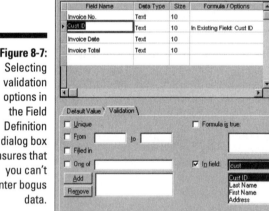

Figure 8-7: Selecting validation options in the Field Definition dialog box ensures that you can't enter bogus data.

✔ We've discovered that our personal capacity for entering bogus data is unsurpassed. We cannot make a dummy-proof database dummy-proof enough for us, but validation options are a step in the right direction.

Part II
Polishing Your Database

The 5th Wave   By Rich Tennant

"I WISH SOMEONE WOULD EXPLAIN TO PROFESSOR JONES THAT YOU DON'T NEED A WHIP AND A LEATHER JACKET TO FIND A LOST FILE."

In this part ...

You can use any database program to perform mundane tasks, such as storing data, sorting and searching records, and printing reports. Boring. What sets Approach 97 apart from other database programs is that it not only lets you do those unimportant things, but it also lets you do the really important stuff, such as changing colors and using great-looking fonts and drop shadows and other neat-looking effects. That stuff is what's *really* important, because in today's world no one gives a whit about content. Who *cares* if the report says that sales are dropping 20 percent each month as long as the report *looks* good. Well, not really, but you can create some pretty spiffy-looking effects using Approach 97.

The chapters in this part help you gussy up your database. You learn how to create fantastic forms and reports that are suitable for royalty, how to draw cute pictures on your views, how to add pictures and sound to your database, and how to work with calculated, date, and time fields. Read on for the details.

Chapter 9
Creating World-Class Forms

• •

In This Chapter

▶ Understanding forms and form objects

▶ Using Design mode

▶ Creating a new form

▶ Designing form fields

▶ Working with field formats

• •

*F*orms. Conjures up images of Olympic gymnasts, striking architecture, and the Internal Revenue Service, right? The default form that Approach 97 conjures up for your use is about as friendly as an IRS form, without the unfortunate checkbook aspect. Through your own creativity and raw talent, you can change your forms into works of art (or at least into something you find usable). It's Kafka's *Metamorphosis* in reverse — you're changing the cockroach of a form into something resembling a familiar object. Cool!

This chapter helps you make your form into one that's more useful and clear. After you throw out the high and low scores, you still find that Chapter 9 has very good form.

Forms, Fields, and Objects

A *form* is a view that enables you to access database records one at a time. Forms are the main portals through which you view and work with database data. You can use forms to enter data into a database, casually browse through the records of a database, or search for records with fields that match your specified search criteria.

Although Approach 97 automatically creates a default form when you create a database, you won't be content to use that form for long. Soon you'll develop the urge to either modify the default form to make it easier to work with or to create additional forms that simplify certain tasks — for example, you may want to create one form to enter comprehensive new customer information and another to quickly update contact information. You can create as many database forms as you want in a single Approach file. To switch from one form to another, just click on the tab that identifies the form you want to call up.

A form (or any other view, for that matter) consists of a *background* and *objects*. The background is just that: the background of the form. You can change the color of the form background, and you can give it a border. Otherwise, you can't do much with it. The more interesting — and more troublesome — part of designing forms is working with objects.

Most objects are field objects that display database data. If you're interested in other types of objects, read the sidebar in this chapter about object types. Otherwise, just plow ahead.

We object to this meaningless drivel about Design objects

We don't really want to do this to you, but we feel compelled to point out that you can use several distinct types of objects on forms.

Field objects: A field object shows the data from the database. Besides run-of-the-mill field boxes that provide an area for the contents of a database field and a label to identify the field, you can also create special types of fields, such as list boxes, radio buttons, and check boxes.

Text objects: A text object is an area that holds text that is displayed on the form. This text is a part of the form, not data obtained from the database. As a result, the same text is shown for every database record. The most familiar text field is the form label that usually appears at the top of the form. If you want to work with text objects on your form, check out Chapter 11.

Repeating panels: A repeating panel is a special area of a form that shows information from databases that are joined in one-to-many fashion. For example, the form for a Customer database can include a repeating panel to show all the customer's invoices that were obtained from a separate Invoice database.

Shape objects: You can add shape objects, such as ellipses, rectangles, and lines. These objects are purely decorative. Chapter 11 covers the procedures for adding these ornaments.

Picture objects: You can also add pictures in several common graphics formats. These pictures are purely decorative, and Chapter 11 also covers them.

OLE objects: An OLE object is a picture, a chart, a portion of a spreadsheet, or some other bit of data created by another program. Chapter 12 covers OLE objects.

Macro buttons: A macro button enables a database user to call up a macro by clicking on the Form button. Macro buttons are often used to invoke predefined Finds, switch from view to view, print reports, or do other useful tricks. Macro buttons are far too nerdy for this chapter, but you can find more information about them in Chapter 19 if you must.

Forget about everything except field objects (and repeating panels) for now. All the other object types are covered in other chapters of this book.

Working in Design Mode

As you undoubtedly know by now, Approach 97 uses several modes, including Browse, Design, Find, and Print Preview. To modify an existing form or to create a new form, you need to switch to the Approach 97 Design mode.

You switch to Design mode in one of four ways:

- Click on the Design button on the Action bar.
- Choose View➪Design.
- Choose Design from the View pop-up menu in the status bar at the bottom of the screen.
- Press Ctrl+D.

When you switch to Design mode, the SmartIcon bar changes to show SmartIcons that are useful when you design forms. Table 9-1 summarizes the most essential Design SmartIcons, along with their keyboard shortcuts.

Table 9-1   Design SmartIcons and Keyboard Equivalents

SmartIcon	Keyboard	What It Does
	Ctrl+S	Saves design changes to the Approach file
	Ctrl+Z	Undoes the most recent design change
	Ctrl+X	Cuts the selection to the Clipboard (deletes the original)
	Ctrl+C	Copies the selection to the Clipboard (leaves the original)
	Ctrl+V	Pastes the contents of the Clipboard on the view
	Ctrl+M	Copies the format of the selected object to other objects
	Ctrl+E	Calls up the Properties dialog box for the selected object. (For details about the Properties dialog box, see the section "Playing with the Properties dialog box" in this chapter.)

The wacky menu

When you work in Design mode, one of the menus on the menu bar — the one to the right of Create — changes, depending on what type of form object you're working with. Do not be alarmed! This change is entirely normal.

Here are some of the the the menus that appear:

Form: Appears when no object is selected and a form view is displayed. (If another type of view is displayed, such as a report or mailing label, this menu changes again.)

Field Object: Appears when an object is selected.

Text Object: Appears when text is selected.

Panel: Appears when a repeating panel is selected.

The commands that appear on the various menus are commands that are appropriate for the type of object you select, and we address them in the context of each of the different objects. For now, just remember that the something-or-another Object menu is immediately to the left of Window on the menu bar.

Using the Tools palette

The programmers who designed Approach 97 wanted to provide so many useful Design icons that they couldn't fit them all on the SmartIcon bar, so they threw in a separate box of icons called the *Tools palette*. The Tools palette, shown in Figure 9-1, consists of Design icons that float about on the screen. Table 9-2 summarizes the functions of the SmartIcons in the Tools palette.

Figure 9-1:
The Tools palette.

Table 9-2	Design Icons in the Tools Palette
SmartIcon	*What It Does*
![arrow]	Changes the mouse pointer back to the standard arrow pointer for selecting objects. Useful after you use one of the other tools
abc	Adds text to a form
▢	Draws squares or rectangles

SmartIcon	What It Does
⬭	Draws squares or rectangles with rounded corners
⬯	Draws circles or ellipses
╱	Draws lines
⊟	Draws a field
☑	Draws a check box field
◉	Draws a radio button
⬜	Draws a macro button
🖼	Draws a PicturePlus field
📇	Calls up the Add Field dialog box to add fields to the form

Here are some juicy tidbits concerning the Tools palette:

✔ The icons on the Tools palette work just like the SmartIcons on the standard SmartIcon bars. To use most of them, you click on a icon to select a drawing tool and then you drag the mouse to draw the selected shape on the form. The only tool that doesn't work this way is Add Field, which calls up a dialog box that enables you to drag database fields onto the form.

✔ If the Tools palette gets in the way, you can move it by dragging it gently by its title bar, just as you can move any window or dialog box.

✔ To really get the Tools palette out of the way, move it down to the bottom of the screen so that only the title bar is visible. Then it doesn't overlap anything except the status bar. You can quickly grab the title bar and drag the Tools palette back into view when you need it.

✔ To get rid of the Tools palette temporarily, choose View➪Show Tools Palette or press Ctrl+L. You can recall it into active service at any time by choosing View➪Show Tools Palette or by pressing Ctrl+L again.

Setting Design mode options

Design mode has a few options that make working with form objects easier. You set these options by using commands on the View menu or SmartIcons on the SmartIcon bar. The following list describes the options and tells you how to activate them.

✔ **Show Data:** This option tells Approach 97 what kind of information to display in fields when you work in Design mode. If Show Data is set, Approach 97 displays actual data from the database. This setting gives you an idea of what the form will look like when you use it in Browse mode. If Show Data is not set, Approach 97 displays the name of the field rather than sample data. Seeing the names of the fields can help you keep track of which field is which. To switch between data and field names, choose View➪Show Data to turn it on or off.

✔ **Show Grid:** If the Show Grid option is set, a pattern of little dots is displayed on the form to help you line up form objects. Initially, 12 of these dots appear per inch. However, you can change the grid spacing by choosing File➪User Setup➪Approach Preferences and looking under the Display tab.

To show the grid, choose View➪Show Grid. To hide the grid, choose View➪Show Grid.

✔ **Snap to Grid:** If you want Approach 97 to force objects to line up with the grid, activate the Snap to Grid option. Then anytime you draw a new object or move an existing object, Approach 97 lines it up with the nearest grid mark. Using this method is the easiest way to create neat-looking forms.

To snap objects to the grid, choose View➪Snap to Grid or press Ctrl+Y. Use the command again to turn off the Snap to Grid option.

✔ **Show Rulers:** The Show Rulers option displays rulers across the top and left edges of the Design window to help you line up objects. This option is useful when you design reports or merge letters, but you probably won't use it when you work with forms.

To display or hide the ruler, choose View➪Show Rulers, press Ctrl+J, or click on the Ruler SmartIcon.

If you find yourself working extensively in the Design mode, you may want to customize a set of SmartIcons to make your life easier. Most of the commands you may want to use are available through a custom set of SmartIcons. See Chapter 21 for the specifics.

Creating a New Form

Approach 97 automatically displays a default form when you create a new database. In many cases, this form is all you need to use the database. However, Approach 97 enables you to create more than one form so that you can access database data in different ways or more easily move around the form. For example, you may want to create a form for a Customer database that shows only the customer name and address fields so that you can easily enter name and address changes.

The easiest way to create a new form is to have the Form Assistant do it for you.

If, at any time, you think you might have made a slight mistake (or a huge oops!), you'll find that Back button at the bottom of each Form Assistant panel mighty handy. Just click on the Back button to return to the scene of the crime and right the wrong.

Just follow this procedure to create a new form:

1. **Open the database for which you want to create the new form.**

   Choose File⇨Open, click on the Open SmartIcon, or select the file from the Welcome to Approach dialog box.

2. **Choose Create⇨Form.**

   The first page of the Form Assistant appears, as shown in Figure 9-2.

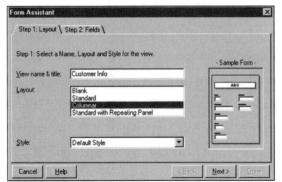

Figure 9-2:
The Form
Assistant,
Step 1.

3. **Change the information in View name & title to something more memorable.**

   Approach 97 suggests a brilliant name, such as *Form 2.* Make your name more descriptive, such as *Customer Info.*

4. **Select the Style.**

   The styles govern the form color and other appearance factors. You can experiment with different SmartMaster styles if you want. The Sample Form box shows you each style after you select it.

5. **Select the Layout.**

   The four layout options are:

   Blank: No fields are added to the form. Choose this option if you plan to extensively customize a form and don't want Approach 97 to help you. If you select this layout, skip ahead to Step 8.

Standard: Fields are added in a horizontal arrangement. This layout is the one that is most compact.

Columnar: Fields are added in a single column. This layout is nifty, but only a few fields fit on the screen without the use of scroll bars.

Standard with Repeating Panel: Use this layout if you want to include fields from a one-to-many join so you can see all of the information associated through joins with a particular record.

6. Click on the Next button.

Page 2 of the Form Assistant appears, as shown in Figure 9-3.

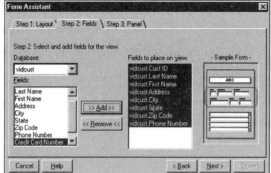

Figure 9-3:
The Form
Assistant,
Step 2.

7. Select the Fields you want to include on the form and click on Add to add them to the list.

To add a field to the form, select it in the Fields list and then click on Add. (Each time you click on Add, the next field in the list is selected. You can quickly add several successive fields by repeatedly clicking on Add.)

To add several fields at the same time, drag over them with the mouse. Or hold down the Ctrl key while you select the fields in the Fields list and then click on Add.

To remove a field from the form, select the field from the Fields to place on view list and then click on Remove.

8. If you are creating a form that has a repeating panel, click on Next; otherwise, skip ahead to Step 10.

Page 3 of the Form Assistant appears, as shown in Figure 9-4.

9. Select the fields you want to include in the repeating panel and click on Add to add them to the list.

Use the same techniques you use to add fields to the form to add fields to the repeating panel.

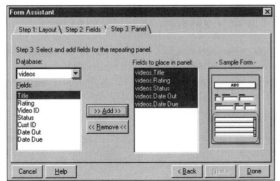

Figure 9-4:
The Form
Assistant,
Step 3.

10. **Click on Done.**

Lean back in your chair (not too far!) while the Form Assistant creates the form for you.

Deleting a Form

If you decide that you no longer need a form, or if you start to customize a form and mess it up so badly that you figure you may as well start over, you can delete a form by switching to Design mode and following this simple procedure:

1. **Select the form you want to delete by clicking on its tab.**

   The desired form comes into view.

2. **Choose Form⇨Delete Form.**

   The confirmation dialog box shown in Figure 9-5 appears.

3. **If you're really absolutely-positively-beyond-a-reasonable-doubt-no-turning-back-now sure that you want to delete the form, click on the Yes button.**

   The form is deleted.

Figure 9-5:
Deleting a
form.

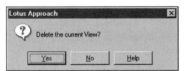

Changing a Form's Name and Title

After you create a form, you may want to change its name or title (the form *name* is what appears in the tabs that you click on to switch from form to form; the *title* is the text object that appears at the top of the form). You may also want to change the name and title of the default form to something more creative and useful than *Blank Database*.

To change the form name, summon the form in Design mode and follow this procedure:

1. Double-click on the form's tab.

The tab widens, and a text insertion point appears in the form name.

2. Type the new name for the form.

3. Press Enter.

To change a form's title field, call up the form in Design mode and follow this procedure:

1. Click on the form's title text a couple of times until an insertion point appears.

This is a finesse move. The first click selects the text object, and the second click enables you to edit the text. Count to three between clicks to avoid double-clicking; if you double-click, the Properties dialog box appears. (For more information about the Properties dialog box, turn to the section, "Playing with the Properties dialog box," in this chapter.)

2. Edit the title text however you like.

3. After you're done, click the mouse anywhere outside the title object.

Working with Fields

Field objects are the heart and soul of forms. The easiest way to make an Approach 97 database more useful is to spend some time in Design mode (both you and Approach 97) beefing up the fields on the database's forms. You can rearrange the fields into a more useful layout, add or remove form fields, change the tab order, and change the field formats. You may want to consider any or all of these options when you customize your forms. The following sections explain how to perform these tasks.

Moving and resizing fields

Often, one of the first things you need to do to a new form is move and resize the form fields. This step is necessary if the fields that the Form Assistant automatically places on the form are not large enough to display the data contained in the field. When you enlarge a field, you often need to move other fields to avoid an overlapped, cluttered, Oscar Madison of the *Odd Couple* appearance.

To move a field, simply use the mouse to drag it to a new location. Move the mouse pointer over the field until the pointer changes to a grabbing hand and then press and hold down the left mouse button. Move the hand to the new location (a rectangle representing the field moves with the hand) and then release the mouse button to move the field.

To resize a field, first select the field by clicking on it. When you click on it, handles (we call them *love handles*) magically appear around the field, shown in Figure 9-6. You can then resize the field by dragging any of its love handles. Carefully position the mouse pointer over one of the handles until the pointer changes to a double-headed arrow. Then press and hold down the left mouse button. Drag the love handle to change the size of the field and then release the button.

Here are some crucial points about moving and resizing fields:

✔ You can move several fields at the same time by holding down the Shift key when you select the fields you want to move. Then when you move any of the selected fields, all of the fields move.

✔ Another way to select several fields is to point to a blank part of the form and then press and hold the mouse button while you drag a rectangle (called a *selection rectangle,* technically) around all the fields you want to select.

✔ Remember to select the field by clicking on it before you attempt to move or resize it. When you see an outline box with love handles surrounding the field, you know that the field is selected.

✔ To maintain a neat, Felix Unger appearance to your form, turn on the Snap to Grid option by pressing Ctrl+Y or choosing <u>V</u>iew➪S<u>n</u>ap to Grid. Then any fields that you move or resize automatically fits neatly into the grid marks.

Figure 9-6:
Love
handles on a
form object.

Adding fields to a form

If you omitted a field from a form when you used the Form Assistant, or if you later add a field to a database and want it included in a form, you can use the following procedure to add a form field from Design mode:

1. **Select the form to which you want to add a field by clicking on the form's tab.**

   The form appears.

2. **Click on the Add Field SmartIcon in the Tools palette.**

   Alternatively, choose Form⇨Add Field (if an object is selected, choose Field Object⇨Add Field instead) or, using the right mouse button, click on any form object to bring up a pop-up menu and then select the Add Field command.

   Either way, the all important Add Field dialog box appears, as shown in Figure 9-7.

3. **If the field you want to add to the form is in a joined database, click on the down-arrow next to the database name (vidcust in Figure 9-7) to reveal a list of joined databases and then select the database you want to use.**

Figure 9-7:
The Add Field dialog box.

4. **Drag the field from the list in the Add Field dialog box to the location on the form where you want the field to appear.**

   The field is added to the form. (You may have to move the field around a little to get it exactly where you want it.)

Here are some important variants to consider when you are adding fields:

- You can define a new database field from the Add Field dialog box by clicking on the Field Definition button. The Field Definition dialog box appears, where you can define new database fields. For details, refer to Chapter 2.

- You can also add a field to a database by following these steps:

   1. **Click on the Field button on the Tools palette or choose Create⇨Control⇨Field Box.**

   2. **Position the mouse on the form where you want to place the field and then hold down the mouse button and drag the mouse across the area where you want the field to appear.**

   3. **Select the database field from the dialog box that appears.**

      After you release the mouse button, the Properties dialog box for the field appears.

   4. **Select the database field you want to assign to the new form field.**

      (Details about using the Properties dialog box are found later in this chapter, under the heading "Playing with the Properties dialog box.")

   5. **Click the Close button in the upper-right corner of the Properties dialog box to dismiss it.**

Deleting fields from a form

To remove a field from a form, follow this procedure:

   1. **Select the form that contains the field you want to remove by clicking on its tab.**

      The form appears.

   2. **Select the field you want to remove by clicking on it.**

      Love handles appear to show that the field is selected.

   3. **Press the Delete or Backspace key or choose Edit⇨Clear.**

      Poof! The field vanishes.

Consider the following:

- If you realize that deleting the field was a foolish thing to do — before you do anything else — press Ctrl+Z, click on the Undo button, or choose Edit⇨Undo to make the field reappear.

- Deleting a field from a form does not delete the field from the database. The field — and data you enter into it — is still safely kept in the database. You just can't see it in the form.

✔ To delete several fields at the same time, hold down Shift while you click
on the fields to select them or drag a selection rectangle around all the
fields by using the mouse. You can choose from three methods to delete
the fields: Press Delete, press Backspace, or choose Edit⇨Clear to delete
all the selected fields.

Changing the tab order

When you work with a form in Browse mode, you bounce from field to field by
pressing the Tab key (or the Enter key if you set the Preferences so that you can
use the Enter key). Normally, the Tab key bounces from field to field in the order
in which you added fields to the form. However, after an exhausting Design
session in which you move fields here and there, you may discover that the Tab
key seems to bounce about the form almost at random. If you have that problem, you need to change the data entry order. Here's how to change it:

1. **Call up the form with the incorrect data entry order.**

2. **Choose View⇨Show Tab Order.**

   A big, boxy number appears next to each form field to indicate the data
   entry sequence (see Figure 9-8). In this example, you can see that pressing
   Tab from the City field bounces the cursor to the Phone Number field, not
   to the State field. This data entry sequence should be changed.

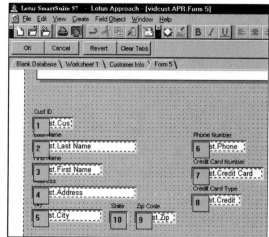

Figure 9-8:
Changing
the tab
order.

3. **Click on the *number* of the field you want to change and then type the
   new number.**

   Aim carefully!

For example, to change the State field to make it sixth in line, click on the *10,* delete the *10,* and then type **6.**

4. **Click on any other number to see the new and improved data entry order.**

   After you click on another number, all of the numbers are updated to show the new order. The old 6 becomes 7, the old 7 becomes 8, and so on.

5. **After you're finished, choose View⇨Show Tab Order again.**

   The numbers disappear, the fields appear in the desired sequence, and you can get back to work.

To totally shake up the data entry order, use this procedure instead:

1. **Call up the form with the data entry order you want to change.**

2. **Choose View⇨Show Tab Order.**

   You can see the data entry sequence.

3. **Double-click on any of the numbered boxes.**

   All of the numbers disappear, but the boxes remain.

4. **Click on the empty boxes in the order you want to establish as the data entry sequence.**

   The new data entry sequence number appears in each field as you click on its box.

5. **After you're finished, choose View⇨Show Tab Order again.**

   The numbers disappear, the fields appear in the sequence you requested, and it's back to work for you.

Changing a Field's Appearance

Approach 97 gives you precise control over the way fields appear on a form. For example, Figure 9-9 shows an Approach 97 form with various kinds of field formats. Of course, you wouldn't want to design a form like this one unless you already had another job lined up. Figure 9-9 is intended only to show that you can vary the font, size, and style of the text used to display the field's contents; the position and style of each field's label; and the border style and background color of the field itself.

Playing with the Properties dialog box

To change the appearance of the field, you must contend with a special dialog box called the *Properties dialog box.* Here is the procedure:

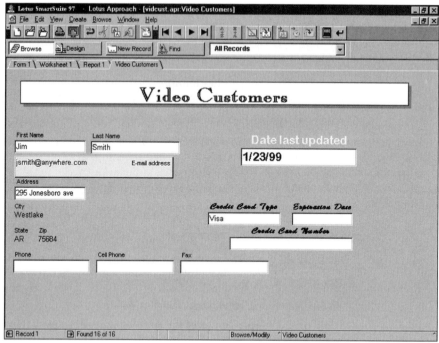

Figure 9-9:
Don't design
a form like
this even
though
you can.

1. Click on the field with the appearance you want to change.

Love handles appear, indicating that the field is selected.

2. Click on the Properties SmartIcon to summon the Properties dialog box.

You can also choose Field Object⇨Object Properties, press Alt+Enter, or
click on the field with the right mouse button and then choose Field
Properties from the shortcut menu that appears. One way or the other, the
Properties dialog box appears, as shown in Figure 9-10.

3. Click on the tab containing the field settings you want to modify.

Because you can use the Properties dialog box to change so many different
settings, the settings are organized into panels. Each panel is identified by
a tab at the top of the Properties dialog box. You click on a panel's tab to
display the panel and its settings. (See Table 9-3 for information on which
field settings appear on each tab.)

Also, you may notice that the tabs shown on the Properties dialog box
vary depending on the type of object you select.

4. Change whatever settings you want.

5. Repeat Steps 3 and 4 to change settings on other panels.

Figure 9-10:
The
Properties
dialog box.

6. **Click on the close control (X) in the upper-right corner of the dialog box to dismiss it.**

The results of the changed settings are immediately apparent.

Table 9-3	Properties Dialog Box Panels
Tab	*Field Setting Display*
	Font, size, style (bold, italic, and so on), color, alignment (left, center, right), and text relief style for field data
	Border width, color, fill color, shadow color, frame style, and border position
	Number format
	Size and position of field
	Database field and field type (text box, radio button, and so on)
	Macros to be run when cursor enters or exits field or when data changes
	Named styles for global control of formatting

Here are some important things to remember when you are working with the Properties dialog box:

✔ You can use two other methods to summon the Properties dialog box. Double-click on the field or point to the field, hold down the right mouse button to summon the pop-up menu, and then choose Field Properties.

✔ You don't have to dismiss the Properties dialog box to select another field. If you call up the Properties dialog box and then click on another form field to select it, the Properties dialog box shows the settings for the second field. (If the dialog box is hiding a field you want to select, move the Properties dialog box by dragging it by its title bar.)

✔ You can shrink the Properties dialog box down to just a strip by double-clicking on the title bar in the dialog box. The Properties dialog box rolls itself up into a nice little package that shows just the title bar and the tabs. To unravel the Properties dialog box, double-click on its title bar again.

✔ Approach 97 has a particularly cool feature called *named styles* that enables you to assign a name to a frequently used combination of Properties dialog box settings. Then you can quickly apply those settings to a field by applying its style. See Chapter 11 for the full scoop on named styles.

Using Fast Format

Approach 97 offers a feature called *Fast Format* that enables you to quickly copy all of the Properties dialog box settings from one field to another. You can use this feature to quickly format all the fields on a form so that their appearance is consistent.

Follow this procedure to Fast Format fields:

1. **Play with the Properties dialog box settings for one of the form's fields until the field is perfect.**

2. **Click on the perfect field to select it.**

3. **Click on the Fast Format SmartIcon.**

   You can also choose Field Object➪Fast Format or press Ctrl+M. Either way, the mouse pointer changes to a paint brush.

4. **Click on the field to which you want to copy the format settings.**

   The format settings from the field you selected in Step 2 are copied to the field you click. The results should be instantly visible.

5. **Click on more fields.**

   The paint brush stays on the screen so you can Fast Format a whole gaggle of fields.

6. **To make the paint brush go away, click on the Fast Format SmartIcon again.**

   You can also choose Field Object➪Fast Format or press Ctrl+M again.

Be sure to eradicate the paint brush before you resume your work. Otherwise, everything you click on will be reformatted!

Chapter 10

Putting Your Database on Report

● ●

In This Chapter

▶ Understanding Approach 97 reports

▶ Creating a report by using the Report Assistant

▶ Discarding an obsolete report

▶ Making sense of report panels

▶ Renaming a report

▶ Changing the heading

▶ Adding more summary fields

▶ Printing a report

● ●

*T*he previous chapters in this book focus on getting information *into* an Approach 97 database. This chapter turns the tables and shows you how to get information *out* of a database by creating reports.

Reports come in many shapes and sizes, ranging from simple listings of database records to complicated listings that group and summarize key data. It's all very interesting, if you're interested in that sort of thing.

Reports can be easy to create, or they can be nightmarish. This chapter focuses on the easy way to create reports, which is to let Approach 97 create reports for you by utilizing a handy feature called the *Report Assistant*. The Report Assistant asks you some questions about what you want your report to look like, and then it goes off and creates it for you. What could be easier?

Throughout this chapter, we work with a sample database that records players' salaries for a fictional professional badminton league. Each record in this database contains four fields: the badminton team name (Team), the player's last name (Last Name), the player's first name (First Name), and the player's salary (Salary). This database is joined to another database that contains contact information for each of the teams.

Understanding Approach 97 Reports

In Approach 97, a *report* is just another view, like a form or a worksheet. Like a worksheet, a report shows data from more than one record on each page. Unlike a worksheet, though, reports have header lines at the top of the page and sometimes have footer lines at the bottom of the page. In addition, reports may have special summary lines that summarize related groups of records.

Although reports are born to be printed, you don't have to send a report to the printer in order for it to be useful. Approach 97 enables you to view a report on-screen by switching to Preview mode, in which you see the report exactly as it will appear if you print it.

Here are some more stunning facts about Approach 97 reports:

✔ One of the weirdest, but sometimes most useful, features of Approach 97 is that you can access most reports in Browse mode, which means that you can add, update, and delete database records from the report. All of the editing techniques you learned in Chapter 4 apply to reports as well as to forms and worksheets.

✔ You can't set a sort sequence for a report to, for example, alphabetize by a particular field. However, you can easily create a macro that sorts the database into whatever sequence you want whenever you call up the report. Chapter 19 offers instructions for creating macros.

✔ The good folks at Lotus realize that when you need to design and create reports you can use a helping hand. So, out of the kindness of their hearts, they endowed Approach 97 with a helpful feature called the *Report Assistant*. The Report Assistant asks you a few simple questions, such as what type of report layout you want, what fields you want to include in the report, and what you had for lunch. Then it magically creates a stunning report for you, right before your very eyes.

✔ After you create a report (or, more accurately, after the Report Assistant creates a report for you), the report appears as a separate view. You can redisplay the report at any time by clicking on its View tab or selecting it from the pop-up View menu in the status bar.

✔ You don't have to use the Report Assistant to lay out your reports if you don't want to. You'd be crazy not to, though. Without the Report Assistant, creating reports is tricky unless you really know what you're doing. With the Report Assistant, it's like falling off a log. Stick with the Report Assistant, at least for now.

✔ The Report Assistant can create five different types of report layouts, which are described, well — oh, here we are! — in the next section.

Considering Approach 97 Report Types

Although Approach 97 enables you to create almost any type of report imaginable, at first you'll probably stick to the six predefined report types described in the following sections. After you get the hang of working with the predefined report layouts, you are ready to venture into changing these reports and designing more complex report layouts, discussed in the "Redesigning a Report" section at the end of this chapter.

Columnar reports

A *Columnar report* is a simple listing of the records in a database, one row per record. The database fields are arranged into columns, which are labeled at the top of each report page. Figure 10-1 illustrates a Columnar report for the badminton players database.

✔ The column headings at the top of each page are initially set to the field names defined for the database. You can change these headings if you want.

✔ You can change the width of each report column. However, Approach 97 usually does a good job of picking the column width so that report data can be properly displayed.

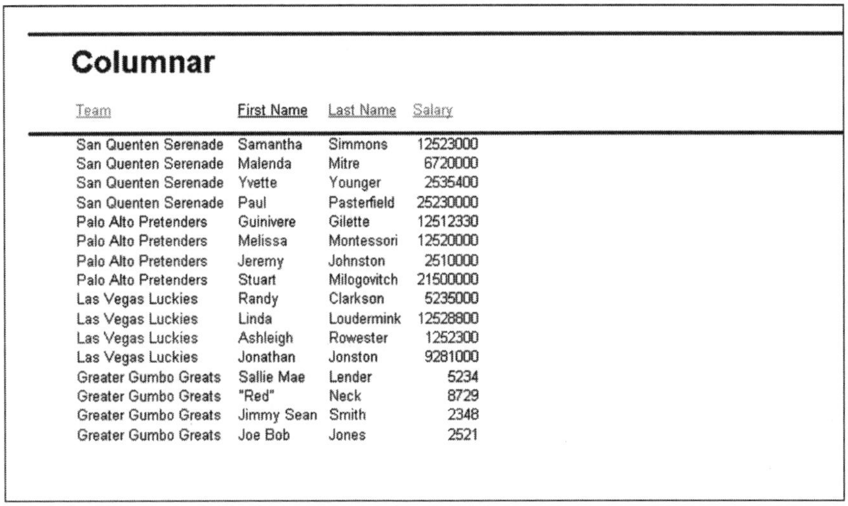

Columnar

Team	First Name	Last Name	Salary
San Quenten Serenade	Samantha	Simmons	12523000
San Quenten Serenade	Malenda	Mitre	6720000
San Quenten Serenade	Yvette	Younger	2535400
San Quenten Serenade	Paul	Pasterfield	25230000
Palo Alto Pretenders	Guinivere	Gilette	12512330
Palo Alto Pretenders	Melissa	Montessori	12520000
Palo Alto Pretenders	Jeremy	Johnston	2510000
Palo Alto Pretenders	Stuart	Milogovitch	21500000
Las Vegas Luckies	Randy	Clarkson	5235000
Las Vegas Luckies	Linda	Loudermink	12528800
Las Vegas Luckies	Ashleigh	Rowester	1252300
Las Vegas Luckies	Jonathan	Jonston	9281000
Greater Gumbo Greats	Sallie Mae	Lender	5234
Greater Gumbo Greats	"Red"	Neck	8729
Greater Gumbo Greats	Jimmy Sean	Smith	2348
Greater Gumbo Greats	Joe Bob	Jones	2521

Figure 10-1:
A Columnar report.

Standard reports

A *Standard report* is a report in which each record is presented as a sort of miniform, with more than one row per record if necessary. Figure 10-2 shows an example of a Standard report.

Standard Report

Team	First Name	Last Name
San Quenten Serenade	Samantha	Simmons
Salary		
12523000		
Team	First Name	Last Name
San Quenten Serenade	Malenda	Mitre
Salary		
6720000		
Team	First Name	Last Name
San Quenten Serenade	Yvette	Younger
Salary		
2535400		
Team	First Name	Last Name
San Quenten Serenade	Paul	Pasterfield
Salary		
25230000		
Team	First Name	Last Name
Palo Alto Pretenders	Guinivere	Gilette
Salary		
12512330		
Team	First Name	Last Name
Palo Alto Pretenders	Melissa	Montessori
Salary		
12520000		
Team	First Name	Last Name
Palo Alto Pretenders	Jeremy	Johnston

Figure 10-2:
A Standard report.

✔ Because data is not necessarily arranged neatly into columns, column headings are not used to identify database fields. Instead, field headings are printed separately for each database record in the body of the report. For this reason, as Figure 10-2 shows, Standard reports are not as concise as Columnar reports.

✔ Standard reports are often used if database records contain more fields than can be printed in a single row in a Columnar report.

✔ Another good use for Standard reports is to provide printed reports on which you can mark data entry changes. For example, you can print a Standard report for an Inventory database before you do a physical inventory count. Then you can mark any discrepancies between the computer inventory and the actual stock on hand on the report, and you can easily enter corrections into the database by using the Standard report view.

Columnar with Groups and Totals reports

A *Columnar with Groups and Totals report* is similar to a Columnar report, with the following differences:

> ✔ Records are sorted into order based on one of the fields.
>
> ✔ All records with the same value for the sort field are grouped together. The sort field value is displayed once, on a separate line just before the group. This line is called the *Leading Summary*.
>
> ✔ A *Trailing Summary* line is displayed after each group of records with the same sort field value. This summary line can include a total that represents the sum, average, or other calculation based on one database field.
>
> ✔ The report also includes a *Grand Summary* that totals a field for the entire report.

Figure 10-3 shows an example of a Columnar with Groups and Totals report. (The figure shows only the beginning of the report, so the Grand Summary isn't visible. Leading and Trailing Summaries are marked so that you can tell which is which.)

Columnar with Grand Totals reports

A *Columnar with Grand Totals report* is a Columnar report with a summary line at the end. The summary line provides a grand total for one of the database fields. Figure 10-4 shows a Columnar with Grand Totals report.

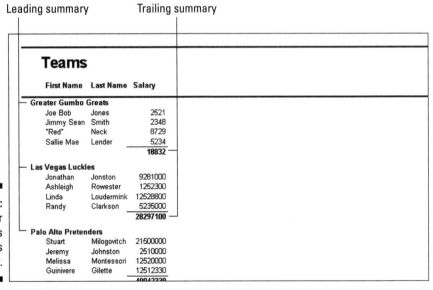

Leading summary   Trailing summary

Teams

First Name	Last Name	Salary
Greater Gumbo Greats		
Joe Bob	Jones	2521
Jimmy Sean	Smith	2348
"Red"	Neck	8729
Sallie Mae	Lender	5234
		18832
Las Vegas Luckies		
Jonathan	Jonston	9281000
Ashleigh	Rowester	1252300
Linda	Loudermink	12528800
Randy	Clarkson	5235000
		28297100
Palo Alto Pretenders		
Stuart	Milogovitch	21500000
Jeremy	Johnston	2510000
Melissa	Montessori	12520000
Guinivere	Gilette	12512330

Figure 10-3: A Columnar with Groups and Totals report.

Figure 10-4:
A Columnar
with Grand
Totals
report.

Summary Only reports

A *Summary Only report* is similar to a Columnar with Groups and Totals report, with one important difference: The database records themselves are not included in the report. In other words, the report shows only the summary lines that give totals for groups of database records with the same value in the sort field. Figure 10-5 shows a Summary Only report.

Figure 10-5:
A Summary
Only report.

Repeating Panel reports

A *Repeating Panel report* resembles a Columnar with Groups and Totals report but also shows all the records from one database and summarizes repeating data across joined databases. For example, Figure 10-6 shows a Repeating Panel report that presents information about each team (in this case, the Web address) and then summarizes the data from a joined database about the team.

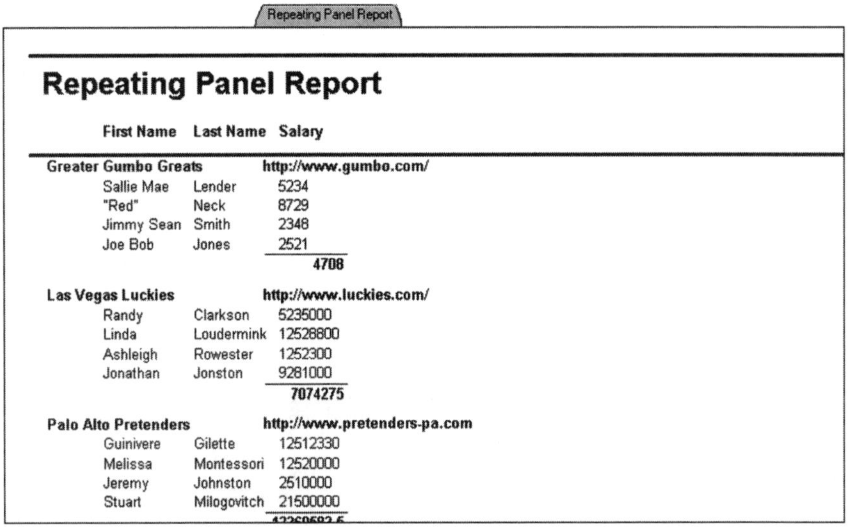

Repeating Panel Report

First Name	Last Name	Salary
Greater Gumbo Greats		**http://www.gumbo.com/**
Sallie Mae	Lender	5234
"Red"	Neck	8729
Jimmy Sean	Smith	2348
Joe Bob	Jones	2521
		4708
Las Vegas Luckies		**http://www.luckies.com/**
Randy	Clarkson	5235000
Linda	Loudermink	12526800
Ashleigh	Rowester	1252300
Jonathan	Jonston	9281000
		7074275
Palo Alto Pretenders		**http://www.pretenders-pa.com**
Guinivere	Gilette	12512330
Melissa	Montessori	12520000
Jeremy	Johnston	2510000
Stuart	Milogovitch	21500000
		42260502.5

Figure 10-6:
A Repeating
Panel
report.

Creating a Report by Using the Report Assistant

The Report Assistant is kind of like your own private computer nerd who already knows how to create Approach 97 reports and is willing to do it for you. All you have to do to keep the Assistant happy is toss him an occasional cupcake or doughnut and make sure that you let him outside twice a day.

The Report Assistant asks you questions about the report you want to create, such as what type of layout to use for the report, what fields to include in the report, and what fields to use to create summary groups and totals. After you answer all the questions, the Report Assistant unbegrudgingly and quickly creates the report for you.

The Report Assistant can automatically create any of the six types of database reports described in the preceding section. In addition, you can use it to create a blank report to which you can add fields in any layout you desire, if you find that the prepackaged reports don't meet your needs.

The following procedure describes how to create a Columnar with Groups and Totals report. The procedure for creating other types of reports is similar, except that you omit certain steps that don't apply. Don't worry, the Report Assistant holds your hand through the whole process so that you don't get lost.

To use the Report Assistant to create a report, follow these steps:

1. **Open the database for which you want to create a report (if it isn't already open).**

   Choose File⇨Open, click on the Open SmartIcon, or select Open an Existing File from the Welcome to Lotus Approach dialog box.

2. **Choose Create⇨Report.**

   The Create⇨Report command is always available, whether you're in Browse, Design, Print Preview, or Find mode. After you choose Create⇨Report, the Report Assistant appears, as shown in Figure 10-7.

Figure 10-7:
The Report Assistant asks what kind of report you want to create.

3. **Type a name for the report in the View name & title box.**

   This name will be used for the report view, so it has to be different from the name of any other view that already exists for the database. The name will also appear as the title at the top of each page of the report. It can be up to 30 characters long, and you can use more than one word. Figure 10-7 shows Salaries as the name.

4. **Select the Columnar with groups & totals design from the Layout drop-down list.**

   The Layout box governs the content of the report. Selecting Columnar with groups & totals enables you to create a report that is sorted and grouped based on one database field. A report with this layout also features a summary line following each group that includes a total calculated from another database field. Whew.

   After you select a layout, the sample report in the Sample Report box changes to give you a preview of what the report will look like.

After you select a layout, the tabs at the top of the Report Assistant dialog box change according to the report layout you selected. For example, after you select Columnar with groups & totals, two additional tabs appear: Step 3: Groups and Step 4: Totals. Not to worry. Remember, the Report Assistant is holding your hand. You won't get lost.

5. Select Default Style from the Style list.

The various styles contained in Approach 97 apply different formatting to the layout you select. Feel free to experiment with the different styles — some are pretty interesting, color-wise.

6. Click on the Next button to move to the next Report Assistant step.

The Report Assistant displays the options on the next tab in line, shown in Figure 10-8.

Figure 10-8:
The Report Assistant asks what fields you want in the report.

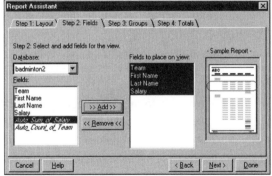

7. Select each field you want to include in the report and click on the Add button.

Each time you click on the Add button, the selected field is copied to the Fields to place on view list, and the next field in the Fields list is selected. To quickly include all database fields in the report, select the first field and then click on the Add button repeatedly until all fields are added. You could also hold down the Ctrl key, click on each of the fields you want to include, and then just click on the Add button once for all of them.

If you're working with joined databases, you can select fields from other databases by selecting a different database from the Database drop-down list.

8. Click on the Next button to move to the next Report Assistant step.

The Report Assistant displays the options on the third tab in line, as shown in Figure 10-9.

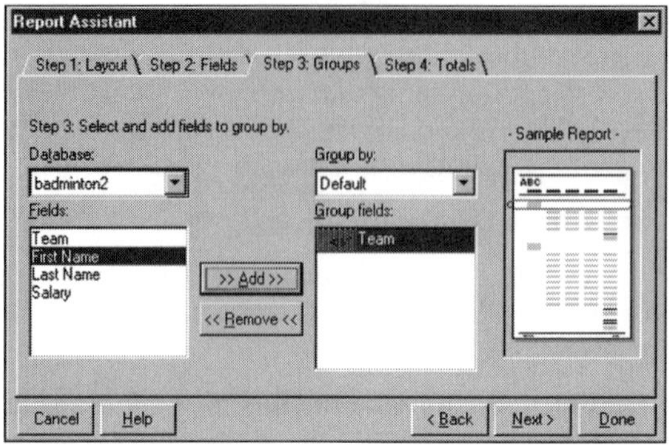

Figure 10-9:
The Report
Assistant
asks what
fields you
want to
group by.

9. **Click on a field in the Fields list.**

   This field will be used to sort and group database records and will be displayed in the leading summary line. For example, to group all players from the same team, select the Team field.

   If you're working with joined databases, you can select fields from other databases by selecting a different database from the Database drop-down list.

10. **Click on the Next button to move to the next Report Assistant step.**

    The Report Assistant displays the options on the fourth tab in line, shown in Figure 10-10.

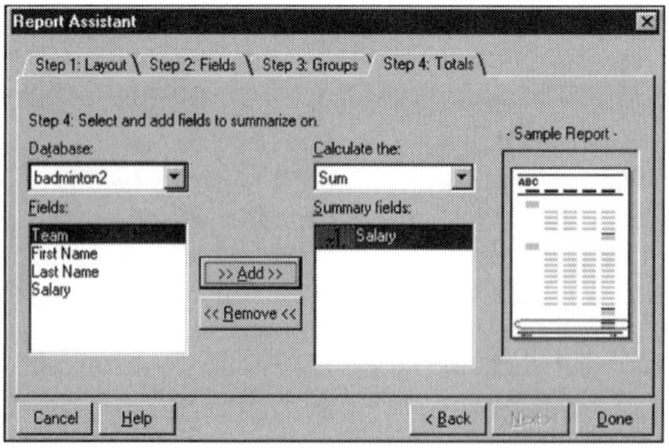

Figure 10-10:
The Report
Assistant
asks what
fields you
want to
summarize.

11. **Indicate what type of calculation you want to include in the trailing summary line and select the field you want to use for the calculation.**

    The Calculate the drop-down list includes several types of calculations (sum, average, standard deviation, and so on). Pick the type of calculation you want and then pick the database field you want to use for the calculation. For example, to total the salaries for each player, choose Sum and then select the Salary field.

12. **Click on the Done button and watch while Approach 97 creates the report.**

    After the Report Assistant is finished, it dumps you into the new report in Design mode.

Here are a few points to ponder during sleepless nights:

✔ The tabs that appear in the Report Assistant, and in some cases the options that appear on each tab, vary depending on the type of report you're creating. For example, Standard Reports do not have leading or trailing summaries, so the Summary tab doesn't appear. Similarly, a Columnar with Grand Totals report has a grand total rather than a leading summary.

✔ If you make a mistake in the Report Assistant before you finish, you can return to any Report Assistant step by clicking on the tab at the top of the Report Assistant dialog box or clicking on the Back button. None of the options you enter are set in stone until you click on the Done button.

✔ Trust us, the Report Assistant saves you a ton of work. Don't take it for granted.

✔ Remember, choose File➪Print Preview, press Ctrl+Shift+B, or click on the Preview SmartIcon to see your report as it will print.

Deleting a Report

The following procedure is useful if you no longer need a report, or (more likely) if you create a beautiful report by using the Report Assistant and then mess it up beyond recognition so that the easiest way to proceed is to delete the report and start over:

1. **Select the report you want to delete by clicking on its View tab.**

   The report is displayed.

2. **In Design mode, choose Report➪Delete Report.**

   Approach 97 displays the confirmation dialog box shown in Figure 10-11.

3. **Click on the Yes button if you think you know what you're doing.**

   The report is deleted.

Figure 10-11:
Deleting a
report.

Redesigning a Report

The Report Assistant does a pretty darn good job of creating reports for you, good enough that you may be content to leave a report well enough alone after the Report Assistant has finished its work. On the other hand, you may want to modify some aspect of the report's appearance to make it even better. The following sections explain how to redesign your reports.

Note: Chapter 9 covers procedures for working with form fields; many of those procedures work equally well with report fields. They don't pay us by the page, so we won't repeat all those procedures here. Refer to Chapter 9 for instructions on changing the size of fields, adding fields, and changing the text font and other field properties.

 The procedures described in the following sections assume that you are working in Design mode. To switch to Design mode, click on the Design button on the SmartIcon bar, choose View➪Design, choose the Design command from the View pop-up menu on the status bar, or press Ctrl+D.

After you switch to Design mode and display a report, the SmartIcon bar changes to provide SmartIcons that are useful when you design reports. Table 10-1 summarizes the most essential design SmartIcons, along with their keyboard shortcuts.

One of the items in the menu bar — the one to the right of the Create menu — has a tendency to change periodically when you're in Design mode. This chameleon menu is nothing to be alarmed about; it provides commands specific to the type of object that's selected.

As when you work with forms in Design mode, you can call up the Properties dialog box to change the properties of any object in a report. See Chapter 9 for details about using the Properties dialog box.

Also, you can call up a pop-up menu that contains commands specific to any report object by pointing the mouse at the object and clicking on the right mouse button.

Table 10-1	Report Design SmartIcons and Keyboard Equivalents	
SmartIcon	*Keyboard*	*Result*
	Ctrl+S	Saves design changes to the Approach 97 file
	Ctrl+Z	Undoes the most recent design change
	Ctrl+X	Cuts the selection to the Clipboard (deletes the original)

SmartIcon	Keyboard	Result
	Ctrl+C	Copies the selection to the Clipboard (leaves the original)
	Ctrl+V	Pastes the contents of the Clipboard on the view
	Ctrl+M	Copies the format of a selected object to other objects
	Ctrl+E	Calls up the Properties dialog box for the selected object
		Inserts a leading summary panel to group records based on the selected field
		Inserts a trailing summary panel to group records based on the selected field
		Creates an automatic sum field to sum the values in the selected field
		Creates an automatic average field to calculate the average of the values in the selected field
		Creates an automatic count field to count the values in the selected field
		Displays or hides panel names
		Switches between a display of actual database data and field names

Understanding panels

The key to working with reports in Design mode is understanding the notion of *panels.* Approach 97 carves up a report into various panels that contain the different pieces that make up the report. These panels serve as templates that govern how Approach 97 prints the various report pieces. Figure 10-12 shows how these panels appear in Design mode.

 If you switch to Design mode for a report view and you still see actual data in the report rather than the field names as in Figure 10-12, click on the Show Field Names button.

The following kinds of panels are shown in Figure 10-12:

- ✔ The *Header panel,* which appears at the top of each report page and includes the report heading and the field headings
- ✔ The *Leading summary panel,* which appears before each group of records
- ✔ The *Body panel,* which displays the fields for each record

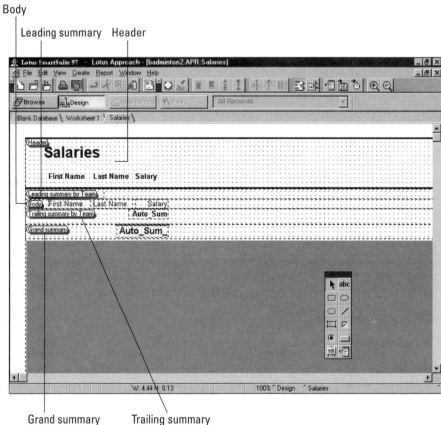

Body

Leading summary   Header

Figure 10-12:
Report
panels.

Grand summary   Trailing summary

▸ The *Trailing summary panel,* which follows each group of records and usually includes a summary field

▸ The *Grand summary panel,* which appears at the end of the report and usually includes a summary field

▸ The *Footer panel,* which appears at the bottom of each report page and usually contains the page number, date, and other information that you want on each page (not actually visible because it extends below the visible portion of the image)

To select a panel, click on the panel outside of a field or other object. If the panel is selected, it will be highlighted. You'll know.

After you select a panel, you can resize it by positioning the mouse pointer directly over the top or bottom border. After the cursor changes from a hand to a double-sided arrow, you can drag the border up or down to increase or decrease the panel size. Increasing the height of a panel adds extra space between report lines.

 If you don't want to see the names of the panels that make up a report, choose View➪Show Panel Labels or click on the Show Report Panel Labels SmartIcon. The bright yellow labels are removed from each panel. The labels have a nasty habit of obscuring important report fields, so we often turn them off.

 Another way to vary the appearance of the report in Design mode is to display the actual database field data rather than field names. You can switch between field names and data by choosing View➪Show Data or by clicking on the Show Data SmartIcon. When you display data, the various report panels are repeated as they will be in the printed report. When you show field names, only one occurrence of each panel is displayed on the report.

Changing a report's name and title

A report's *name* is the identifying text that appears in the View tabs that you click on to switch from form to form; the *title* is the text object that appears in the heading at the top of each report page. You can assign a more meaningful name and title than "Report 1" if you use the Report Assistant to create a report. However, if you want to change the name or title later, you can follow the procedures outlined in this section.

To change the report name, follow this procedure:

1. **Double-click on the report's View tab.**

   The tab widens, and a text insertion point is placed in the report name.

2. **Type the new name for the report.**

3. **Press Enter.**

   Or call up the Properties dialog box for the report and change the report name there.

To change a report's title, switch to Design mode, call up the report, and then follow this procedure:

1. **Click on the report's title text a couple of times until an insertion point appears.**

   Count to three between clicks to avoid double-clicking, which would bring up the unwanted Properties dialog box.

2. **Edit the title text however you want.**

3. **After you're done, click the mouse anywhere outside the title.**

Changing report headings

The Report Assistant always uses the database field names for column headings. If a field name is cryptic, like "Custno," you may want to change it to something a little more English-like, such as "Customer Number." Call up the report in Design mode and then follow this procedure:

1. **Click twice on the report heading you want to change.**

   Don't double-click, or you'll call up the Properties dialog box. Click on the heading once to select the text object and then click again to edit it. Count to three between clicks.

2. **Edit the heading text however you want.**

3. **After you're done, click the mouse anywhere outside the title.**

Using PowerClick reporting

What happens if you finish your report and your boss announces that you need to include additional summaries? Do you have to redo the whole thing? No problem. That's what PowerClick reporting is for. Just call up the report in Design mode, show your data (choose <u>V</u>iew⇨<u>S</u>how Data), and then follow these simple steps to add additional total or summary fields:

1. **In the Body panel, click on the field for which you want to create an additional total field.**

   For example, if the report is missing a total of the Sales field, click on the Sales field in the Body panel.

2. **Select the kind of total field you want to create by choosing <u>C</u>olumn⇨Groups & <u>T</u>otals and selecting an option or by clicking on the appropriate PowerClick SmartIcon.**

   You can use the PowerClick SmartIcons or their corresponding menu commands shown in Table 10-2 for creating total fields.

Table 10-2	PowerClick SmartIcons and Menu Equivalents	
PowerClick Icon	*Result*	*Menu choice*
$\frac{1}{+2}$	Adds up all of the field values	<u>C</u>olumn⇨Groups & <u>T</u>otals⇨<u>S</u>um
	Calculates the average value	<u>C</u>olumn⇨Groups & <u>T</u>otals⇨<u>A</u>verage

PowerClick Icon	Result	Menu choice
	Counts the values	Column⇨Groups & Totals⇨Count
	Calculates the minimum value	Column⇨Groups & Totals⇨Minimum
	Calculates the maximum value	Column⇨Groups & Totals⇨Maximum
	Calculates the standard deviation	Column⇨Groups & Totals⇨ Standard Deviation
	Calculates the variance	Column⇨Groups & Totals⇨Variance
	Calculates the leading summary	Column⇨Groups & Totals⇨Leading Summary
	Calculates the trailing summary	Column⇨Groups & Totals⇨Trailing Summary

After you click on the SmartIcon, a field is added to the summary panel. You may need to adjust the position of the field a bit to get things lined up correctly.

Some of the SmartIcons aren't visible by default, so you may need to customize your SmartIcon groupings if you'll be using the icons regularly. See Chapter 21 for details on customizing your SmartIcon groupings.

Printing a Report

Printing a report is fairly simple: You just call up the report and click on the Print SmartIcon. However, to print a report *properly,* you need to attend to a few preliminaries. Here's the complete list:

1. **Call up the report you want to print.**

2. **Sort the records if you want (you must switch into Design mode by pressing Ctrl+D).**

 To sort records into ascending sequence, click on the field by which you want to sort the records and then click on the Ascending Sort SmartIcon.

 To sort records into descending sequence, click on the field by which you want to sort the records and then click on the Descending Sort SmartIcon.

For more complicated sorts, see Chapter 6.

3. If you want, you can use a find to select records you want to include in the report.

To include all records in the report, select All Records from the drop-down list on the Action bar.

To include just certain records in the report, change into Browse mode (press Ctrl+B), click on the Find button, type search criteria into the database fields, and then click on the OK button.

For more information about finding records, see Chapter 5.

4. Switch to Print Preview mode to check the report.

 Click on the Print Preview button, choose File⇨Print Preview, or press Ctrl+Shift+B. This step helps preserve the rain forest.

5. If the report is up to snuff, you can print the report.

 Choose File⇨Print, press Ctrl+P, or click on the Print SmartIcon.

Chapter 11
Drawing on Forms and Reports

• •

In This Chapter

▶ Drawing simple lines and shapes

▶ Drawing text objects

▶ Creating drop shadows, embossed effects, and other fancy looks

▶ Understanding layers and groups

▶ Lining things up

▶ Stealing pictures from other programs

• •

*A*rt time! Everybody get your crayons and glue and don an old paint shirt. You're going to cut out some simple shapes and paste them onto your Approach 97 views so that people either think you are a wonderful artist or scoff at you for not using clip art.

This chapter covers the crude but useful drawing features in Approach 97. Approach 97 isn't equipped with the artist's tools that you need to draw fancy pictures, but it does give you some rudimentary drawing tools to spice up your forms with a bit o' something here and a bit o' something there.

Some General Drawing Tips

The Approach 97 drawing tools aren't as powerful as the tools provided with a full-blown drawing program such as CorelDraw! or Illustrator, or even Lotus's own Freelance Graphics 97, but they are powerful enough to create serviceable pictures to add some pizzazz to your views. Before we get into the specifics of how to use these drawing tools, here is a handful of general tips for drawing pictures for your views.

Start in Design mode

 Before you jump in, make sure you're in Design mode. The procedures you'll see in the following sections assume that you are starting in Design mode. To switch to Design mode, just click on the Design button in the Action bar, choose View➪Design, choose the Design command from the View pop-up menu in the status bar at the bottom of the screen, or press Ctrl+D. Take your pick.

Display the Drawing SmartIcons

 Technically, SmartIcons are hiding in Chapter 21 back with the rest of the customizing Approach 97 fun stuff. However, you'll be much more productive in this chapter if you can see the Default Drawing SmartIcons (also visible hanging out in the margin next to this paragraph). They may be up at the top in the SmartIcon bar, or they may be out in your working area.

 To display the Default Drawing SmartIcons, right-click on the SmartIcon bar and then left-click on Default Drawing. For a better long-term solution, choose File➪User Setup➪SmartIcons Setup to bring up the SmartIcons Setup dialog box. Under Bar name, select Default Drawing and then check the Bar is enabled to display during its context check box. Click on the OK button to return to your regular programming.

If the Drawing SmartIcons are visible in the SmartIcon bar, but are way off to the side and only a couple are in sight, you can click in the blue area to the left of the SmartIcon bar and drag the icons down into your workspace, or right-click on the SmartIcon bar and uncheck a different bar (to make room for the drawing SmartIcons), or click in the blue area to the left of the SmartIcon bar and drag the bar to the left.

Zoom in

When you work with the Approach 97 drawing tools, you need to increase the zoom factor so that you can draw more accurately. Approach 97 usually displays views full size (100 percent), but you can change the zoom factor to 25, 50, 75, 85, 100, or 200 percent. For precision drawing, you should switch the zoom factor to 200 percent.

From Design mode, you can use any of the following techniques to change the zoom setting:

✔ Click on the zoom setting in the status bar at the bottom of the screen to pop up a menu of allowable zoom settings and then choose the zoom factor you want.

 ✔ Click on the Zoom In SmartIcon or choose View⇨Zoom In to zoom in to the next higher zoom setting.

 ✔ Click on the Zoom Out SmartIcon or choose View⇨Zoom Out to zoom out to the next lower zoom setting.

✔ To switch back to full size, choose View⇨Zoom To⇨100% or press Ctrl+1.

After you zoom in, you may have to play with the scroll bars a bit to find the portion of the view that you want to draw on.

Display the rulers

 If you want to be precise about lining up objects, consider activating the rulers. If the rulers aren't displayed already, choose View⇨Show Rulers, press Ctrl+J, or click on the Rulers SmartIcon to show the rulers. To make the rulers go away, repeat the command.

When you edit a text object, the ruler indicates the text margins and tab positions.

Use the grid

The grid is a pattern of dots that are superimposed on a view to help you line things up. You can use the grid as a visual guide to help you place objects, or you can activate the Snap to Grid feature to cause Approach 97 to automatically align any object you draw with the nearest grid point.

To display the grid, choose View⇨Show Grid. To hide the grid, choose the command again. (The View⇨Show Grid menu item is checked when the grid is visible.)

To force any objects you draw to line up with the grid, choose View⇨Snap to Grid or press Ctrl+Y. To disable the Snap to Grid option, use the command again.

 One thing to be aware of when you use the grid is that objects that have been automatically placed on a form by the Form Assistant (or on a report by the Report Assistant) are not necessarily aligned to the grid. As a result, any objects that you draw when the Snap To option is on may be misaligned with objects that are already on the screen. To rectify this situation, simply click on each object that's out of alignment (no, not your tires) and nudge it toward the nearest grid point.

Save frequently

 Drawing can be tedious work. You don't want to spend an hour working on a particularly important drawing only to lose it all just because a comet strikes your building or the cat sits on the power strip and turns your computer off. You can prevent catastrophic loss of your work by pressing Ctrl+S, by clicking on the Save SmartIcon, or by selecting File⇨Save frequently as you work. And always wear protective eyewear.

Don't forget Ctrl+Z

 Don't forget that you're never more than one keystroke away from erasing a boo-boo. If you do something silly — such as hitting Delete when you have your entire drawing selected — you can always press Ctrl+Z (or choose Edit⇨Undo) to undo your last action. Ctrl+Z is our favorite and most frequently used key combination. (For left-handed mouse users, Alt+Backspace does the same thing.)

Drawing Simple Lines and Shapes

The Approach 97 drawing tools are limited to lines and basic geometric shapes such as circles and rectangles. Yet with these simple shapes, you can create some very good effects. For example, have a look at Figure 11-1. Here, we use a rectangle to group the customer name and address information together. Then we use a circle, two lines, and a text object to draw attention to a field that we don't want the user to overlook. (The box that contains the title was added by Approach 97 when it created the form.)

The icons used to draw these shapes are found on the floating drawing Tools palette and are summarized in Table 11-1. You can summon the Tools palette by choosing View⇨Show Tools Palette or pressing Ctrl+L.

 Make sure you're in Design mode before you start trying to draw. To switch to Design mode, just click on the Design button in the Action bar, choose View⇨Design, or press Ctrl+D. Take your pick.

Table 11-1	Drawing Icons
Drawing Icon	*What It Does*
▲	Not really a drawing tool, but rather the generic mouse pointer used to choose objects.

Drawing Icon	What It Does
abc	Adds a text object. Used to add explanatory text, instructions, or lawyer jokes to forms or reports.
▢	Used to draw rectangles. To make a perfect square, hold down Shift while you draw.
⬭	Draws circles and ovals. To create a perfect circle, hold down Shift while you draw.
▢	Draws a rectangle with rounded corners. To draw a square with rounded corners, hold down Shift while you draw.
╱	Adds a line. You can later change the attributes of the line to make the line thicker or add a dashed pattern. To force the line to be horizontal, vertical, or 45-degree diagonal, hold down Shift while you draw.

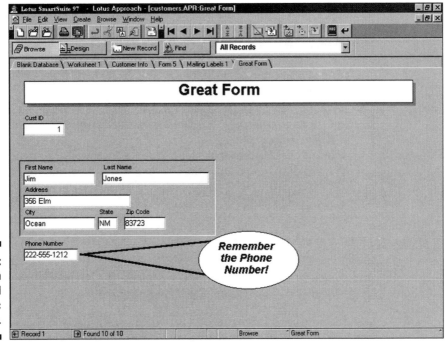

Figure 11-1:
A form embellished with graphic shapes.

To draw an object, follow this procedure:

1. **Click on the icon for the shape you want to draw.**

2. **Point (with your cursor, not your finger) to where you want the object to start.**

3. **Click and drag the mouse button to where you want the object to end.**

   Approach 97 stretches the object as you move the mouse.

4. **Release the mouse button when you reach your destination.**

Here are some pointers to keep in mind when you are drawing lines and shapes:

- ✔ If the floating drawing palette has mysteriously disappeared, you can call it back into view by choosing <u>V</u>iew⇨Show Tools <u>P</u>alette or by pressing Ctrl+L.

- ✔ Hold down Shift while you draw to force the object to be a perfect square or circle or to restrict lines to 45-degree angles. This step makes it much easier to create accurate and useful drawings, as opposed to drawing like Salvador Dali.

- ✔ After you draw a shape, you can adjust it by clicking on it to select it and then dragging one of the love handles that appear at the object's corners. (The official term for these love handles is just *handles,* but our term is more colorful, don't you think?)

- ✔ If you know in advance that you want to draw more than one object of the same type, double-click on the drawing tool button. Then you can keep drawing objects of the selected type 'til the cows come home. To stop drawing, click on the arrow icon or any of the other drawing icons. (The icon you double-click on turns blue in the face to remind you that you've selected it. It returns to normal color when you select another icon.)

Drawing Text Objects

A text object is a bit of text that's displayed in a view. Text objects are useful for displaying instructions, explanatory notes, or jokes.

Be sure not to confuse text objects with database fields, which display text contained in database records. Text objects are a fixed part of the view, not the database. Therefore, the text does not change as different database records are retrieved.

To add a text object to a view when you're in Design mode, follow these steps:

1. **Click on the Text Object icon in the floating Tools palette.**

   As soon as you move the mouse away from the floating Tools palette, the pointer changes to a funky abc icon.

2. **Click and drag in the view where you want the text object to appear.**

   A default-style text object appears on the screen.

3. **Type whatever text you want to appear on the view.**

   As you type, the borders of the text object expand to accommodate the text.

4. **Click outside the text object when you're finished entering your text.**

Here are a few important pointers to keep in mind when you are working with text objects:

- ✔ As you type text into a text object, Approach 97 expands the object to accommodate the text. After you're finished, you may want to resize the object if you don't like the way the text fits. Click on the text object to select it and then drag any of the love handles that appear at the corners of the object.

- ✔ To edit the text in an existing text object, click on the text object to select it and then click again to edit the text. Take your time between clicks — if you click too quickly, Approach 97 thinks you're double-clicking on the object, and it brings up the Properties dialog box instead of placing your cursor so you can edit the text.

- ✔ The default text style places text on a white background and uses a border style that creates a recessed appearance. To change the appearance, call up the Properties dialog box by selecting the object and pressing Ctrl+E, choosing Text Object➪Object Properties, or clicking on the Properties dialog box SmartIcon. Then play with the settings until you're satisfied.

- ✔ Figure 11-2 shows several text fields that have different formats to give you an idea of the effects that are possible. The formats shown in Figure 11-2 represent different combinations of text font and style, border style, background and shadow color, and text color (to create the white-on-black text). For the specifics on setting these options, see the following sections of this chapter.

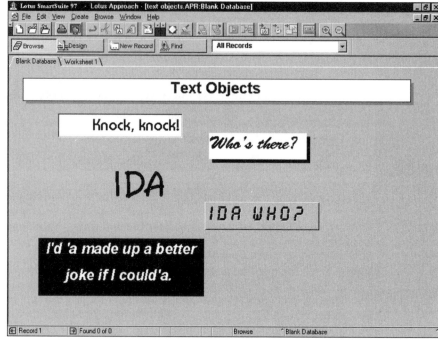

Figure 11-2:
Text
objects,
complete
with fancy
formatting.

Improving an Object's Appearance

No matter what they say, appearances do count. To create geometric objects that look as good (!?) as the circle and lines in Figure 11-1, you have to spend some time tweaking the object settings.

The procedure for modifying an object's appearance is the same as the procedure for setting a field's appearance. The following is a summary of the procedure; if you want more detailed information, refer to Chapter 9.

1. **Click on the object whose appearance you want to change.**

   Love handles appear, indicating that the object is selected.

2. **Call up the Properties dialog box by clicking on the Properties SmartIcon.**

   Or choose Object⇔Object Properties, press Alt+Enter, or double-click on the object. Any way you do it, the Properties dialog box appears, as shown in Figure 11-3.

Note that the actual name of the Object menu includes the type of object, as in Text object, Rectangle object, and so forth with all other objects. Handy, huh?

3. **Click on the Properties dialog box tab that contains the settings you want to modify.**

4. **Change whatever settings you want.**

   The results of the settings changes are immediately apparent on your form.

5. **Repeat Steps 3 and 4 to change settings on other Properties dialog box tabs.**

6. **Click on the Properties dialog box's Close button (in the upper-right corner of the dialog box) to dismiss it.**

Figure 11-3:
The
Properties
dialog box.

Table 11-2 summarizes the settings that are displayed for each of the Properties dialog box tabs.

Table 11-2	Properties Dialog Box Tabs
Tab	*Field Settings It Displays*
	Used for text objects to change the font, size, style (bold, italic, and so on), color, alignment (left, center, right), and text relief style
	Border width, color, fill color, shadow color, frame style, and border position
	Size and position of object
Basics	Stuff that's not very important for drawn objects, like whether it should or should not print, and if the users should be able to tab to it
Macros	Names a macro to be run when the user clicks on the object
	Allows you to create and use named styles (so you don't have to reapply formatting characteristics — you just select the style name)

Here are some important points to ponder when working with the Properties dialog box:

✔ You don't have to dismiss the Properties dialog box to select another object. If you call up the Properties dialog box and then click on another object to select it, the Properties dialog box changes to show the settings for the second object. (If the Properties dialog box is in the way of an object that you want to select, just move the dialog box by dragging it by its title bar.)

✔ If the Properties dialog box is *really* in the way, you can shrink it down to just a strip by double-clicking on its title bar. The dialog box rolls itself up into a nice little package that shows just the title bar and the tabs, as shown in Figure 11-4. To unravel the Properties dialog box, double-click on the title bar again or click on one of its tabs.

Figure 11-4:
The
Properties
dialog box,
rolled up.

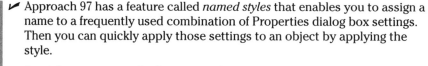

✔ Approach 97 has a feature called *named styles* that enables you to assign a name to a frequently used combination of Properties dialog box settings. Then you can quickly apply those settings to an object by applying the style.

✔ A quick way to copy the Properties dialog box settings from one object to another is to use the Fast Format command. Click on an object that's formatted the way you want and then click on the Fast Format SmartIcon, press Ctrl+M, or choose Object➪Fast Format. Next, click on any objects to which you want to copy the formatting from the first object. When you're done fast-formatting your objects, click on the Fast Format SmartIcon or press Ctrl+M again.

The following sections outline the procedures for creating particular effects.

Creating a drop shadow

To create a shadow behind an object, as in the *Who's there?* object in Figure 11-2, select the object, call up the Properties dialog box, and click on the Border tab. Set the Style to None, and then set the Shadow Color to black. (You can use any color you want for the shadow, but black usually works best.) To get rid of a shadow, set the shadow color to Transparent (represented by a *T* in the color box).

Creating embossed effects

To create an embossed effect for an object, as in the *Ida who?* object in
Figure 11-2, select the object, call up the Properties dialog box, and click on the
Border tab. Then set a Style — one of them creates a raised effect, the other a
recessed effect; you can tell which style is which by the picture. Next, set the fill
color to Transparent or to the same color as the view background. (You can use
an embossed frame style with any fill color, but the effect is most pronounced
when you use the view background color.)

Creating simple text with no border

To create simple text displayed without a border, as in the *Ida* object in
Figure 11-2, select a text object, call up the Properties dialog box, and apply
these formats:

 ✔ Set the Style to None.

 ✔ Set the fill color to the same color as the view background or make it
   transparent (represented by a *T* in the color box).

 ✔ Set the shadow color to the same color as the view background or make it
   transparent.

 ✔ Set the Color (for the border, at the lower center of the dialog box) to
   Transparent or to the same color as the view background.

Creating white-on-black text

To create white-on-black text, as in the *I'd 'a made ...* object in Figure 11-2, click
on a text object, call up the Properties dialog box, and then apply these formats:

 ✔ On the Border panel, set the Style to the simple rectangle outline.

 ✔ Set the Fill color to black. The text disappears temporarily, but it reappears
   when you set the Color setting.

 ✔ Set the Shadow color to Transparent.

 ✔ Set the Color to black.

 ✔ On the Text panel, set the text color to white.

Drawing Complicated Pictures

When you add more than one object to a view, several problems are bound to come up. What happens when the objects overlap? How do you line up objects so that they don't look as if they were thrown from a passing car? And how do you keep objects together that belong together, short of locking them in a closet?

This section explains how to use Approach 97 to handle overlapped objects, align objects, and group objects.

Make sure you're in Design mode before you start the procedures in this section. To switch to Design mode, click on the Design button in the Action bar, choose View⇨Design, or press Ctrl+D. Take your pick.

Changing layers

Whenever you have more than one object on a view, the potential exists for objects to overlap one another. Like more sophisticated drawing programs, Approach 97 handles this problem by layering objects like a stack of plates. The first object you add to a view is at the bottom of the stack; the second object is on top of the first one; the third object is on top of the second one; and so on. If two objects overlap, the one that's at the higher layer is the one that wins; objects below it are partially covered.

So far, so good — but what if you don't remember to draw the objects in the correct order? What if you draw an object that you want to tuck behind an object that you've already drawn, or what if you want to bring an existing object to the top of the pecking order? No problem. Approach 97 enables you to change the stack order by moving objects toward the front or back so that they overlap just the way you want them.

Approach 97 provides four commands for changing the stacking order:

- **Object⇨Arrange⇨Bring to Front:** Brings the chosen object to the top of the stack.

- **Object⇨Arrange⇨Send to Back:** Sends the chosen object to the bottom of the stack.

 - **Object⇨Arrange⇨Bring Forward:** Brings the chosen object one step closer to the front of the stack. The Bring Forward SmartIcon has the same effect.

 - **Object⇨Arrange⇨Send Backward:** Sends the chosen object one step closer to the top of the stack. The Send Backward SmartIcon has the same effect.

To use any of the preceding commands, first select Object⇨Arrange. A submenu then appears, listing the Bring to Front, Send to Back, Bring Forward, and Send Backward commands. Just click on the command of your choice.

Layering problems are most obvious when objects have a fill color. If an object is transparent, any objects behind it show through, and only the border overlaps objects that are beneath it.

To bring an object to the top of another object, you may have to choose Object⇨Arrange⇨Bring Forward several times. The reason is that even though the two objects may appear to be adjacent, other objects may occupy the layers between them.

Line 'em up and spread 'em out

Few things look more amateurish than objects that have been dropped randomly on a view with no apparent concern for how they line up with one another. Approach 97 provides several features, some of which you already know about, that enable you to line up objects as you draw them:

- ✔ **Show Grid:** When Show Grid is on, a grid of dots, spaced 12 per inch, appears on the screen. You can use this grid to align objects. To turn the grid display on or off, choose View⇨Show Grid or click on the Grid SmartIcon, if it's visible.

- ✔ **Snap to Grid:** When Snap to Grid is on, any object you create or move automatically sticks to the nearest grid point. To turn Snap to Grid mode on or off, choose View⇨Snap to Grid or press Ctrl+Y.

- ✔ **Show Rulers:** Choose View⇨Show Rulers or press Ctrl+J to show or hide a ruler to help line things up.

- ✔ **Align command:** The Multiple Objects⇨Align command enables you to choose several objects at a time and then line them up or space them out evenly. You can align objects horizontally to the left, center, or right of the objects, or vertically to the top, center, or bottom. You can also spread objects out evenly.

To align or distribute objects, follow this procedure:

1. **Select the objects that you want to align by clicking on them while holding down Shift.**

   Alternatively, hold down the mouse button while you draw a selection rectangle that encloses all of the objects that you want to align. When you release the mouse button, all the objects are selected.

2. Choose Multiple Objects⇨Align.

Or summon the Properties dialog box by clicking on the Properties SmartIcon, by pressing Alt+Enter, or by choosing Multiple Objects⇨Object Properties. In the dialog box, click on the Object alignment tab. You'll see the Properties dialog box with the Object alignment tab selected, as shown in Figure 11-5.

Figure 11-5: The Object alignment panel from the Properties dialog box.

3. Select the horizontal or vertical alignment options you want.

As you select alignment options, the alignment of the objects changes on the form. If you want to align only horizontally or vertically, make sure that you do not click on a button for alignment that you don't want. To space objects out, select either the Space Horizontally or Space Vertically option.

The Align To each other option just moves the objects in relation to the others in the group you selected. The Align To grid option moves them to the nearest grid points.

4. Click on the Close control at the top right of the dialog box to dismiss the Properties dialog box when you are finished.

Figures 11-6 and 11-7 show how these Align commands work. Figure 11-6 shows three objects as they were originally drawn. Figure 11-7 shows the result of selecting all three objects and choosing various Align options. The labels in the figure describe the selections.

Unfortunately, Approach 97 has no keyboard shortcuts or SmartIcon shortcuts for the Align command.

Group therapy

A *group* is a collection of objects that Approach 97 treats as if they were one object. Using groups properly is one key to putting simple shapes together to make complex pictures without becoming so frustrated that you have to join a therapy group.

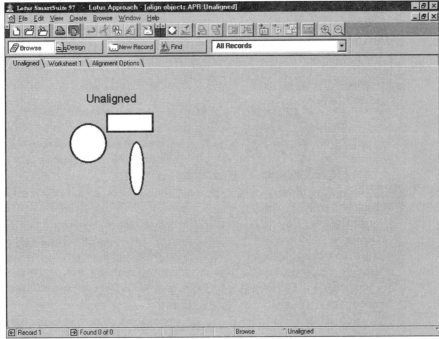

Figure 11-6:
Unaligned
shapes, as
seen in
Browse
mode
(because
that's how
your
database
users will
see them).

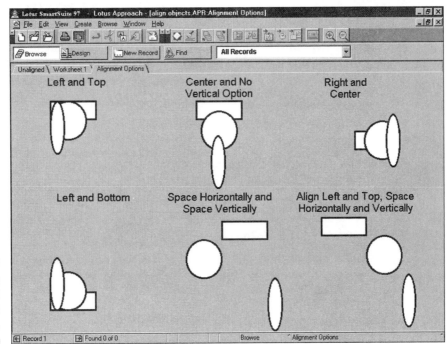

Figure 11-7:
Several
alignment
options.

To create a group, follow these steps:

1. Select all objects that you want to include in the group.

2. Choose Multiple Objects⇨Group.

Or press Ctrl+G or click on the Group SmartIcon.

To take a group apart so that the objects are treated as individuals again, follow this procedure:

1. Select the object that you want busted apart.

2. Choose Multiple Objects⇨Ungroup.

Or press Ctrl+U or click on the Ungroup SmartIcon.

Approach 97 even lets you create groups of groups. This capability is useful because you can work on one part of the view, group it, and then work on the next part of the view without worrying about accidentally disturbing the part you've already grouped. After you have several such groups, choose them all and group them. You can create groups of groups of groups of groups, and so on, and so on, and so on, and so on.

Stealing Pictures from Other Programs

This chapter wouldn't be complete if we didn't point out that, frankly, the Approach 97 drawing tools leave something to be desired. Sometimes using another program to create a picture is easier — even the simple Paintbrush program that comes free with Windows 95 has some advantages over the Approach 97 drawing tools. After you create the picture elsewhere, you can copy the picture from the drawing program to the Clipboard, switch to Approach 97, and paste the picture into Approach 97.

Make sure you're in Design mode before you start the procedures in this section. To switch to Design mode, click on the Design button in the Action bar, choose View⇨Design, or press Ctrl+D.

Here's the procedure for pasting in a picture from another program:

1. Draw a picture using your favorite drawing program.

Make sure that the background color of the picture matches the background color of the Approach 97 view that you're going to paste the picture onto.

2. **Select the portion of the picture that you want to copy into Approach 97.**

3. **Press Ctrl+C or choose Edit⇨Copy to copy the picture to the Clipboard.**

4. **Switch to Approach 97.**

   If Approach 97 is already running, press Alt+Tab until Approach 97 appears. Otherwise, go to the Start menu, start Approach 97, and open the database that you want to paste the picture into.

 5. **Press Ctrl+V, choose Edit⇨Paste, or click on the Paste SmartIcon.**

   The picture is pasted into the view.

6. **Grab the picture with the mouse and move it to the location where you want it.**

   The picture starts out in the upper-left corner of the view, which probably isn't where you want it to stay. Click on the picture to select it and then move the mouse pointer over the picture. When the pointer changes to a hand, drag the picture to its new location.

7. **Resize the picture, if necessary.**

   It's probably too big. Click on the picture and then position the mouse pointer over one of its love handles. When the arrow pointer changes to a double-arrow pointer, drag the love handle to resize the picture.

Using Named Styles

After you've formatted any object to your satisfaction, you can assign a name to the formatting so you can format similar objects in a jiffy. These names are called *styles* in Approach 97 and are good for any kind of objects.

 Make sure you're in Design mode before you start the procedures in this section. To switch to Design mode, click on the Design button in the Action bar, choose View⇨Design, or press Ctrl+D.

Creating a named style

Approach 97 doesn't supply pre-made named styles, so you're on your own for creating them. Here's the procedure for creating a named style.

1. **Format an object (using the other formatting information in this chapter).**

2. **Select the object by clicking on it.**

3. **Call up the Properties dialog box by clicking on the Properties SmartIcon.**

   Or choose Object⇨Object Properties, press Alt+Enter, or double-click on the object. Any way you do it, the Properties dialog box appears.

 4. **Click on the Named Styles tab.**

5. **Click on the Create Named Style button to bring up the Create Named Style dialog box.**

6. **Type a descriptive name in the Style name text box, tab to the Description text box, and type in a Description. Click on the OK button when you're finished.**

Applying a named style

After you've created a named style, you can use it to quickly format any other objects that should look like the named style. Here's the process to apply a named style to an object.

1. **Select the object you want to format by clicking on it.**

2. **Call up the Properties dialog box by clicking on the Properties SmartIcon.**

   Or choose Object⇨Object Properties, press Alt+Enter, or double-click on the object. Any way you do it, the Properties dialog box appears.

 3. **Click on the Named Styles tab (the far right one).**

4. **Click on the Style name you want to apply.**

   Presto chango! Your object is all formatted, and it only took a second!

Here are a few additional notes about using named styles:

 ✔ If you decide that you want to change one of your named styles, just format an object as you usually would, and then bring up the Properties dialog box, Named Styles tab, and click on Redefine Style. Finally, click on the OK button in the Redefine Style dialog box to reset your style.

 ✔ If you really get into using these named styles, call up the Properties dialog box, click on the Named Styles tab, and click the Manage Styles button. You'll see all kinds of options (some leading to other dialog boxes) in which you can, for example, Edit, Copy, and Delete your named styles. Have fun!

Chapter 12

Adding Pictures and Sounds to a Database

· ·

In This Chapter

▶ Using PicturePlus fields

▶ Adding pictures to a database record

▶ Adding sound to a PicturePlus field

▶ Adding video to a PicturePlus field

· ·

*W*hat's all the rage about multimedia these days? You'd think that some computer geek in Sunnyvale had just invented talking movies. Multimedia technology has progressed almost to the point where a $2,000 computer can *both* belch realistically and play six seconds of *The African Queen* almost as well as a $159 VCR can.

Oh, well. Computer technology is a trendy business. Multimedia features have infected just about every type of computer program you can buy, and database programs are no exception. We wouldn't be caught dead not including a chapter about multimedia in an Approach 97 book, especially not when Approach 97 devotes an entire database field type to multimedia gags: PicturePlus fields. You can use PicturePlus fields, as the name suggests, to store pictures or other "plus" stuff, such as sounds and videos.

Actually, as you see in this chapter, these fields do have some very real uses (not that we'll quit poking fun at them).

What Is a PicturePlus Field?

A *PicturePlus* field is a special type of database field that is designed to store objects created by other programs. The most common type of object stored in a PicturePlus field is a picture created by a drawing program or, more likely, scanned in with a scanner. For example, you can use a scanner to scan photo-graphs of your employees to store in an employee database or photos of your products to store in an inventory database.

The contents of the PicturePlus fields in your database are part of the data you collect, just like names and dates. Pictures drawn on views, as we describe in Chapter 11, are decorations for the different views of the database, but they don't affect the actual data.

Here are some important points to remember about PicturePlus fields:

- ✔ A PicturePlus field can contain a picture drawn in a graphics program or an object created by a program that supports OLE. See the sidebar "Stop me before I tell you about OLE" if you're interested in OLE.

- ✔ You can use a PicturePlus field to insert many different kinds of objects into a database record. You can insert a spreadsheet created by a spreadsheet program, a bit of text or a whole document created by a word-processing program, a sound or a video clip, and who knows what else.

Stop me before I tell you about OLE

Microsoft introduced OLE, which can be pro-nounced *oh-el-ee* or *ohlay!* (like the shout at a bullfight), as part of Windows 3.1 and continues to develop and improve it. Of course, the capa-bilities are built into Windows 95 as well.

OLE stands for *Object Linking and Embedding.* OLE enables you to create documents that contain different kinds of data. For example, you may want to include some spreadsheet data in a word-processing document. OLE enables you to simply insert a spreadsheet object into the word-processing document. OLE remembers that the data was originally created by your spreadsheet program. If you want to edit the spreadsheet data, you just double-click on it. OLE magically conjures up your spreadsheet pro-gram so that you can edit the data.

With regular OLE, a new window appears when you double-click on an embedded object to edit it. Microsoft has also introduced a new flavor of OLE, called OLE 2.0, in which embedded objects are not edited in separate windows. Instead, when you double-click on an embedded object, the menus and toolbars from the embedded object's program appear, replacing the main program's menus and toolbars. You can then edit the object without switching to another window. Not all applications let you do this fun OLE stuff, but, of course, Approach 97 does.

In OLE terminology, the document that contains an embedded object is called a *container,* and a program that creates a container document is called a *client.* An embedded object is called a *component,* and the program that creates it is called a *server.* These terms are important to the people who write OLE programs, but they're completely unimportant to normal people like us.

Adding PicturePlus fields to a database

To use a PicturePlus field, you need to define a PicturePlus field in the database. If you didn't include a PicturePlus field when you created the database, you can add one later by following this procedure:

1. **Open the database to which you want to add the PicturePlus field.**

   Choose File⇨Open, press Ctrl+O, click on the Open SmartIcon, or pick Open an Existing Approach File from the Welcome to Lotus Approach dialog box.

2. **Switch to Design mode, if you aren't already in it.**

   Press Ctrl+D, choose View⇨Design, select Design from the View pop-up menu in the status bar at the bottom of the screen, or click on the Design button.

3. **Choose Create⇨Field Definition.**

   The Field Definition dialog box, which is shown in Figure 12-1, appears.

Figure 12-1: The Field Definition dialog box.

Field Name	Data Type	Size	Formula / Options
City	Text	20	
State	Text	2	
Zip Code	Text	10	
Phone Number	Text	14	
Credit Card Number	Text	20	
Credit Card Type	Text	4	
Customer Pet	PicturePlus	Fixed	OLE Enable -

4. **Scroll to the bottom of the field list, type a field name in the first blank Field Name space, and press the Tab key.**

   Choose a good name for the PicturePlus field. The database shown in Figure 12-1 is for a vet, so an appropriate name for that PicturePlus field is Customer Pet.

5. **Select PicturePlus for the Data Type.**

   You can click on the arrow that appears when you click on the Data Type column to drop down the list of data types and then click PicturePlus or press P to quickly select PicturePlus.

6. **Click on the Options button.**

   The Field Definition dialog box expands to reveal the PicturePlus field options, shown in Figure 12-2.

Figure 12-2:
The Field
Definition
dialog box
with the
PicturePlus
field options
displayed.

7. **Uncheck the A_llow OLE objects check box if you want to restrict the field to pictures only (no OLE objects).**

   This choice is boring, but probably acceptable, and a good idea if you know that you only want to store pictures in this field. However, if you restrict the field to pictures only, you also lose the ability to update the drawings from within Approach 97 — you must revise the drawing and reimport it into your database to update it.

8. **Select an option in the D_efault object type menu if the field will usually contain a particular type of OLE object.**

   For example, if the field will usually hold a sound object, select Wave — Sound as the D_efault object type. (If you unchecked the A_llow OLE objects check box, skip this step.)

9. **Click on the OK button.**

   You're done!

Adding a PicturePlus field to a view

After you add a PicturePlus field to the database, you'll probably want to add it to one or more of your views. Follow these steps:

1. **Switch to the view to which you want to add the PicturePlus field.**

   Click on the view's tab or select the view from the View pop-up menu on the status bar at the bottom of the screen.

2. Switch to Design mode, if you are not already in it.

Press Ctrl+D, choose View⇨Design, select Design from the View pop-up menu in the status bar at the bottom of the screen, or click on the Design button.

3. If the Add Field dialog box is not visible, click on the Add Field SmartIcon in the floating icon palette.

The Add Field dialog box appears, as shown in Figure 12-3.

Figure 12-3:
The Add
Field dialog
box.

4. Drag the PicturePlus field from the Add Field dialog box onto the view.

If the PicturePlus field isn't visible, make sure that the correct database is selected in the drop-down menu at the top of the dialog box.

When you release the mouse button, the PicturePlus field is added to the view at the mouse location.

5. If you added the field to a form, you can resize the PicturePlus field if you want to.

The default size is appropriate for most pictures, but you may want a different size or shape. If so, just click once on the field to select it, and then click and drag the love handles until the box is the right shape and size.

6. That's it!

You're done.

Adding a Picture to a Database Record

After you create a PicturePlus field and add it to a database view, you can use any of the following procedures to add a picture to the field. (To add an OLE object, see "Talking Fields" and "Let's Go to the Movies" later in this chapter.) You can paste the picture from a file or from the Clipboard.

Inserting a picture from a file

If the picture you want is already stored in a file, follow this procedure:

1. In Browse mode, call up the record to which you want to add the picture.

2. Click on the PicturePlus field.

3. Choose Edit⟿Picture⟿Import.

The Import Picture dialog box appears, as shown in Figure 12-4.

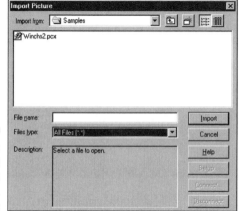

Figure 12-4:
The Import
Picture
dialog box.

4. Select a file and click on the OK button.

You may need to rummage around your hard disk until you find the file you're looking for. If necessary, change the Files type field to show the file type you're looking for (BMP, PCX, and so on).

The rest of the dialog box contains the standard drive, directory, and file settings. Find the file that contains the picture you want to paste into the PicturePlus field. Then click on the Import button.

The picture is pasted into the PicturePlus field.

5. Admire the picture.

Figure 12-5 shows a possible real-world application for these fields.

Table 12-1 summarizes some of the most common graphic file types Approach 97 can work with.

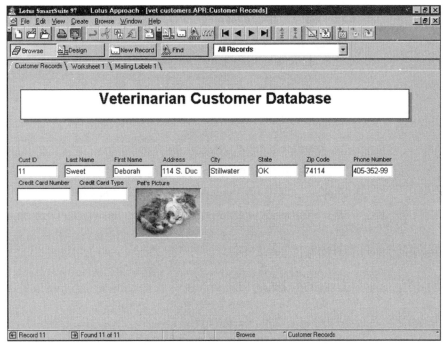

Figure 12-5:
An actual
PicturePlus
field in use!
Believe it or
not!

Table 12-1	Graphic File Types
File Extension	*File Type*
BMP	Windows Bitmap file created by Paintbrush
WMF	Windows Metafile, often used to exchange graphic data between Windows applications
TIF	Tagged Image File Format file, used by high-end paint programs, such as Adobe Photoshop
PCX	Another graphics format, also used by Paintbrush
GIF	Yet another graphics file format, this one frequently found in documents on the Internet and also used by online services such as CompuServe or America Online
JPG	JPEG, still another graphics file format that you also find on the Internet
TGA	Targa, still another relatively obscure graphic file format
EPS	Encapsulated Postscript File, used by high-end drawing programs such as Adobe Illustrator

Pasting a picture from the Clipboard

Another way to insert a picture into a PicturePlus field is via the Clipboard. This technique is useful when the picture is in a file format that you can't directly import into Approach 97, such as a drawing you created in PageMaker or in Microsoft PowerPoint.

Here's the procedure:

1. **Use your favorite program to draw a picture.**

2. **Select the portion of the picture that you want to copy into Approach 97.**

3. **Choose Edit⇨Copy to copy the picture to the Clipboard.**

    Or use the keyboard shortcut, Ctrl+C, or click on the Copy SmartIcon.

4. **Switch to the Approach 97 database to which you want to add the picture.**

   If Approach 97 is already running, press Alt+Tab until Approach 97 appears. Otherwise, head for the Start menu, start Approach 97, and open the database into which you want to paste the picture.

5. **In Browse mode, switch to the record to which you want to add the picture and then click on the PicturePlus field to select it.**

6. **Choose Edit⇨Paste, press Ctrl+V, or click on the Paste SmartIcon to paste the picture into the field.**

   Whichever way you choose, the picture is pasted into the PicturePlus field.

 If you choose Edit⇨Paste Special to paste your graphic into the Approach 97 database, a dialog box appears that lets you select two options: a preferred file type and, depending on the application from which you pasted, Paste Link. If you select Paste Link, you'll be able to update the drawing in the original file and have the change automagically appear in the Approach 97 database field.

Talking Fields

It used to be that the only sound you could get from your computer was a sterile *beep*. Nowadays, you can make your computer talk almost as well as the computers in the *Star Trek* movies. Or you can give it a sophomoric sense of audible distaste. At last, the computer can be as obnoxious as the user!

There's a catch. Your computer has to be equipped with a sound card to play these kinds of sounds. Apple Macintosh users love to brag that every Macintosh ever made has had sound capabilities built right in while poor PC users still have to purchase a separate sound card to make their computers burp as well as a Mac. Fortunately, sound cards are getting less and less expensive and are very frequently included in new PCs. Most newer PCs have sound cards, or you can buy one for under $100.

All about sound files

Computer sounds are stored in sound files, which come in many flavors, including these two popular varieties:

- ✔ **WAV files (WAV):** Contain digitized recordings of actual sounds, such as Darth Vader saying, "I find your lack of faith disturbing," or Dr. McCoy saying, "He's dead, Jim." Windows 95 comes with a slew of recordings in WAV format.

- ✔ **MIDI files (MID):** Contain synthesized sounds or music stored in a form that the sound card's synthesizer can play. Windows 95 comes with a bunch of MIDI files, including classics such as Beethoven's *5th Symphony* and Bach's *Brandenburg Concerto Number 3*.

To find the WAV or MIDI files on your computer, root around for them by using Windows Explorer. *Tip:* You can find most of them in your C:\windows\media folder.

To insert a sound into a database record, all you have to do is paste one of these sound files into a PicturePlus field. Then you can play the sound by double-clicking on the field.

You're more likely to use WAV files than MIDI files in an Approach 97 database. MIDI files are great for playing music, but WAV files enable you to incorporate a voice or other actual recording into the database.

 WAV files consume large amounts of disk space. A typical two-second sound clip can take up 25K of precious disk real estate. That amount doesn't seem like much, but it adds up. (The main reason that we use DoubleSpace — a disk compression program that works with Windows 95 — is to make room for the huge collection of *Schoolhouse Rock* sound files.)

Inserting a sound in Approach 97

To add a sound to an Approach 97 database record, follow these steps:

1. **Call up the record to which you want to add the sound.**

2. **Click on the PicturePlus field.**

Where to get great sounds

The WAV files that come with Windows are pretty boring, but fortunately the nation isn't suffering a shortage of sound files. You can download them from the Internet or from just about any online service such as CompuServe or America Online. You can purchase them in collections from computer software stores, or you can beg, borrow, or steal them from your computer geek friends. Most computer geeks will gladly offer you a disk full of their favorite sounds in exchange for a large bag of potato chips and a six-pack of their favorite beverage.

If you have a microphone, you can plug it into your sound card and record your own sounds. Move your computer into the living room some weekend and rent the following movies:

✔ *Star Wars*

✔ Any *Pink Panther* movie

✔ *Jaws*

✔ *When Harry Met Sally*

✔ Any Bruce Willis shoot-em-up

✔ *2001: A Space Odyssey*

✔ *Annie Hall, Bananas,* or *Sleeper*

These films should give you a good assortment of sounds to incorporate into your databases. For more information about recording sounds, check out *MORE Windows For Dummies* or *Multimedia and CD-ROMs For Dummies,* both by Andy Rathbone, published by IDG Books Worldwide, Inc.

3. **Go to the the Start menu and choose Programs⇨Accessories⇨ Multimedia⇨Sound Recorder to start the Sound Recorder application.**

   Breathe deeply and relax after the excursion through all those menu levels.

4. **Stare at the Sound Recorder window a minute to get your bearings.**

   Figure 12-6 shows what the Sound Recorder looks like. The wavy line in the middle of the recorder in Figure 12-6 is an image of the current sound file. (You won't see a wavy line on your screen because you haven't yet opened a sound file.)

Figure 12-6:
The Sound Recorder window, complete with Chimes.WAV sound.

5. **Choose File⇨Open or press Ctrl+O to bring up the Open dialog box.**

6. **Select the sound file you want to insert and click on the OK button.**

   You may have to rummage through your hard disk until you find the file. Keep looking; it's there somewhere — probably in C:\windows\media if the file came with Windows 95, and somewhere else if it didn't.

7. **Click on the Play button (the one with the right-facing arrow on it) to make sure that you found the right sound.**

   Repeat this step until you tire of the sound or your family starts trying to turn the TV up loud enough to drown you out.

8. **Choose Edit⇨Copy, use the familiar keyboard shortcut, Ctrl+C, or click on the Copy SmartIcon to copy the sound to the Clipboard.**

9. **Pop over to Approach 97; press Alt+Tab until Approach 97 comes back to life or just click on the Approach 97 button in the Taskbar.**

10. **Choose Edit⇨Paste Special.**

    The Paste Special dialog box appears.

11. **Click on the Paste or Paste Link radio button and then click on the OK button.**

    If you want to just include the file in your database, choose Paste. If you want changes in the source sound file to also show up in the file in the database, choose Paste Link.

    The sound is pasted into the PicturePlus field, and a microphone icon appears in the field.

    By choosing Paste Link, you are actually pasting a *link* from the sound file to the database, which is good for saving disk space. If you use the regular Edit⇨Paste command (or choose Paste in the Paste Special dialog box), the sound file itself is copied into the database, which wastes a great deal of disk space.

Playing a sound

After you paste a sound into a PicturePlus field, you can play the sound easily. Just follow this procedure:

1. **Double-click on the microphone icon in the PicturePlus field.**

2. **Listen.**

If you don't hear the sound, several things could be wrong:

> ✔ Your computer doesn't have a sound card.
>
> ✔ The sound card isn't working properly.
>
> ✔ The sound card is working, but the speakers are unplugged or turned off, or the volume control is turned down too low.
>
> ✔ The kids are yelling too loudly in the other room for you to hear anything.

Removing a sound

 If you decide that sounds are a bit frivolous, you can easily remove them. To remove a sound from a PicturePlus field, click on the field to select it and press Ctrl+X, choose Edit➪Cut, or click on the Cut SmartIcon.

Let's Go to the Movies

Welcome to the MTV era of computing. If your computer has the chutzpah, you can add small video clips to your database records and play them at will. This stuff is pretty exotic, but what the heck. It's fun.

Adding a video clip to a PicturePlus field is similar to adding a sound clip. The crucial difference, however, between video clips and sound bites is that video clips are meant to be seen as well as heard.

Oh, and you think sound files are big? Wait until you see how big video files are. Ha! The whole multimedia revolution is probably a conspiracy started by hard disk manufacturers.

> ✔ As we said, video clips are big, big, big. Sure, you can find them on the Internet, but you can grow old waiting for them to download. Your best bet is to buy them in a collection from a computer store.
>
> ✔ To find out more about video and multimedia in general, check out *Multimedia and CD-ROMs For Dummies,* by Andy Rathbone, published by IDG Books Worldwide, Inc. We don't get a nickel for this endorsement, but we figure you can probably use some more help here.

Adding a video clip

To add a video clip to a database record, follow these steps:

1. **Call up the record to which you want to add the video clip.**

2. **Click on the PicturePlus field.**

3. **Go to the Start menu and choose Programs⇨Accessories⇨Multimedia⇨ Media Player to start the Media Player.**

   Figure 12-7 shows what the Media Player looks like. The buttons that look like the buttons on your VCR work like the buttons on your VCR. Too bad Microsoft didn't throw in a blinking 12:00 to complete the VCR look.

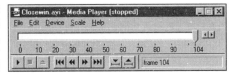

Figure 12-7: The Media Player, ready for action!

4. **Choose File⇨Open or press Ctrl+O to bring up the Open dialog box.**

5. **Select the video file that you want to insert and click on the OK button.**

   Video files have names that end in AVI. If you can't find the movie you want, hunt around until you locate it. If you just need a sample to play with, look in C:\windows\help — boring, but functional.

6. **Click on the Play button to make sure that you found the right video clip.**

7. **Choose Edit⇨Copy Object to copy the video to the Clipboard.**

   Or use the familiar keyboard shortcut, Ctrl+C, or click on the Copy SmartIcon.

8. **Pop over to Approach 97; press Alt+Tab until Approach 97 comes back to life or choose Approach 97 from the Taskbar.**

9. **Choose Edit⇨Paste Special to bring up the Paste Special dialog box and then click on the OK button.**

   Approach 97 pastes the video into the PicturePlus field, and one frame of the video is visible. If you want the video frame to appear as an icon, check the Display as Icon option in the Paste Special dialog box and a film reel icon appears in the field.

Playing a video

After you have pasted a video clip into a PicturePlus field, you can play the video at any time by following this procedure:

1. **Make some popcorn.**

2. **Turn down the lights.**

3. **Double-click on the film icon in the PicturePlus field.**

4. **Watch.**

5. **Marvel. (Ooooos and ahhhhhs go here.)**

Chapter 13

Using Calculated Fields

A calculated field is a database field that contains a formula that automatically calculates the field's value. For example, if a database has an
invoice subtotal field, you can use a calculated field to figure the sales tax as a
percentage of the subtotal. Then you can use another calculated field to
produce the invoice total by adding the sales tax to the subtotal.

Chapter 2 briefly introduces calculated fields. This chapter dives headfirst into
the depths of creating formulas for calculated fields. If the water gets too deep
here, you can use your mouse pad as a flotation device.

Using Simple Arithmetic

Approach 97 uses a formula to figure out the value of a calculated field.
Formulas can be simple or complex, depending on what value you want
Approach 97 to calculate for the field. The simplest Approach 97 formulas use
ordinary arithmetic — addition, subtraction, multiplication, and division. Here
are some sample formulas that use nothing more than sixth-grade math:

`TotalParts + TotalLabor`	Calculates an invoice total for an auto repair shop
`Subtotal * .0725`	Calculates the sales tax assuming a tax rate of 7.25 percent
`AtBats / Hits`	Calculates a batting average for a Little League baseball database

Notice that all the database field names in the preceding formulas consist of one word. To use a field name that consists of two or more words with intervening spaces, you have to type a quotation mark on either side of the field name. For example, if the TotalParts and TotalLabor fields in the first example were named Total Parts and Total Labor, the formula would require quotation marks, like this: `"Total Parts" + "Total Labor"`.

Table 13-1 summarizes the *operators* (that is, math symbols) that you can use to create simple arithmetic functions.

Table 13-1	Simple Arithmetic Operators
Operator	*What It Does*
+	Addition
–	Subtraction
*	Multiplication
/	Division

Crazy but unavoidable formula jargon

After you start working with formulas, you inevitably bump up against some pretty confusing terminology. These terms were originally the result of a conspiracy between computer science majors and math majors to prevent outsiders from understanding their secret language. Here are the terms you need to know:

Expression: Nothing more than a computer and/or math geek's way of saying *formula*. Technically, an expression is a combination of operators and operands that yields a single result. Approach 97 enables you to use three kinds of expressions: arithmetic expressions (math, like adding and multiplying), comparison expressions ("which one of these is not like the other"), and logical expressions (yes, no, true, false).

Operand: A value that is used in an expression. An operand can be a number, such as 23 or 689.58, or a database field, as in InvoiceAmount or TaxRate.

Operator: A symbol that tells Approach 97 what to do with a pair of operands. For example, the Addition operator (+) tells Approach 97 to add two operands.

Arithmetic expression: An expression that produces a numeric result by adding, subtracting, multiplying, dividing, or using special functions such as `Sqrt(64)` or `PMT (Principal, Rate,Months)`.

Comparison expression: An expression that produces a Yes or No result by comparing two values, such as `State = 'CA'`.

Logical expression: An expression that produces a Yes or No result, usually by combining the results of several comparison expressions, such as `State = 'CA' OR State = 'NV'`.

Creating simple formulas

To create a calculated field that uses a simple arithmetic formula, follow these steps:

1. **Choose Create➪Field Definition to call up the Field Definition dialog box.**

   If the Field Definition dialog box is already visible, skip this step.

2. **Type a name for the calculated field in the Field Name column.**

   You may have to scroll down the field list to find a blank row in which to create the new field.

3. **Select Calculated as the new field's Data Type from the drop-down list.**

   When you select the Data Type, the Field Definition dialog box expands to show the field options for the calculated field, as shown in Figure 13-1.

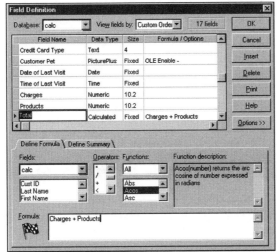

Figure 13-1:
Creating a
calculated
field.

4. **Create the formula for the field by double-clicking on the Fields, arithmetic Operators, and Functions that you want to include in the formula.**

   For example, to create the formula Charges + Products (if you have Charges and Products in your database), double-click on Charges in the Fields list, double-click on the Addition operator (+) in the Operators list, and then double-click on Products in the Fields list.

You can type numeric constants when you need them. For example, to create the formula Subtotal * 0.0725, double-click on Subtotal, double-click on the Multiplication operator (*), and then type **0.0725** directly in the Formula field.

5. After you have created the formula, click on the OK button.

Or type another field name in the next blank row at the top of the dialog box to create another field.

Here are some things to watch for when you create simple formulas:

✔ Notice the checkered flag at the lower-left of the Field Definition dialog box. The flag has a red stroke through it if the formula is incomplete. As soon as you complete the formula, the red stroke disappears, and the checkered flag lights up. (When you create more complex formulas, the stroke may turn on and off several times. Don't panic; this behavior is entirely normal.)

✔ When you double-click on a field name to add it to the formula, Approach 97 automatically adds quotation marks if they are needed.

✔ If the Approach 97 file includes joined databases, the joined databases are listed in the drop-down list box above the field names.

✔ If you prefer to type the formula yourself in the Formula field instead of hunting and pecking for fields and operators, feel free to do so. Just make sure that you type the field names correctly and don't forget to use quotation marks when necessary.

Creating fancy formulas with parentheses

Formulas can get more complicated than simple addition and subtraction. You can also use parentheses to make formulas that look like the kind of math you've been trying to forget since high school algebra. For example, consider how the parentheses affect the results of these two formulas:

✔ 5 + 3 * 2 equals 16, because Approach 97 first adds 5 to 3 to get 8, and then it multiplies 8 by 2 to get 16.

✔ 5 + (3 * 2) equals 11, because Approach 97 first multiplies 3 by 2 to get 6, and then it adds 6 to 5 to get 11.

Approach 97 normally calculates formulas from left to right, but parentheses change that order. Approach 97 always calculates values within parentheses first and works from the innermost set of parentheses out.

If you really want to impress your friends who think they know more about math than you do, try using parentheses within parentheses, as in 5 * (3 + (2 * 3)), which equals 45. (2 × 3 = 6; 6 + 3 = 9; 9 × 5 = 45.)

Here are some vital facts concerning parentheses:

- ✔ Sometimes parentheses do *not* affect the results of a calculation. For example, the formulas 5 + 3 * 2 and (5 + 3) * 2 both give the same result: 16.

- ✔ To add parentheses to a formula, click on the left and right parentheses in the list of operators in the Field Definition dialog box or type the parentheses yourself.

- ✔ Make sure that you always use parentheses in matched pairs — one left parenthesis for every right parenthesis. If parentheses aren't properly matched, the red stroke appears over the checkered flag to indicate that the formula isn't finished. (Too bad they didn't also include a yellow caution flag, because crashing into the wall is pretty easy when you are creating formulas.)

Working with Functions

You can do a great deal with formulas that use only the basic math operators, but formulas get even more interesting when you start using functions in them. Functions perform a whole sequence of calculations to come up with a result, such as finding the square root of a number or determining the monthly payment for a loan, given the loan amount, interest rate, and number of payments.

To use a function in a formula, you double-click on the function in the F̲unctions list (each function has its own name) from the Field Definition dialog box, followed by a left parenthesis, usually one or more *arguments* (which is a fancy way of saying additional pieces of information), and a right parenthesis. Each function requires either no arguments at all or a specific number of arguments. Usually, the arguments are field names or constant values, such as numbers or text strings:

```
Sqrt(64)
PMT(Principal,Rate,Months)
```

Some functions do not use arguments. Even so, the parentheses are still required, as in the following example:

```
Pi()
```

If you really want to get ambitious, you can use another function as a function argument, as in the following example:

```
DayOfWeek(Today())
```

In this example, the argument for the DayOfWeek function is the value of the Today function.

If you see a function and you aren't quite sure what it does, just click once on the name and read the Function description box. If you still don't understand what it does, call your old math teacher and grovel.

You can also combine functions with other calculations. The following are examples:

```
PMT(Principal,Rate,Months) / 2
Today() + 30
```

The following section outlines the more useful Approach 97 functions.

Many of the program's functions are designed for playing with date and time values. These functions are covered in Chapter 14 rather than here. Skip ahead to Chapter 14 if you're after that information.

Mathematical functions for eggheads

If you are the type of person who loved using a slide rule (or fancy calculator, depending on your age) in high school, you'll love the math functions in Approach 97. They let you calculate stuff that most of us have been trying to forget for years. Table 13-2 summarizes the basic math and trigonometry functions in Approach 97. You can find these functions in the Functions list in the Field Definitions dialog box on the Define Formula tab.

Table 13-2	Math Functions
Function	*What It Does*
Abs(*number*)	Calculates the absolute value of *number*
Acos(*number*)	Calculates the arc cosine of *number*
Asin(*number*)	Calculates the arc sine of *number*
Atan(*number*)	Calculates the arc tangent of *number*
Atan2(*number1,number2*)	Calculates the arc tangent of *number1/number2*

Function	What It Does
Cos(*angle*)	Calculates the cosine of *angle*
Degree(*radians*)	Converts *radians* to degrees
Exp(*number*)	Calculates *e* to the power of *number*
Factorial(*number*)	Calculates the factorial of *number* (1*2*3 and so on, all the way up to *number*)
Ln(*number*)	Calculates the natural logarithm of *number*
Log(*number*)	Calculates the logarithm (base 10) of *number*
Mod(*number1,number2*)	Calculates the remainder when *number2* is divided into *number1*
Pi( )	Returns the value of pi: 3.14159265
Pow(*number1,number2*)	Calculates *number1* raised to the power *number2*
Radian(*degrees*)	Converts *degrees* to radians
Random( )	Returns a random number between 0 and 1
Round(*number,precision*)	Rounds off *number* to the number of decimal places indicated by *precision*
Sign(*number*)	Returns –1 if *number* is negative, 1 if *number* is positive, or 0 if *number* is zero
Sin(*angle*)	Calculates the sine of *angle*
Sqrt(*number*)	Calculates the square root of *number*
Tan(*angle*)	Calculates the tangent of *angle*
Trunc(*number,precision*)	Truncates *number* to the number of decimal places indicated by *precision*

Of the functions listed in Table 13-2, the only one that doesn't require a pocket protector and a love of higher mathematics is Round( ). You can use Round( ) whenever a monetary calculation involves division to avoid charging a customer $10.9863. The first argument that you use with Round( ) is the number that you want rounded; the second argument is the number of decimal places that you want to preserve. For example, if the field Credit has a value of 10.9863, the formula `Round(Credit,2)` returns the value 10.99.

Trunc( ) is similar to Round( ), but with a crucial difference. Round( ) rounds a number up if the first unused digit is 5 or greater, but Trunc( ) simply lops off unwanted digits. Thus, if the value of Credit is 10.9863, the function `Trunc(Credit,2)` returns the value 10.98, not 10.99. For most business purposes, Round( ) is the one you want. Use Trunc( ) if you're trying to embezzle millions of dollars, half a penny at a time.

Conjuring conversion functions

Conversion functions, as shown in Table 13-3, change one type of data to another type. This process may make your (increasingly pocket-protector-equipped) life a little easier by eliminating manual calculations or the need to convert different types of information.

Table 13-3	Conversion Functions
Function	*What It Does*
DateToText(*date,format*)	Converts *date* to a text string with the *format* you specify
NumToText (*number,format*)	Converts *number* to a text string with the *format* you specify
NumToWord (*number,precision*)	Converts *number* to a text string with the specified *precision*
TextToBool(*text*)	Returns No if the first character in the *text* is F, f, N, n, or 0 (zero); otherwise, returns Yes
TextToDate(*text*)	Converts *text* to a date value
TextToTime(*text*)	Converts *text* to a time value

Interesting financial functions

If your idea of good reading is an amortization table, you'll love the financial functions that Approach 97 offers, which Table 13-4 summarizes.

Table 13-4	Financial Functions
Function	*What It Does*
FV(*payment,rate,periods*)	Tells you the future value of *payment* invested at a given interest *rate* for a certain number of *periods*
NPeriods (*rate,principal,payment*)	Tells you how many periods are necessary to pay off *principal* at a given interest *rate* and *payment*
PMT(*principal,rate,periods*)	Tells you what the payment is if you borrow *principal* at a given interest *rate* for a certain number of *periods*
PV(*payment,rate,periods*)	Tells you the present value of an annuity with a given *payment*, interest *rate*, and number of *periods*
SLN(*cost,salvage,life*)	Calculates straight-line depreciation for an asset with a given *cost*, *salvage* value, and *life*

Notice that several of these functions use the same arguments — *principal, rate,* and *periods* — but in different orders. For example, the NPeriods function is NPeriods(*rate,principal,payment*), but the PMT function is PMT(*principal,rate, periods*). Very confusing. You have to check for the correct sequence of arguments when you use one of these functions because Approach 97 doesn't know and cannot tell you if you list the arguments in the wrong order.

When you use these financial functions, you need to keep in mind that the interest rate is the rate *per period.* Thus, if you make payments once per month, the interest rate argument must provide the monthly interest rate. For example, perhaps you want to know the monthly payment for a three-year (36-month) loan of $15,000 at an annual interest rate of 12 percent. In this case, the monthly interest rate is 1 percent, so you use the PMT function like this:

```
PMT(15000,.01,36)
```

If you don't deal much with financial calculations, you won't need these functions. If you do, you may be better off using a spreadsheet program such as Lotus 1-2-3, which has more powerful financial functions and provides more ways to manipulate and analyze financial data.

Using logical functions

Logical functions are the weirdest functions in the program's function goody box. They return one of two different values, depending on the results of a conditional test. These logical functions can help make decisions, depending on specific conditions. For example, you can calculate sales tax, but only for people living in a particular state, completely automatically. Table 13-5 summarizes the logical functions.

Table 13-5	Logical Functions
Function	*What It Does*
If(*condition,true value,false value*)	Evaluates the *condition* expression and then returns *true value* if the condition is true or *false value* if the condition is false
Blank(*field,value*)	Returns the value of *field,* unless *field* happens to be blank, in which case *value* is returned instead
IsBlank(*field*)	Returns Yes if *field* is blank; otherwise, returns No
IsLastRecord()	Returns Yes if the record is the last record as the set is currently sorted; otherwise, returns No

The If function is the main logical function in Approach 97. You use it to set a field to one of two different values depending on the result of a conditional test. For example, suppose that you need to charge 7.5 percent sales tax for sales to customers who live in California (as indicated by a field named State) but no sales tax for customers who live outside of California. You can use an If function:

```
If(State = 'CA',.075,0)
```

In this example, the *condition* argument is `State = 'CA'`. Approach 97 analyzes this comparison expression to see whether the State field is indeed equal to CA. If it is, the If function uses the true value, .075. If it is not, the false value, 0, is used. (Also, notice how we use apostrophes to mark the value CA. Double-quotation marks (") are used to enclose field names that include spaces; apostrophes are used to enclose all text field values.)

You can use the preceding If function to set the value of a Tax Rate field, or you can use it as a part of a more complicated formula to calculate a sales tax amount:

```
Subtotal * If(State = 'CA',.075,0)
```

In this example, the value of the Subtotal field is multiplied by .075 or 0, depending on whether the State field equals CA.

You can use the Blank function to set a value for fields that are blank. For example, perhaps you want to charge $2 shipping and handling if no other value is typed in the Shipping field. In that case, you can use a formula such as `Blank(Shipping,2.00)`. This formula returns the value of the Shipping field as long as the Shipping field is not blank. If the Shipping field *is* blank, 2.00 is used.

The IsBlank function provides a convenient way to test whether a field has a blank value. The formula `IsBlank(State)` returns a value of Yes if the State field is blank, or No if the State field is not blank.

You can use IsBlank within an If function, as in the following:

```
If(IsBlank(State),.075,0)
```

In this example, .075 is used if the State field is blank; otherwise, 0 is used.

You can see from the preceding examples that you can really get yourself tied up in knots if you overuse these logical functions. Use them only if you must and be extra careful when you do. Make sure that you thoroughly test them with every possible combination of field values to make sure that they work the way you expect them to work.

Functions for doing funny things with text fields

Some of the Approach 97 functions enable you to do strange things with text fields, such as extracting characters from the left, right, or middle of a text field; combining text fields; or capitalizing each word in a text field. These functions are too numerous for us to describe all of them, but most of them are reserved for computer nerds. Table 13-6 lists the functions that ordinary mortals commonly use.

The text function that you're most likely to use is Combine( ). This text function gangs up two or more strings to create a single string, and it is most often used to combine a first and last name to create a full name:

```
Combine("First Name", ' ', "Last Name")
```

This function produces results such as the following:

```
John Smith
Mary Hernandez
Sylvia Hancock
```

Notice that *three* arguments are used in the preceding Combine( ) function: the first name, a space, and the last name. If you omit the space between the first and last names, the names are jammed together.

If you want to list names last name first, use a Combine( ) function such as this one:

```
Combine("Last Name", ', ', "First Name")
```

This function produces results such as the following:

```
Smith, John
Hernandez, Mary
Hancock, Sylvia
```

In this example, the second argument is a text constant that consists of a comma and a space.

Table 13-6	Text Functions
Function	*What It Does*
Asc(*character*)	Gives you the ASCII numeric value of the *character*
Chr(*number*)	Tells you the ASCII character for the *number*
Combine(*list of strings*)	Combines all the text strings that you give it to create a single text string
Exact(*text1,text2*)	Compares the two text fields exactly (if the strings match exactly, Approach 97 returns Yes; otherwise, returns No)
Fill(*text,number*)	Repeats *text* as many times as indicated by *number*
Lead(*text*)	Capitalizes the first letter in the *text*
Left(*text,number*)	Returns *text* with the specified *number* of characters from the text specified, starting from the left
Length(*text*)	Returns the total number of characters in the specified *text*, including all spaces, numbers, and special characters
Like(*text1,text2*)	Compares the two text fields, ignoring case — you can use the wildcards * and ? to stand for multiple or single characters (returns Yes if the strings match; otherwise, returns No)
Lower(*text*)	Changes all the characters in *text* to lowercase.
Middle(*text,start,size*)	Returns a string extracted from *text*, beginning at the *start* position and including the number of characters *size* specifies
Position(*text,search string,start*)	Returns the position of the first occurrence of the *search string* in the *text* from the *start* position
Prefix(*text1,text2*)	Returns Yes if the characters in *text1* match the same number of characters at the beginning of *text2*; otherwise, returns No
Proper(*text*)	Converts the first letter of each word in *text* to uppercase; converts all other letters to lowercase
Replace(*original text,start, size,replacement text*)	Replaces *size* characters in the *original text*, beginning at *start*, with the *replacement text*
Right(*text,number*)	Returns *text* with the specified *number* of characters from the text specified, starting from the right
Soundslike(*text1,text2*)	Compares two text fields to see whether they are phonetically similar (returns Yes if they are or No if they are not)

Function	What It Does
Span(*text1,text2*)	Returns the number of characters in *text1* that match *text2* up to the first character that doesn't match
SpanUntil(*text1,text2*)	Returns the number of characters in *text1* that do not match *text2*, up to the first character that does match
Translate(*text, character1,character2*)	Replaces all occurrences of *character1* with *character2* in *text*
Trim(*text*)	Removes extraneous spaces from the left and right of *text*
Upper(*text*)	Converts *text* to all uppercase

Statistical functions

Approach 97 only provides the very basics as far as statistical functions are concerned. If you need more, you could either build the formulas (a hard, time-consuming, and boring task) or just use Lotus 1-2-3, which does a far better job.

The summary functions are listed in Table 13-7.

Table 13-7	Statistical Functions
Function	**What It Does**
Avg(*list of numbers*)	Calculates the average of however many numbers you give it
STD(*list of numbers*)	Calculates the standard deviation of however many numbers you give it
Var(*list of numbers*)	Returns the variance of however many numbers you give it

Summary functions

The last group of functions that we want to present in this chapter is summary functions. These functions are applied to field values from more than one record. Usually, you use these summary functions when you create a form that includes a repeating panel or a report that includes summary totals. However, you can also use summary functions when you define fields by using the Field Definition dialog box.

The summary functions are listed in Table 13-8.

Table 13-8	Summary Functions
Function	*What It Does*
SAverage(*field*)	Calculates the average value for *field* in a range of records
SCount(*field*)	Counts the number of records that have a value for *field* in a range of records
SMax(*field*)	Tells you the largest value for *field* in a range of records
SMin(*field*)	Tells you the smallest value for *field* in a range of records
SNPV(*value, discount rate*)	Tells you the net present value of an investment based on a series of periodic cash flows (*value*) and a *discount rate*
SSTD(*field*)	Calculates the standard deviation for *field* in a range of records
SSUM(*field*)	Adds up the values for *field* in a range of records
SVAR(*field*)	Calculates the variance for *field* in a range of records

Chapter 14

Working with Date and Time Fields

*I*f you've ever been late for a very important date, you'll be relieved to know that Approach 97 is quite sophisticated at working with date and time fields. This chapter covers the ins and outs of working with these kinds of fields. You find out how to enter values into date and time fields and how to perform various calculations on these fields.

Entering Values into Date and Time Fields

Aside from simply being able to type a date or time into a date or time field, you need to know about several techniques that enable you to enter date and time values more efficiently. The following sections cover these techniques.

Entering values into date fields

To enter a date into a date field, type the month, day, and year, using numbers separated by non-numeric characters. For example, you type **5/02/97** or **12-31-97.** You can use any non-numeric character you prefer to separate the month, day, and year, but slashes or hyphens are the most common. Approach 97 uses slashes whenever it displays a date field.

If you leave out the month and year, Approach 97 assumes that you mean the current month and year. For example, if you type **20** in a date field during November 1997, Approach 97 assumes that you mean November 20, 1997.

You can type two or four digits for the year. If you type two digits, Approach 97 assumes that you mean the twentieth century. Thus, **97** is interpreted as 1997. If you type four digits, Approach 97 accepts whatever year you type. (If you type just one digit, Approach 97 also assumes the twentieth century. Thus, **5** is interpreted as 1905.)

For the months January through September, you can type a single digit (**1** through **9**) or two digits (**01** through **09**). It doesn't matter.

If you defined a fancy date format for a date field, the format of the date changes the moment the insertion point leaves the date field. For example, if you type **5-02-96** into a date field, the date may change to something such as Monday, May 02, 1996, when you move the cursor out of the field. Do not be alarmed; this behavior is normal. The date is supposed to do that. (For more information about using fancy date formats, see the section "Using Fancy Date and Time Formats" in this chapter.)

If the Show data entry format option is selected for the field (via the Properties dialog box), slashes and underlines appear on-screen to indicate how to type the date. To enter a date into this type of field, you type only the month, day, and year values; you do not need to type any separator characters.

Entering values into time fields

To enter a time into a time field, type the hours and minutes, using a normal person's 12-hour clock or a military-style 24-hour clock. Either way, you have to type the hour and minutes as numbers separated by colons. For example, you type **12:15** or **19:30**.

If the hour is 12 or less, Approach 97 assumes that you mean morning. To type an afternoon or evening time when you are using a 12-hour clock, you have to type **PM,** as in **6:00 PM.**

If you're into precision, or if you're recording information about Swiss train schedules, you can type seconds and even hundredths of seconds. For example, you can type **11:30:45** or **11:30:45.99.**

On the other hand, if all you're interested in is the hour, just type the hour. Approach 97 assumes that a single number typed by itself is an hour. Thus, when you type **8**, it appears as 8:00 and **12** appears as 12:00.

Note that if you define a time format for a time field, the time that you enter into the field is reformatted the moment the cursor leaves the time field. For more information about time formats, see the section "Using Fancy Date and Time Formats" later in this chapter.

If the Show data entry format option is selected for the field (via the Properties dialog box), colons and underlines appear on-screen to indicate how to type the time. To enter a time into this kind of field, you type only the hours, minutes, and seconds. Approach 97 supplies the colons, so you don't have to type them.

Automatically entering the current date and time

You can quickly enter the current date in a date field by using one of the following techniques:

 ✔ Click on the field and then click on the Insert Today's Date SmartIcon.

 ✔ Click on the field and then press Ctrl+Shift+D.

 ✔ Click on the field and then choose Browse⊃Insert⊃Today's Date.

To enter the current time in a time field, use one of the following techniques:

 ✔ Click on the field and then click on the Insert Current Time SmartIcon.

 ✔ Press Ctrl+Shift+T.

 ✔ Choose Browse⊃Insert⊃Current Time.

If your computer's system clock has the wrong date or time setting, these techniques put the wrong date or time values into the database. To check and correct the system clock, move your cursor over the time display in the Taskbar at the bottom right of your screen. Right-click on the time and select Adjust Date/Time. Adjust the date and time settings if necessary and then click on the OK button.

Using Fancy Date and Time Formats

Date and time fields would be pretty boring if the only ways to format them were 05/02/96 and 12:30 PM. Fortunately, Approach 97 gives you a plethora of choices for formatting dates and times on forms, reports, and other views. If you prefer, you can display a date as May 02, 1996, or even Thursday, May 02, 1996. You can even leave parts of the date off, such as May 02 or just May.

Times aren't quite as flexible as dates, but you can use a 12-hour or 24-hour clock; specify which suffixes to use (AM and PM, am and pm, or whatever), and decide whether to include all of the time, just the hours and minutes, or just the hours.

Keep in mind that these date and time formats apply only to how the date or time is displayed on a form, report, or other view. The format does not affect how the date or time is actually stored in the database.

Setting a fancy date format

To set a fancy date format, follow this procedure:

1. Switch to Design mode and select the view that you want to modify.

To switch to Design mode, click on the Design button, choose Design from the View pop-up menu in the status bar, choose View➪Design, or press Ctrl+D. My, aren't there a lot of ways to switch to Design mode?

To select the view, click on the appropriate view tab or choose the view from the View pop-up menu in the status bar.

2. Click on the date field you want to modify.

You should really set the field to be a Date field if that's all you'll be using it for, but you can set date formatting for other types of fields. Refer to Chapter 2 for more information about creating fields.

3. Call up the Properties dialog box.

Click on the Properties SmartIcon, press Ctrl+E, or double-click on the field. The Properties dialog box for the date field appears.

4. Click on the Number Format tab (#) in the Properties dialog box.

The date format options appear, as shown in Figure 14-1.

Figure 14-1:
The date
format
options in
the
Properties
dialog box.

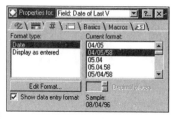

5. Change the Format type from Display as entered to Date.

When you click on the Number Format tab, most of the formatting options shown in Figure 14-1 are unavailable until you change the Format type to Date.

6. **Select a date format in the Current format box.**

   As you scroll through the Current format box, you may notice that you have several — tons, actually — of format types from which to choose. To see what each format looks like, look at the Sample displayed at the bottom of the dialog box or see how the format looks in the Date field itself (if the field contains data).

7. **Close the Properties dialog box by double-clicking on the control box (in the upper-left corner) or by clicking on the Close button (in the upper-right corner).**

Here are some points to consider when you define date formats:

✔ You can edit the format you choose by clicking on the Edit Format button. In the Edit Format dialog box that appears, use the Format Code area to change, for example, the separator character or capitalization so that the date appears exactly as you want.

✔ You can edit the format of periods (like quarters and trimesters) by clicking on the Edit Format button. For more information, see the sidebar called "All about periods, period" in this chapter.

Setting a fancy time format

Mercifully, you don't have as many options for setting time formats as you do for setting date formats. Here's the procedure:

1. **Switch to Design mode and select the view that you want to modify.**

   To switch to Design mode, click on the Design button, choose Design from the View pop-up menu in the status bar, choose View➪Design, or press Ctrl+D.

   To select the view, click on the appropriate view tab or choose the view from the View menu or the View pop-up menu in the status bar.

2. **Click on the time field whose format you want to modify.**

3. **Summon the Properties dialog box.**

   Click on the Properties SmartIcon or press Ctrl+E. The Properties dialog box appears.

4. **Click on the Number Format tab (#) in the Properties dialog box.**

   The time format options appear, as shown in Figure 14-2.

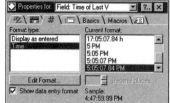

Figure 14-2:
The time
format
options
in the
Properties
dialog box.

5. Change the Format type from Display as entered to Time.

Most of the formatting options shown in Figure 14-2 are unavailable until
you change the Format type to Time.

6. In the Current format area, select a time format you like.

As you scroll through the Current format box, you notice that you have
several types of formats from which to choose. To see what each format
looks like, look at the Sample displayed at the bottom of the dialog box or
see how the format looks in the Date field itself.

**7. Exit the dialog box by double-clicking on the control box (in the upper-
left corner) or by clicking on the Close button (in the upper-right corner).**

That's all there is.

Here is a timely thought: You can usually coax your friendly computer guru into
formatting time fields for you by offering a six pack of his or her favorite
beverage as a bribe. On the other hand, given the slew of formats provided and
the fact that you can click on the Edit Format button and edit the samples
yourself, why bother?

Using Dates and Times in Calculations

Besides storing and displaying dates and times, Approach 97 enables you to
perform various calculations on date and time fields. For example, you can use
a date field in an Invoice database to calculate the age of an invoice so that you
can send annoying collection notices to customers who have overdue bills. Or
you can calculate the number of days since the last time a customer ordered or
the date on which a bill will be due.

Chapter 13 covers calculations in detail; feel free to refer to that information if
this section seems rather cryptic and arcane.

All about periods, period

Approach 97 enables you to use all kinds of fancy or customized date formats, including ones that show periods of the year, such as quarters, trimesters, and halves. For example, Approach 97 can display the date 6/20/98 as 2Q98, First half of 1998, or 2nd trimester, 1998. Most of the usual (and unusual) options you may want are already available to you, but if your boss strongly prefers to include the quarter along with the month, date, and year, you can accommodate. (Deciding if you *want* to do so is a topic for discussion in a different book.)

To use these special periods, you have to edit one of the existing date formats. You can include any text in the format, plus any of the following special codes:

Code	What It Stands for
4	The quarter, as a number (1, 2, 3, or 4)
44	The quarter, as an ordinal number (1st, 2nd, 3rd, or 4th)
444	The quarter, spelled out (First, Second, Third, or Fourth)
3	The trimester, as a number (1, 2, or 3)
33	The trimester, as an ordinal number (1st, 2nd, or 3rd)
333	The trimester, spelled out (First, Second, or Third)
2	The half, as a number (1 or 2)
22	The half, as an ordinal number (1st or 2nd)
222	The half, spelled out (First or Second)
DD	The date, two digits
DDD	The day of the week, abbreviation
DDDD	The day of the week, spelled out
MM	The month, two digits
MMM	The month, abbreviation
MMMM	The month, spelled out
YY	The year, two digits (as in *97*)
YYYY	The year, four digits (as in *1997*)

Here are some sample formats that use the above codes:

Format Code	Example with Date 6/20/97
4QYY	2Q94
222 half of YYYY	First half of 1997
DDDD, DD. MMMM	Saturday, 12. March
33 trimester, YYYY	2nd trimester, 1997

Simple date and time calculations

You can use date and time fields in simple formulas, but you need to be aware of a few key points when you use dates and times in calculations:

- ✔ If you subtract one date from another, the result is a number that represents the number of days between the dates. For example, the formula `Today()-InvoiceDate` tells you how many days old an invoice is.

- ✔ If you add or subtract a number to or from a date, the result is another date. Thus, to determine the date 30 days from today, you can use the formula `Today()+30`.

- ✔ Although Approach 97 can do it, multiplying or dividing date or time values makes no sense. It won't give you more hours in a day, so don't even think about it.

- ✔ To incorporate a constant date value into a formula, you have to use the `TextToDate( )` function, which is described in the next section, "Functions for date and time calculations."

- ✔ If you subtract one time value from another, the result is the difference between the two times in hundredths of seconds. For example, suppose that the value of a field named Time1 is 4:30:00 PM, and the value of another field, named Time2, is 4:30:15 PM. The formula `Time2 — Time1` gives the result 1,500.

  To determine the number of seconds between two times, divide the result by 100, as in the formula `(Time2 — Time1) / 100`.

- ✔ To add or subtract a value to or from a time, express the value in hundredths of seconds. Thus, to add 10 seconds to a field named Time, use a formula such as `Time + 1000`.

Functions for date and time calculations

Approach 97 provides several functions that you can use with Date and Time values to make date and time calculations easier. The date functions are summarized in Table 14-1, and Table 14-2 summarizes the Time functions.

Table 14-1	Date Functions
Function	*What It Does*
Today()	Returns the current date
Date(*month,day,year*)	Converts separate *month*, *day*, and *year* values to a date value

Function	What It Does
Month(*date*)	Returns the month for *date*
Day(*date*)	Returns the day of the month for *date*
Year(*date*)	Returns the year for *date*
DayOfWeek(*date*)	Returns the day of the week (1 – 7) for *date*
DayOfYear(*date*)	Returns the day of the year (1 – 365) for *date*
WeekOfYear(*date*)	Returns the week of the year (1 – 52) for *date*
DayName(*number* or *date*)	Returns the name of the day for *number* (1 – 7) or *date*
MonthName(*number* or *date*)	Returns the name of the month for *number* (1 – 12) or *date*
DateToText(*date*)	Converts *date* to a text string that can be displayed.
TextToDate(*text*)	Converts a *text* string to a date

Table 14-2	Time Functions
Function	**What It Does**
CurrTime()	Returns the current time
Time(*hours,minutes, seconds,hundredths*)	Converts separate *hours, minutes, seconds,* and *hundredths* to a time value
Hour(*time*)	Returns the hour for *time*
Minute(*time*)	Returns the minute for *time*
Second(*time*)	Returns the second for *time*
Hundredth(*time*)	Returns the hundredths of a second for *time*

The two functions that you are most likely to use are Today( ) and CurrTime( ), which tell you the current date and time. The other functions are useful for special types of date calculations, most of which are best performed while you are wearing a propeller cap and a pocket protector. Having summarized these functions in Tables 14-1 and 14-2, we therefore guiltlessly leave the task to you to figure out how and when to use them.

Part III
Getting Real Work Done

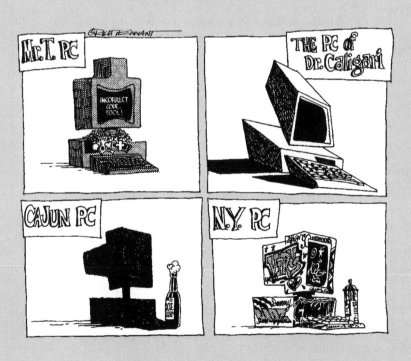

In this part ...

Database, shmatabase. What the heck can you do with an Approach 97 database to help you out in the real world? Well, you will be happy to know that an Approach 97 database can make grueling tasks easy — such as creating form letters and their corresponding envelopes and/or labels, summarizing database data, and generating beautiful charts and graphs to knock them dead at presentations. So read this part of the book and get to work.

Chapter 15

Creating Form Letters

*F*orm letters let you send junk mail to the unsuspecting people who are on file in your Approach 97 database. Of course, so many other people are sending those same people form letters every day that probably no one will even open your letter. So you may as well not bother. But in case you're more optimistic than we are, this chapter shows you how to use Approach 97 to create form letters.

In the old days, creating form letters was about as much fun as having oral surgery. If you've ever done a mail merge with WordPerfect, you know what we're talking about. You started by creating a primary document that was filled with a bunch of weird codes. Then you had to create a secondary document that contained all the names and addresses plus more weird codes. Then you had to spread votive candles about the room and offer a sacrifice to the Mail Merge gods. Then you had to . . . well, you get the idea.

Approach 97 makes creating and printing form letters easy. In fact, a built-in Form Letter Assistant does most of the dirty work for you. All you have to do is answer a few questions, type the letter, and — voilà! — you're in the junk mail business.

After your friends find out that you know how to create form letters on your computer, they will assume that you are a computer expert and will come to you with their computer problems until you eventually decide to leave town and begin a new life. A word of advice: Don't let on that you know the first thing about creating form letters. Tell them that you paid Ed McMahon to do it for you.

Seeing the Big Picture

Suppose that you weren't at the Parents Club meeting last night, so the members elected you secretary. Now you have the job of sending a letter to all the parents at the school begging them to join the Parents Club. The Parents Club decided that sending a note home with the kids isn't good enough; a *personalized* letter must be sent to each parent's home.

Preparing a personalized form letter is a three-step affair:

1. **Collect the names and addresses in an Approach 97 database.**

   Hope that someone has already typed the names and addresses of all the parents into a computer. In the best of all worlds, that person typed the names into an Approach 97 database, so you're all set. In the OK-but-still-unlikely world, someone has already entered the names, but they were entered in PC CheaperBase or something worse, such as Microsoft Access. You then have to figure out a way to convert the data into a format that you can use with Approach 97. Chapter 22 can help you convert the data.

   Most likely, though, you have to plead with the principal to get permission for the kids to take home a form on which parents can write their names and addresses, with a request that the kids bring back the forms the following day. If you're lucky, about half of the forms come back within a week. You can safely figure that the other half probably got turned into paper airplanes or spit wads and never arrived home, so you have to send reminder notes home a week later, hoping — as they say in the direct-mail business — to improve your response rate. After two or three weeks, you have a stack of 400 forms with barely legible names and addresses just waiting to be typed into your computer. Oh, the joys of database.

   Now you go through the process of defining an Approach 97 database and spending two or three evenings entering the names and addresses when you could be watching reruns of *Seinfeld*.

2. **Create the form letter.**

   Next, you have to figure out what to say to all those unsuspecting parents. You can use the Form Letter Assistant to create a skeleton form letter that contains the special codes necessary to insert database fields in the letter for the inside address and the salutation (Dear John, not bringing your right hand up to your forehead).

   Then you get to toil over the body of the letter for hours, trying to be firm yet inoffensive. To come up with the body of the letter, you use Approach 97 as if it were a word-processing program. On occasion, you may wish that Approach 97 were a word-processing program, which it isn't, so don't get all excited.

The most important thing to remember about this step is that a form letter is nothing more than a special type of database view, just like a form or report. The step-by-step procedure for creating a form letter is in the section "Creating a Form Letter" in this chapter.

3. **Print the form letters.**

This part is easy. After you create the database records with the names and addresses, and after you create a form letter, all you have to do is click on the Print button, and away she goes. (If you want to send the letters to only a certain privileged few, you can use the Find command before you print the form letters.)

Creating a Form Letter

So your database is stuffed full of names and addresses, and you're dying to drop some junk mail on those poor unsuspecting folk. No problem. Just summon the Form Letter Assistant, which promptly asks you about the details of the letter you want to create and then creates the letter for you — no fuss, no muss.

Open the database that contains the names and addresses to which you want to send junk mail and then follow these steps:

1. **Choose Create▷Form Letter.**

The Form Letter Assistant appears, as shown in Figure 15-1.

As you can see, the Form Letter Assistant contains six tabs, corresponding to six steps for creating form letters. If you realize that you made a mistake in any of these steps, you can go back by clicking on the Back button or by clicking directly on the tab to which you want to return.

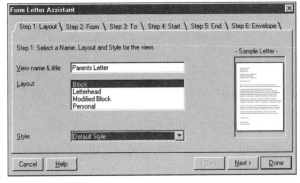

Figure 15-1:
Form Letter
Assistant,
at your
service.

2. **If you prefer, you can change the View name & title to something more meaningful than Form Letter 1.**

3. **Select the Layout.**

   In the Layout box, you can select the Block, Letterhead, Modified Block, or Personal letter layout. Pick the layout that suits your fancy — we chose Block for our letter. You see a vague approximation of your choice, in Lilliputian size, in the Sample Letter box.

   Note that the tabs and the numbers of tabs change according to the letter style you select.

4. **Select the Style.**

   You use the Style setting to pick one of four styles for the letter: Default Style (a generic, inoffensive layout), Business, Classic, and Informal. (All this setting does is change the font.)

5. **Click on the Next button or click on the Step 2: From tab.**

   The Form Letter Assistant return address options appear, as shown in Figure 15-2.

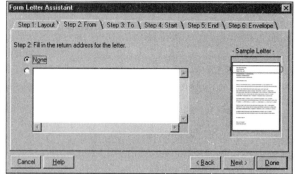

Figure 15-2:
Return address options.

6. **If you want to include a return address in the letter, type the address in the box. Otherwise, click on the None radio button.**

   Omit the return address if you plan to print the form letters on preprinted letterhead, or if you don't want people to know where you live. (Actually, if you're using letterhead, you should probably be using the Letterhead layout.)

7. **Click on the Next button or click on the Step 3: To tab.**

   The Form Letter Assistant inside address options appear, as shown in Figure 15-3.

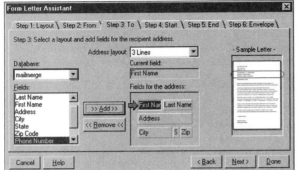

Figure 15-3:
Inside
address
options.

8. Select the Address layout.

This option lets you pick the number of lines to include in the inside address. When you are mailing to residences, three lines are usually adequate. For business mailings, you may need to use four or five lines.

9. Select the Fields that you want to appear in each portion of the inside address.

When you pick the address layout, the boxes in the Fields for the address section of the Form Letter Assistant dialog box change to indicate where you can insert fields in the inside address. For the three-line layout, the first line contains two fields (typically, first name and last name), the second line contains one field (the street address), and the third line contains three fields (city, state, and zip code). Other layouts have similar field arrangements.

To add a field to the inside address, click on the field in the Fields list and then click on the Add button. The field name appears in the field for the inside address box, and the next box in the inside address is selected. Continue until all the address fields have been added to the inside address. If you goof up and want to delete a field from the address box, click on the specific field box and then click on the Remove button.

10. Click on the Next button or click on the Step 4: Start tab.

The Form Letter Assistant Start options (salutation options) appear, as shown in Figure 15-4.

11. Select one or two fields to include in the salutation.

If you want to include, for example, only the parent's first name, you select First Name from the left box and (None) from the right box. If you want to include both a first and last name, you select First Name from the left box and Last Name from the right box.

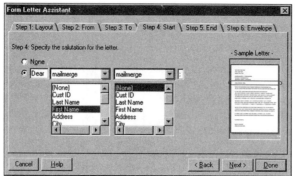

Figure 15-4:
Start
options.

12. Click on the Next button or click on the Step 5: End tab.

The Form Letter Assistant End options (closing options) appear, as shown in Figure 15-5.

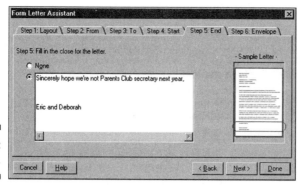

Figure 15-5:
End options.

13. Edit the close however you choose.

The closing initially says "Sincerely yours," but you can edit it to say anything you choose. You should also probably include your name in the closing.

If you want to edit the "Sincerely yours," to say something like, "Sincerely hope I'm not Parents Club secretary next year," all you have to do is select the text and fill in what you want to say.

14. Click on the Next button or click on the Step 6: Envelope tab.

The Form Letter Assistant's envelope options appear, as shown in Figure 15-6.

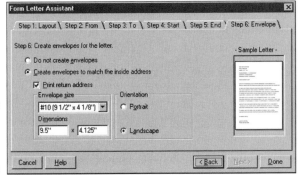

Figure 15-6:
Envelope
options.

15. **Select the envelope options you want.**

Be sure to select the envelope size before running off and printing your letters and envelopes. If you don't want to create envelopes at all, select the Do not create envelopes option. If it's July 15 and bored kids are lying around the house, hand-addressing the envelopes should stave off the boredom complaints for a week or two.

16. **Click on the Done button.**

Approach 97 spins and whirs for a few moments, and then it spits out a skeleton form letter similar to the one shown in Figure 15-7.

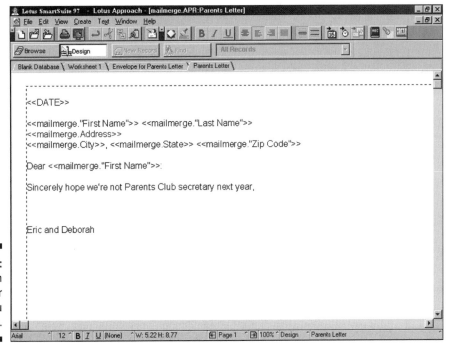

Figure 15-7:
A skeleton
form letter
for you
to fill in.

17. Type the body of the form letter.

Sending out form letters that don't say anything is pretty silly, so you undoubtedly want to add some text to the letter. Just move the pointer to the end of the salutation, click to position the insertion point there, press the Enter key to create a new line, and start typing.

After you're done, the letter should look something like the one in Figure 15-8.

18. You're done!

Here are a few important points to ponder when you create form letters:

- ✔ On the right side of the Form Letter Assistant dialog box is a Sample Letter, which shows you the result of different format options. As you move through the steps, take a look at the Sample Letter to compare how the different options look.

- ✔ Within the text of a form letter, database fields appear between two angle-brackets (for example, <<FirstName>>). Do not be alarmed. Actual database data replaces the brackets and the field name when you print the form letters.

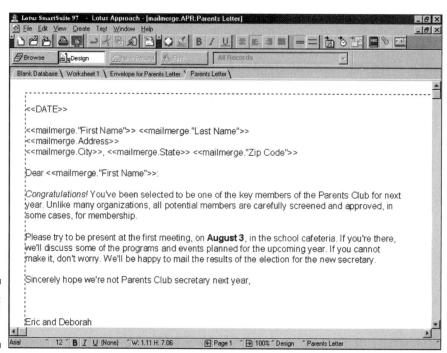

Figure 15-8:
A completed
form letter.

✔ To apply formatting to portions of text, highlight the text with the mouse and then use the Te<u>x</u>t commands listed in Table 15-1 to apply the formatting.

Table 15-1   Commands for Formatting Text in Form Letters

Command	*What It Does*
Te<u>x</u>t⇨<u>N</u>ormal	Removes character formats
Te<u>x</u>t⇨<u>A</u>ttributes⇨<u>B</u>old	Makes the text bold
Te<u>x</u>t⇨<u>A</u>ttributes⇨<u>I</u>talic	Makes the text italic
Te<u>x</u>t⇨<u>A</u>ttributes⇨<u>U</u>nderline	Underlines the text
Te<u>x</u>t⇨<u>A</u>ttributes⇨<u>S</u>trikethrough	Draws a strikethrough line through the text
Te<u>x</u>t⇨<u>A</u>lignm<u>e</u>nt	Enables you to pick left, right, center, or justified alignment
Te<u>x</u>t⇨<u>L</u>ine Spacing	Enables you to pick single, 1.5, or double line spacing

✔ To add a field to the body of the letter, click on where you want the field to be added and then choose Te<u>x</u>t⇨<u>I</u>nsert⇨<u>F</u>ield Value. Select the field that you want to insert and then click on the OK button.

✔ You can also choose Te<u>x</u>t⇨<u>I</u>nsert⇨Today's <u>D</u>ate to insert the (duh!) date. Te<u>x</u>t⇨<u>I</u>nsert⇨Current <u>T</u>ime puts in the time.

✔ Don't embarrass yourself by sending out 1,000 letters that contain a simple spelling error! Spell check your letters before printing them. See Chapter 7 for more information about the spell checker.

✔ You can always choose <u>F</u>ile⇨<u>P</u>rint Preview or press Ctrl+Shift+B to see what your letters will look like after you print them.

Printing Form Letters and Envelopes

You can print form letters pretty much the same way you print a report. Just follow these steps:

1. **If you want to print letters for only certain records, use the Find command to find the records for which you want to print letters.**

   Chapter 5 contains the lost secrets of finding records.

2. **If you want the letters printed in a certain order, sort the database.**

   See Chapter 6 for orderly instructions on sorting.

3. Make sure that the printer is on, ready, and loaded with the right paper.

If you're printing on letterhead, insert the letterhead into the printer. Make sure that you have extra letterhead — placing the letterhead in the printer so that the letterhead doesn't appear upside down at the bottom of the page always takes a couple of tries.

4. Click on the Print SmartIcon, choose File⇨Print, or press Ctrl+P.

After the Print dialog box appears, resist the urge to play with its settings. Usually, the Print dialog box is already set up just right.

5. Click on the Print button.

Away you go!

If you choose to create envelopes too, it's time to print them next.

6. Click on the Envelope tab that was created by the Form Letter Assistant.

Everything should look just right here, because the address came directly from the inside address of the letters you just printed. If you want to tweak the formatting, go ahead and do so, using the formatting commands you used on the letter. We'll wait.

7. Make sure that your printer is properly set up with envelopes.

8. Click on the Print SmartIcon, choose File⇨Print, or press Ctrl+P.

Here are a couple of other things to think about for your venture into mass mailing.

✔ If you aren't satisfied with the envelopes that you get from the Form Letter Assistant, choose Create⇨Envelope and follow the instructions you see on the screen to create envelopes of your own. The process is very much like creating form letters, so it should seem familiar.

✔ Although form letters aren't nearly as difficult as they could be, we strongly recommend finding someone else to do them, sticking a bookmark in this chapter, and loaning them the book.

Chapter 16

Printing Mailing Labels

In This Chapter

▶ Creating mailing labels

▶ Using the Mailing Label Assistant

▶ Creating your own label formats

▶ Printing mailing labels

*I*f you've ever spent 20 minutes printing 100 form letters and then spent two hours hand-addressing the envelopes, you'll appreciate that Approach 97 can prepare mailing labels for your database quickly. You'll never hand-address an envelope again, even if the envelopes are too big for your printer, or if your printer (like ours) eats envelopes for dinner.

As you read this chapter, keep in mind that although the mailing labels feature is usually used to create, well, *mailing* labels, you can use it for other kinds of labels as well. For example, you can create a file folder label for each of your customers. Or you can create floppy disk or videotape labels, or even name tags, or, if you're pretty into this labeling stuff, you can make inventory labels for the contents of your under-bed storage boxes.

Creating Mailing Labels

Approach 97 provides a Mailing Label Assistant to help you create mailing labels easily. Like forms, reports, and form letters, mailing labels are another type of database view in Approach 97. The Mailing Label Assistant merely sets up this mailing label view for you.

The Mailing Label Assistant stayed up all night memorizing the Avery label catalog. Thus, the feature already knows the exact size of each type of label created by Avery, a popular label manufacturer. All you have to do is specify the Avery label number and the fields you want to include on the labels. Producing labels couldn't be easier.

Although Approach 97 is designed to work best with Avery brand labels, you can use other brands. Some brands include Avery numbers on their packages. If you can find an Avery number on the package, use it. Otherwise, you can create a custom label format that fits your labels perfectly. See the section "Using a Custom Label Format" in this chapter if you must.

To create mailing labels, open the database that contains the names and addresses you want to use. Then follow these steps:

1. **Choose Create⇨Mailing Label.**

   The Mailing Label Assistant appears, as shown in Figure 16-1.

Figure 16-1: The Mailing Label Assistant, at your service.

Unlike many other Approach 97 assistants, the Mailing Label Assistant offers only two tabs: Basics and Options. Better yet, you usually only have to mess around with the settings on the Basics tab. You use the Options tab only for oddball labels that don't match any of the predefined Avery label types, and if you've ever looked at an Avery catalog, you know there aren't many labels that don't match an Avery type.

2. **Change the Mailing label name field to something more meaningful than Mailing Labels 1 if you're compulsive about such things or if you plan to prepare several sets of labels for different purposes.**

3. **Select an address layout.**

   In the Select an address layout field, you pick the number of lines to include on the label. When you are mailing to residences, three lines are usually adequate. For business mailings, you may need to use four or five lines. The other layouts are for oddball uses.

4. Select the database and fields that you want to appear in each portion of the address.

When you pick the address layout, the boxes in the Field placement box change to indicate where you can insert fields on the label. For the three-line layout, the first line contains two fields (typically, first name and last name), the second line contains one field (street address), and the third line contains three fields (city, state, and zip code). Other layouts have similar arrangements of fields.

To select the database, select the database name from the Database drop-down list. To add a field to the address, click on the field in the Fields list and then click on the Add button. You can double-check which field you selected by looking at Current field, and you can control where the data appears on the label by clicking on the fields provided in the Field place-ment area. *Note*: The arrow points to the area to which the field will be added.

If you goof up and select a field that you don't want printed on the mailing label, click on the field in the Field placement box and then click on the Remove button. Otherwise, keep adding fields until you have added all the fields you want to place on the label.

5. Pick a Label type.

The drop-down list in the Label type field lists a whole bunch of Avery label formats. If you're using Avery labels, check the package of labels to find the label number and then pick that number from the list. If you're not using Avery labels, check the package anyway. Sometimes other compa-nies list Avery numbers on their packages if the labels are the same size. If you don't find Avery label sizes on your package, you may consider creating a custom label format, which we discuss in the next section.

6. Click on the Done button.

After a few moments, the labels appear on-screen, shown in Figure 16-2. You're done!

That's all there is to it, although you should keep the following points in mind:

✔ When you view mailing labels in Browse mode, the fields on the labels are spaced out — that is, the display shows too much space between the fields (not that they're off in La La Land). For example, look at the labels in Figure 16-2. Way too much space separates the first and last names and the city and state fields. Don't worry; this extra space disappears when you print the labels. For a sneak peek at what the labels will look like with the extraneous space removed, choose File➪Print Preview, click on the Print Preview SmartIcon, or press Ctrl+Shift+B to switch to Preview mode.

✔ You may need to visit the Options tab in the Mailing Label Assistant to arrange the labels row by row across the page, rather than column by column down the page. Click on the Left to right or Top to bottom radio

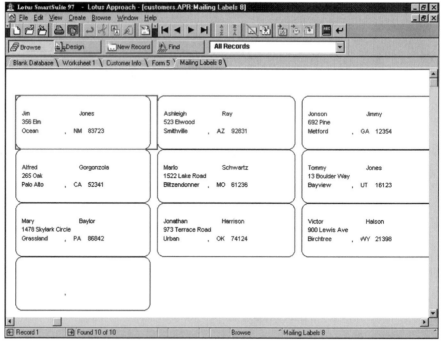

Figure 16-2:
Mailing labels created by the Mailing Label Assistant.

button, depending on your mood. If you already clicked on the Done button, you can return to the Options dialog box by switching to Design mode (Ctrl+D) and choosing Mailing Label⇨Properties.

✔ When you work in Browse mode, you can actually enter and edit data through a mailing label view. Just click on the field you want to enter or edit and start typing.

✔ Unfortunately, the default arrangement of fields on mailing labels some-times doesn't leave enough room to print longer city names. If you encoun-ter this problem, switch to Design mode and drag the state and zip code fields a bit to the right. Then grab the edge of the city field and extend it to the right to fill up the space that you opened up between the city and state fields. You should have enough room to print the names of most American cities. You may have trouble with addresses in Germany, though, where city names such as Garmischpartenkirchen are common.

✔ If the labels shown in Figure 16-2 are too plain for you, switch to Design mode and make whatever changes you want. If more than one label appears when you switch to Design mode, choose View⇨Show Data to display field names rather than actual database data. Then the display should look something like Figure 16-3. With this display, you can custom-ize the label format easily by changing the size of fields, moving fields around, adding additional text, or drawing objects on the label. See Chapter 9 for a refresher look at Design mode.

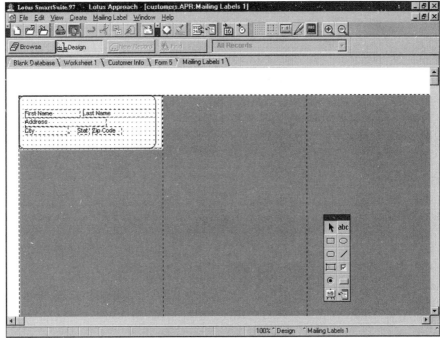

Using a Custom Label Format

Skip this section if you possibly can. Stick to Avery labels or labels that have equivalent Avery numbers and all shall go well for you, your children, and your children's children. If you're stuck with using nonstandard labels because your cheapskate boss got a great deal on a case of them at the local office warehouse store, you must design a custom layout or find a new job. Here's the procedure for designing a custom layout (the getting a new job procedure is outlined in *Job Hunting For Dummies,* by Joyce Lain Kennedy, published by IDG Books Worldwide, Inc.):

1. **Find a ruler and measure the labels.**

   Make a note of the following measurements:

   Top margin: The space between the top of the page and the top of the top row of labels

   Left margin: The space between the left edge of the page and the left edge of the leftmost column of labels

   Width: The width of each label

   Height: The height of each label

Vert. gap: The amount of vertical space between the bottom of each label and the top of the label beneath it.

Horiz. gap: The amount of space between the right edge of each label and the left edge of the label next to it.

2. Choose Create⯈Mailing Label and then click on the Options tab.

The Mailing Label Assistant Options tab appears, as shown in Figure 16-4.

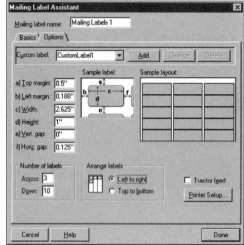

Figure 16-4:
The Mailing
Label
Assistant
Options tab.

3. Type a name for the custom label format in the Custom label field.

4. Type the measurements from Step 1 in the appropriate fields.

5. Type the number of labels across and down each page in the Across and Down text boxes.

6. Select the printing order (Left to right or Top to bottom).

If you select Left to right, the labels print across the page, filling up one row before starting the next. If you select Top to bottom, the labels print down the page, filling up the first column before starting the second, and so on.

7. If the labels are on continuous-feed paper for use in an old-fashioned dot-matrix printer, check the Tractor feed box.

If you check Tractor feed, Approach 97 ignores the top and bottom margins because continuous feed labels print right to the very top and bottom of each sheet of labels.

8. **If you think that you need to use this label format again, click on the <u>A</u>dd button.**

   From then on, the custom label appears as one of the label format options on the Basics tab, so you won't have to return to the Options tab again to set the same specifications.

9. **Click on the Done button.**

Keep the following two points in mind when customizing label formats:

✔ After you create a mailing label view, you can change the layout options. You can change them in Design mode or by using the Properties dialog box (press Ctrl+E, click on the Properties SmartIcon, or choose <u>M</u>ailing Label⇨Mailing Label <u>P</u>roperties).You can change background color, borders, margins, and even find your way back to the Options tab in the Mailing Label Assistant (Basics tab, Edit Label Options button). Close the Properties dialog box (Alt+F4 or click on the Close control button in the top-right corner of the box) after you finish.

✔ You can remove a custom label setting by calling up the Mailing Label Assistant Options panel again, selecting the custom layout that you want to delete, and clicking on the <u>D</u>elete button. Also, if you create a custom label and you want to modify it, make the changes and then click on the <u>C</u>hange button.

Printing Mailing Labels

You print mailing labels the same way that you print reports or form letters. Here's the procedure:

1. **If you want to print labels for only certain records, use the Find command to collect the records for which you want to print labels.**

   See Chapter 5 for more information about finding records.

2. **If you want the labels printed in a certain order, sort the database.**

   See Chapter 6 for information about sorting.

3. **Make sure that the printer is on, ready, and loaded with the correct labels.**

4. **Click on the Print SmartIcon, choose <u>F</u>ile⇨<u>P</u>rint, or press Ctrl+P.**

5. **Click on the Print button.**

   TaDaaaaaaa! Your labels print.

If you're unsure about the label format, try printing the labels on plain paper first. Then you can hold up the names and addresses printed on plain paper to a blank sheet of labels to see whether everything lines up correctly. Of course, if you were subjected to the cheap labels that made your life difficult, not testing on plain paper helps you use up the labels that much faster.

Chapter 17

Working with Worksheets and Cursing at Crosstabs

A *worksheet* is a special type of database view that you can use to display the fields and records in an Approach 97 database in an arrangement that is similar to a spreadsheet program, such as Lotus 1-2-3. In a worksheet view, each database record is represented as a row in the worksheet, and each field is represented as a column. The intersection of a row and column is called a *cell*.

Worksheets are simple enough. Crosstabs are harder to swallow. A *crosstab* is a special type of view in which each cell shows summary information — such as a total, an average, or a count — for a group of database records. For example, you can use a crosstab to summarize information from a Sales database by sales district, salesman, or product.

This chapter shows you how to work with worksheets and how to set up simple crosstabs.

Working with Worksheets

When you create an Approach 97 database, a default worksheet view named Worksheet 1 is automatically created for you. To switch to this worksheet view, click on the tab labeled Worksheet 1 at the top of the work area. Figure 17-1 shows a worksheet view of a database.

Unlike forms, which show one database record at a time, worksheets show as many database records as can fit on the screen, with each record in a separate worksheet row. If the database contains more records than can fit on the screen at one time, use the scroll bars to display them all.

- ✔ If you are experienced with Lotus 1-2-3 (or any other spreadsheet program), you're already way ahead of the worksheet game. The basics of finding your way around Approach 97 worksheets — such as using the arrow keys to move from cell to cell — are the same.

- ✔ You can change database fields while you are working in worksheet view. Just click on a cell and start typing to replace the contents or double-click to edit.

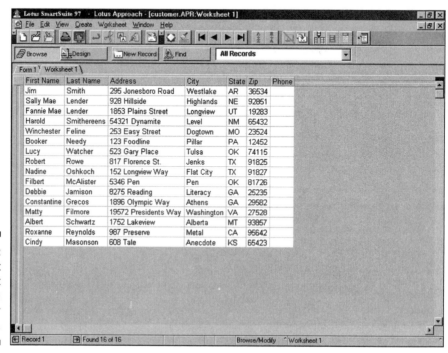

Figure 17-1:
A default worksheet view of a customer database.

✔ Inserting a new record in worksheet view is the same as inserting a new record in a form. Click on the New Record button, choose Worksheet⇨ Records⇨New, or press Ctrl+N. Approach 97 inserts a new row for the new record.

✔ To change the text in a column heading, triple-click on the header and then type the new text — click, click, click!

✔ To change the name of the worksheet on the tab, double-click on the tab in Design mode and type the new name.

✔ The default worksheet for a new database includes a column for each database field. The column headings are the field names, and each column is wide enough to accommodate the longest entry in the field. If you're picky, you can change many aspects of this basic layout: Rearrange columns, remove columns you don't need or want, change the column width, change the column headings, and so on. You see how to make these changes in settings later in this chapter.

Creating additional worksheets

Approach 97 automatically creates a worksheet for you when you create a new database. For most databases, one worksheet is more than enough. If you need to create an additional worksheet, perhaps to show just a portion of the data, follow this procedure:

1. Open the database for which you want to create a new worksheet.

Choose File⇨Open, click on the Open SmartIcon, use the keyboard shortcut Ctrl+O, or select Open an Existing File from the Welcome to Lotus Approach 97 dialog box.

2. Choose Create⇨Worksheet.

The Worksheet Assistant appears, as shown in Figure 17-2.

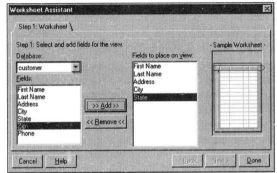

Figure 17-2:
The
Worksheet
Assistant.

3. **Select the fields you want to include on the worksheet and click on the Add button to add them to the list.**

   To add a field to the worksheet, select it in the Fields list and then click on the Add button. (Each time you click on the Add button, Approach 97 selects the next field in the list. You can quickly add several successive fields by repeatedly clicking on the Add button or just by double-clicking on the fields.)

   To add several fields at the same time, hold down the Ctrl key while you select them in the Fields list and then click on the Add button. Or you can hold down the Shift key to mark a range of fields or click on the first field and then hold down the left mouse button and drag to select a range of fields.

   To remove a field from the worksheet while you're in the Worksheet Assistant, select the field in the Fields to place on view list and then click on the Remove button or double-click on the field in the Fields to place on view list.

4. **Click on the Done button.**

   Approach 97 creates the worksheet.

Moving around in a worksheet

One of the most common ways to move around in a worksheet is to use the arrow cursor-control keys. Pressing one of these keys moves the cell pointer up, down, left, or right one cell.

If you're semipermanently attached to your mouse, you can also move directly to any cell by clicking on it with the mouse. If the cell you want to move to isn't visible, use the scroll bars to bring the cell into view.

Use the following keyboard shortcuts for moving about the worksheet:

- **Tab:** Moves to the next cell
- **Shift+Tab:** Moves to the previous cell
- **PgDn:** Scrolls the worksheet forward one screen
- **PgUp:** Scrolls the worksheet backward one screen
- **Ctrl+Home:** Moves to the first record
- **Ctrl+End:** Moves to the last record

Selecting worksheet cells

Here are the all-important techniques for selecting cells in a worksheet:

- To select a single cell, click on it.

- To edit a cell, double-click on it.

- To select a range of cells, point to the cell at one corner of the range, press and hold the left mouse button, and drag the mouse to highlight the cell range.

- To select an entire column of cells, click on the column heading.

- To select several columns, point to the column heading of the first column you want to select and then press and hold the left mouse button as you drag the mouse to select additional columns.

- To select an entire row of cells, click on the border immediately to the left of the row.

- Unfortunately, accidentally moving a field or creating a crosstab is all too easy when you are mousing around with the column headers. Be careful not to release the mouse button after first selecting the column and then clicking. If the mouse pointer changes to a hand, release the mouse button immediately.

- To select several rows, point to the border immediately to the left of the first row you want to select, press and hold the left mouse button, and drag the mouse to select additional rows.

- To select the entire worksheet, click on the box at the upper-left corner of the worksheet.

Resizing a column or row

When Approach 97 creates worksheet columns, it sets the column width so the column is just wide enough to display the original contents of the field that is displayed in the column. If you later add information that is longer than will fit in the existing cells, you'll probably want to change the width of one or more columns so that the column is wide enough to display the data.

To resize a column, position the mouse pointer at the border between the heading of the column you want to change and the heading of the column immediately to its right. When you get the mouse in the right spot, the arrow pointer changes to a funny-looking double arrow. After the double arrow appears, you can click on the left mouse button and drag the column to a new width.

If the worksheet rows are not high enough to display your data — perhaps because you increased the size of the font in the field — you can increase the row height. Just position the mouse pointer at the border to the left of the rows until the arrow pointer changes to a double arrow. Then click on the left mouse button and drag the row to new heights.

Although each worksheet column can be a different width, all rows in the worksheet are the same height. So when you adjust the height of any worksheet row, the height of all rows is automatically adjusted.

Adding a column to a worksheet

You can add a new column to a worksheet to contain a field you accidentally omitted when you created the worksheet. You can also add a column that contains a formula.

If you left out a field when you created a worksheet and you want to add it later, follow this procedure:

1. **If the Add Field dialog box is not already visible, choose Worksheet⇨Add Field.**

   The Add Field dialog box appears, as shown in Figure 17-3.

Figure 17-3:
The Add Field dialog box.

2. **Point the mouse pointer at the field you want to add to the table and then click on the left mouse button and hold it down while you drag the field to the position among the column headings where you want to add the new column.**

   As you drag the field, the mouse pointer turns into a hand and the field name follows the handy little mouse pointer.

3. Release the mouse button.

A new column is added to the worksheet.

To add a column that contains a formula, follow these steps:

1. Position the mouse just above the column heading area, between the columns where you want to insert the new column.

When you get the mouse at the right spot, the arrow pointer changes to a wedgie. You'll know.

2. Click the mouse.

A blank column is inserted in the worksheet, and the Formula dialog box, shown in Figure 17-4, appears.

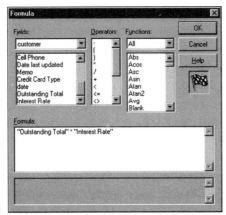

Figure 17-4:
The Formula
dialog box.

3. Build a formula for the column by clicking on the various pieces you want to include in the formula or by typing the formula in the Formula text box.

For more information about creating formulas, see Chapter 13.

4. Click on the OK button.

The results of the formula appear in each cell of the new column.

You can change the formula for a formula column by double-clicking on any cell in the column. This action calls forth the Formula dialog box, wherein you can edit to your heart's content.

Removing a column from a worksheet

To remove a column, click on the column heading and press the Delete key. The column is removed from the worksheet. (Don't worry. The data is not deleted from the database. It's just removed from the worksheet view.)

Rearranging columns

You can change the order of columns in a worksheet by clicking on the heading for the column you want to move. The mouse pointer quickly changes to a grabbing hand. Then you can drag the column to its new location.

Be careful when you drag the column heading. If you drag it beyond the left or top border of the worksheet, a crosstab is created, jumbling up your worksheet, possibly beyond repair. If that happens, your best bet is to delete the worksheet and create a new one, or if you think fast enough, try choosing Edit➪Undo or pressing Ctrl+Z to undo the goof.

Printing a worksheet

Printing an Approach 97 worksheet is just like printing any other view, except that you may need to set certain printing options before you begin. To set the printing options, follow this procedure:

1. **Switch to the worksheet view and press Ctrl+E, click on the Properties SmartIcon, or choose Worksheet➪Worksheet Properties while no worksheet cell is selected.**

   The Properties dialog box appears.

2. **Click on the Printing tab.**

   The printing options come forward, as shown in Figure 17-5.

Figure 17-5:
The Properties dialog box printing options for a worksheet.

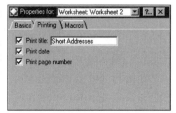

3. **Select the printing options you want to use.**

   Print title: Prints a title in the header of each page

   Print date: Prints the date in the footer of each page

   Print page number: Prints the page number in the footer of each page

4. **Double-click on the control box in the upper-left corner of the Properties dialog box or click on the Close button in the upper-right corner (the button with the X on it) to dismiss the Properties dialog box.**

Now you can use the program's normal printing techniques to print the worksheet:

- ✔ Choose File⇨Print.

- ✔ Press Ctrl+P.

 ✔ Click on the Print SmartIcon.

Cursing at Crosstabs

A *crosstab* is similar to a worksheet, but instead of displaying each database record in a separate row, each crosstab row represents summary values for a group of related records.

For example, consider a database for a toy manufacturer. Each record contains information about a toy: cost of development, quantity on hand, and the sales representative who sells the toy. You can use a crosstab to summarize the cost of development for each sales representative's products, as shown in Figure 17-6.

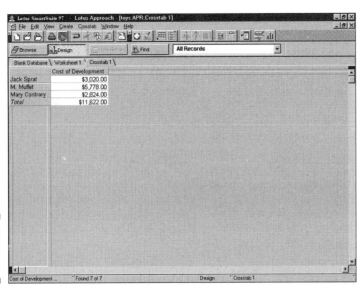

Figure 17-6:
A simple
crosstab.

The crosstab in Figure 17-6 is simple — as crosstabs should be. You can create crosstabs that summarize data based on several fields, and you can summarize not only rows but columns as well. For example, you can use a sales database to create a crosstab that summarizes sales by product within sales district for each sales representative. The columns can summarize the products and sales districts, and the rows can summarize sales by individual sales reps. Such complex crosstabs can easily get out of control, so you can leave them to the computer nerds to figure out. In the rest of this chapter, you find out how to work with simple crosstabs — simple, of course, is relative. Crosstabs are not the easiest Approach 97 feature to master, but they're doable, nonetheless.

Creating a simple crosstab

To create a simple crosstab, such as the one shown in Figure 17-6, use the Crosstab Assistant. Here's the procedure:

1. **Decide which fields' data you want to summarize.**

   This step is the most important one in creating a crosstab. Fields that you use to summarize crosstab data should be fields that contain repeating data — that is, exactly the same value in multiple fields — that can be used to categorize the records.

   A field that contains only a limited number of values is usually best. For example, a limited number of sales representatives exists, so the sales representatives' names are good choices. The field with toy names probably contains no repeating values; each record contains a different toy name. Therefore, the toy field would *not* be good to summarize on.

   For more complex crosstabs, you can categorize records based on two or more fields at once.

2. **Choose Create⇨Crosstab.**

   This command summons the Crosstab Assistant, which handles most of the dirty work of creating crosstabs for you.

   Figure 17-7 shows the Crosstab Assistant. Like most Approach 97 Assistants, the Crosstab Assistant breaks the task of creating crosstabs into simple steps. The first step is to tell Approach 97 which fields you want to use in summarizing the rows. If you decide that you need to return to a step to correct a mistake, you can click on the Back button or click on the tab for the step to which you want to return.

3. **Click on the Step 1: Rows tab.**

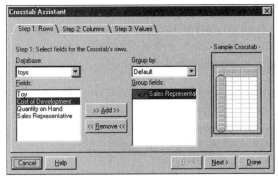

Figure 17-7:
The
Crosstab
Assistant
displaying
its Step 1:
Rows tab.

4. **In the Fields list, select the field you want to use in summarizing the rows and then click on the Add button.**

   The field appears in the Group fields list. Although you can select more than one field, simple crosstabs require only a single field to summarize rows. Using only a single field, at least at first, tends to reduce frustration as well.

5. **If you want to organize different values together, select a grouping from the Group by drop-down list.**

   Different field types allow you to group in different ways, including by month or quarter for date fields or just alphabetically for text fields.

6. **Click on the Next button.**

   The Columns settings for the Crosstab Assistant are displayed, as shown in Figure 17-8.

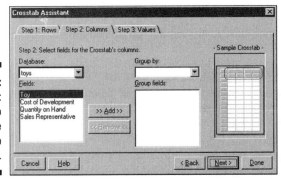

Figure 17-8:
The Step 2:
Columns tab
from the
Crosstab
Assistant.

7. Skip the Columns settings for simple crosstabs.

If you want to summarize data that is grouped by more than one field, select the additional fields here. Otherwise, do not select additional fields.

8. Click on the Next button.

The Values settings for the Crosstab Assistant are displayed, as shown in Figure 17-9.

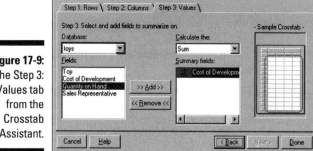

Figure 17-9:
The Step 3:
Values tab
from the
Crosstab
Assistant.

9. Select the type of calculation you want Approach 97 to perform and the database field you want Approach 97 to perform it on.

This step is where you tell Approach 97 which database field you want summarized in the body of the crosstab. In Figure 17-9, we told Approach 97 to calculate the sum of the Cost of Development fields for each group of records.

10. Click on the Done button.

The Assistant dutifully prepares the crosstab for you.

Creating crosstabs looks easy, but messing up the task is easy, too. Here are some thoughts that may alleviate your suffering:

✔ If you mess up a crosstab by telling the Assistant to group by the wrong fields or by using the wrong formula for the calculation, deleting the view and starting over is usually easier than trying to correct the crosstab. To delete a crosstab, switch to Design mode and choose Crosstab➪Delete Crosstab.

✔ Notice that the Crosstab Assistant inserts a Total row at the bottom of the crosstab, summarizing totals for the entire database. If you don't want this row, click on the Total row heading and press Delete or choose Edit➪Cut.

✔ Another way to create a crosstab is to call up a worksheet view and then drag one of the column headings over to the row heading area. The field you drag is used to group summary data for rows, and the remaining worksheet columns are converted to Sum or Count formulas.

Adding more columns to a crosstab

You can add more columns to the crosstab after you create the crosstab. For example, in a simple crosstab of a sales database that summarizes sales amounts grouped by sales representative, you may also want to see a summary of the sales commission field so that you know how much commission each salesperson earned. For the additional summary, you create a new column that sums the sales commission field.

Or you may want to see a count of how many toys are in each sales representative's portfolio. You create a new column that contains a count of the Toys field.

Here is the procedure for adding a new summary column to a crosstab:

1. **Call up the Add Field dialog box by choosing Crosstab⇨Add field or clicking on the Add Field SmartIcon in the toolbar or the Tools palette.**

   The Add Field dialog box appears, listing all of the fields in the database.

2. **Drag the field you want to add into the body of the crosstab and place it at the location where you want to insert the new column.**

   Approach 97 adds the new column. If the field is a text field, the Count function is used to indicate how many records in each grouping contain a value for that field. For numeric fields, a Sum function is used. For instructions on changing the function, see the section "Changing a crosstab formula" in this chapter.

   That's all! You're done.

Be careful not to drag the field into the column heading area! If you drag the field into this area, Approach 97 regroups the crosstab, using the field you added as a category field. If that happens, quickly choose Edit⇨Undo or press Ctrl+Z to remove the field.

Changing a crosstab formula

If you want to change the formula used to calculate the summary values that appear in a crosstab column, follow this procedure:

1. **Click on the heading of the column with the function you want to change.**

2. **Press Ctrl+E or click on the Properties SmartIcon to bring up the Properties dialog box for the column.**

3. **Click on the Formula tab to call up the column's formula.**

   See Figure 17-10.

4. Click on the formula you want to use to calculate the summary values.

Table 17-1 lists the formulas you can use to calculate summary values.

5. Double-click on the Properties dialog box's control box in the upper-left corner or click on the Close button (the button with the X on it) in the upper-right corner of the dialog box.

The Properties dialog box disappears, and you're done.

Figure 17-10:
The
Properties
dialog box
shows the
crosstab
formula.

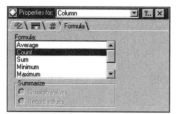

Table 17-1   Summary Formulas for Crosstab Calculations

Formula	What It Does
Average	Adds up the total value of the fields and then divides the result by the number of records in the summary group that have a value for the field. (Note that a value of zero is different from no value at all. Zero is considered to be a value, but Average ignores records for which the field has no value.)
Count	Counts the number of records in the summary group that have a value for the field
Sum	Adds up the values of the field for all records in the summary group
Minimum	The smallest value for the field from all records in the summary group
Maximum	The largest value for the field from all records in the summary group
Standard deviation	The standard deviation of the field values for all records in the group
Variance	The variance of the field values for all records in the group

Chapter 18
Charting Your Course

· ·

In This Chapter

▶ Understanding charts

▶ Creating a chart by using the Chart Assistant

▶ Changing to a different chart type

▶ Making your chart look better

▶ Changing chart text

· ·

Numbers, numbers, numbers. If a database contains too many numbers, pretty soon all the numbers start to look the same. When you can't tell one number from the next, the time has come to put the numbers into a chart. Charts turn numbers into pictures, which have been the preferred mode of communication since Ross Perot ran for president or, more likely, since the ancients started drawing on cave walls in France.

Approach 97 charts are actually drawn by a thingamabob called Lotus Chart, which works the same way with other Lotus programs such as 1-2-3, Word Pro, and Freelance Graphics. The charting features may look a bit different in those programs, but all of them are based on Lotus Chart. If you're already familiar with creating charts in any of those programs, this chapter will be a piece of cake.

Understanding Charts

If you've never worked with a charting program, creating a chart can be a daunting task. Approach 97 takes a series of numbers from a database and renders them as a graph. Many different kinds of charts are possible, from simple bar charts, to pie charts, to exotic high-low-open-close charts and scatter charts. Very cool, but a little confusing to the uninitiated (and occasionally the authors). We stick with pretty simple charts — the most effective kind — in this chapter.

We start demystifying this chart business by letting you know some of the jargon that you must contend with when you're working with charts:

Chart or graph: Same thing. These terms are interchangeable. A chart or graph is nothing more than a bunch of numbers turned into a picture. After all, a picture is worth a thousand numbers, or something like that.

Chart type: Approach 97 supports several different chart types: bar charts, area charts, pie charts, line charts, and others. Different kinds of charts are better suited to displaying different kinds of data.

3-D chart: Some charts have a three-dimensional effect that gives them a jazzier look. Nothing special here — the effect is mostly cosmetic. (Rumor has it that Lotus has hired world-renowned physicist Stephen Hawking to create 4-D charts in an effort to stay one dimension ahead of Microsoft.)

Data window: If you use Lotus Chart from Word Pro or Freelance Graphics, you use a special data window to enter the values to be plotted on the chart. Approach 97 doesn't have a data window; we just threw it in here in case you are a Word Pro or Freelance Graphics user, and you're stumped because you can't find it. In Approach 97, the data comes directly from the database, so the data window isn't necessary.

Series: A collection of related numbers to be plotted. Simple charts use only one series, in which each value is usually plotted along the X-Axis. More complicated charts, such as the chart in Figure 18-1, can use more than one series. In this case, by displaying information from each of four quarters, Approach 97 is showing four series of data. Approach 97 allows you to use up to 23 series, which is more than anyone other than the Rainman can comprehend.

Axis: This term has nothing to do with the bad guys in World War II. The X-Axis is the line along the bottom of a chart; the Y-Axis is the line along the left edge of a chart. The X-Axis usually indicates categories. Actual data values are plotted along the Y-Axis. Lotus Chart automatically provides labels for the X-Axis and the Y-Axis, but you can change them.

Legend: A box that identifies the various series plotted on the chart. Lotus Chart creates a legend automatically.

Creating a Chart

Creating a chart of your database data is a pretty straightforward matter as soon as you realize that Approach 97 comes with a Chart Assistant that does all the work for you. All you have to do is tell the Assistant what to do, and it gladly obliges. You don't even have to leave a tip.

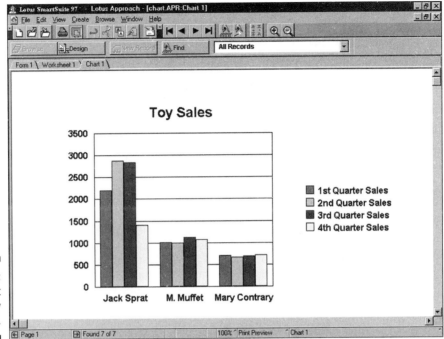

Figure 18-1:
A chart
created by
Approach 97.

To create a chart, just follow these steps:

1. **Open the database for which you want to create a new chart.**

   Choose File⇨Open, click on the Open SmartIcon, or select the file from the Welcome to Lotus Approach dialog box.

2. **Choose Create⇨Chart.**

   You see the first tab of the Chart Assistant (shown in Figure 18-2), in which the Assistant asks some basic questions about the chart.

3. **If the suggested name bores you, you can type something else in the View name & title text box.**

4. **From the Layout list, select a chart type.**

   The Sample Chart box shows a sample of the selected chart type to help you decide. We selected a bar chart. (Note that the tabs on the Chart Assistant vary depending on the chart type you pick; pie charts don't require as many choices.)

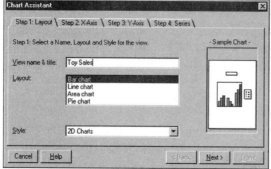

Figure 18-2:
The Chart
Assistant
asks some
basic
questions
about the
chart.

5. Pick a style from the Style list.

In general, we recommend that you stick to 2-D charts. Although 3-D charts look cool, they can often distort information. For example, the small slices of a pie chart can appear bigger in 3-D than they do in 2-D because that third dimension adds volume to the slice. So, even if the slice represents 5 percent of the total pie, the slice may appear bigger than the actual figure represents.

6. Click on the Next button.

The second tab of the Chart Assistant appears, in which the Assistant becomes more stern as it asks you what field to use for the X-Axis. See Figure 18-3.

Figure 18-3:
The Chart
Assistant
sternly asks
about a field
for the
X-Axis.

7. Click on the field that you want to use for the X-Axis field.

The X-Axis is the field you want to use to group data along the horizontal border of the chart. For the chart shown in Figure 18-1, the X-Axis is the Sales Representative field.

8. **Leave the <u>G</u>roup by list set at Default because the choices, for text fields, are all the same.**

   This option isn't much fun on text fields — you get to group your choices alphabetically or alphabetically using only the first characters.

   If the field you're using for your X-Axis is a numeric field, you can group the items by 10s, 50s, 100s, and so forth.

9. **Click on the <u>N</u>ext button.**

   The Chart Assistant now has the nerve to ask about the Y-Axis, as shown in Figure 18-4.

Figure 18-4: The Chart Assistant boldly asks what field to use for the Y-Axis, as well as what to chart.

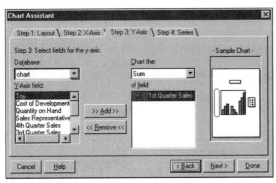

10. **In the <u>Y</u>-Axis field box, click on the field you want to use for the Y-Axis field.**

    The Y-Axis represents the field with the value you want to have plotted on the chart. Approach 97 groups all the records that have the same value for the X-Axis field, and then the program performs the calculation you choose here to determine what value to plot on the Y-Axis.

11. **In the <u>C</u>hart the box, select what Approach 97 should chart.**

    Table 18-1 lists the calculations you can use for the Y-Axis. For the chart in Figure 18-1, the Y-Axis is the Sum calculation for each of the Sales fields. You can use as many or as few fields on the Y-Axis as you choose.

12. **Click on the <u>N</u>ext button.**

    The Chart Assistant demands to know whether you want to use an additional series to plot the data, as you can see in Figure 18-5.

    Use an extra series when you want to plot an additional set of data for each value that appears on the X-Axis.

    To use an additional series, check the <u>S</u>how a new series for box and then select the field by which you want to group the new series.

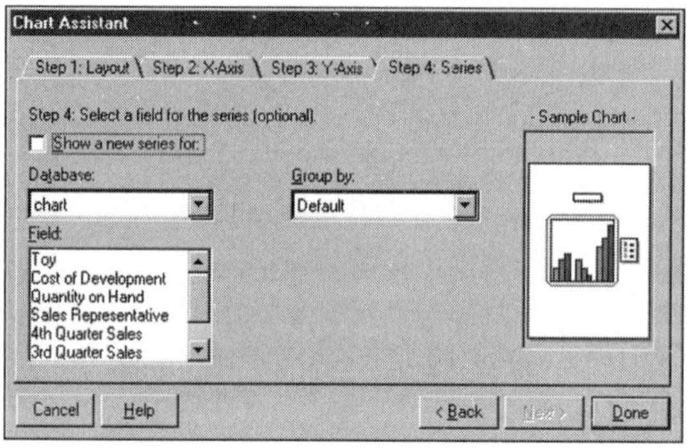

Figure 18-5:
The Chart
Assistant
asks if you
want an
additional
series.

13. Click on the Done button.

Stand back and watch Approach 97 create the chart.

After the chart is finished, Approach 97 displays it for you. If you don't like the chart, switch to Design mode and fiddle around with it, following the procedures presented in the following sections of this chapter.

Table 18-1 lists the calculations that you can use for the Y-Axis.

Table 18-1	Calculations You Can Use in Charts
Calculation	**What It Does**
Average	The average value of the field
Count	The number of records that have a value for the field
Sum	The sum of the field values for each record
Smallest item	The smallest value for the field
Largest item	The largest value for the field
Standard deviation	The standard deviation of the field values
Variance	The variance of the field values

Here are some points to ponder before you get too carried away with creating charts.

✔ If you want to change the database field used for the X-Axis, the Y-Axis, or the series, click once on the chart in Design mode and then choose Chart Object⇨Chart Data Source. This command calls up the Chart Data Source Assistant, which is identical to the Chart Assistant except that the first step, in which you identify the chart type, is omitted. You use the Chart Data Source Assistant just as you use the Chart Assistant, and with the same good results.

✔ Another way to create a chart is to first create a crosstab that summarizes the data that you want to chart. Choose Crosstab⇨Chart this Crosstab. Approach 97 then automatically creates a chart. For more information about crosstabs, see Chapter 17.

Changing the Chart Type

You can create scads of charts in Approach 97. Each chart type conveys information with a different emphasis. For example, sales data plotted in a column chart may emphasize the relative performance of different regions, whereas the same data plotted as a line chart may emphasize the increase or decrease of sales over time. The kind of chart that's best for your data depends on the nature of the data and on which aspects of it you want to emphasize.

Fortunately, Approach 97 doesn't force you to decide on the final chart type up front. You can easily change the chart type at any time without changing the chart data.

These steps explain how to change the chart type:

1. **Double-click on the chart to call up the Properties dialog box.**

   The Chart Properties dialog box appears, as shown in Figure 18-6. If the dialog box doesn't look quite like the one in Figure 18-6, some element of the chart, such as the legend or title, may have been selected when you double-clicked. Click on the drop-down list at the top of the dialog box (labeled Title, Legend, X-Axis, Y-Axis, or whatever) and select Chart from the list that appears.

Figure 18-6:
The Chart
Properties
dialog box.

2. **Select the chart type from the Chart type list.**

3. **To the right of the Chart type list, you see a selection of buttons. Click on the button that represents the layout for the chart type that you selected.**

   Each of the chart types offers several layout variations. For example, Figure 18-6 shows the layout options for bar charts. Pick the one you like best.

4. Double-click on the control box in the upper-left corner or click on the Close button (the button with the X on it) in the upper-right corner to dismiss the Properties dialog box.

You're done!

Improving a Chart's Appearance

Approach 97 enables you to tweak a chart's appearance in many ways. In fact, you could probably spend the rest of the decade exploring the various bells and whistles that accompany charts.

You control chart ornamentation through the Properties dialog box for charts, which differs slightly from the Properties dialog box you encounter elsewhere in Approach 97:

- ✔ The drop-down list at the very top of the dialog box activates a menu that lets you select the chart element with which you want to fiddle. The regular Approach Properties dialog box doesn't often offer this menu.

- ✔ The drop-down menu at the top of the Properties dialog box lets you select different parts of the chart (Title, Legend, Y-Axis, and so on). After you select a part of the chart, you see controls to change characteristics such as the text color, font and style, line width, or fill color.

Feel free to experiment with the Properties dialog box for your chart. After you get a feel for it, you'll have no trouble with any of the following procedures.

You can bring up the Properties dialog box for a chart in several ways:

- ✔ Click on the Properties SmartIcon.
- ✔ Double-click on the chart.
- ✔ Choose Chart⇨Chart Properties.
- ✔ Right-click on the chart to bring up the quick menu and then choose Chart Properties.
- ✔ Press Alt+Enter.

After you summon the Properties dialog box, use the drop-down menu at the top of the dialog box to select the chart element that you want to adjust. Table 18-2 lists the various chart options that you can control from the Properties dialog box.

Table 18-2	Chart Elements You Can Adjust from the Chart Properties Dialog Box
Chart Element	*Options You Can Set*
Chart	Changes the chart type and layout
Title	Changes the position of the title; adds a subtitle; or changes the text color, style, and font for the title text
Legend	Changes the position and text style for the legend
X-Axis	Adds elements, such as tick marks and grid lines, to the X-Axis; changes the scale for the X-Axis
Y-Axis	Adds elements, such as tick marks and grid lines, to the Y-Axis; changes the scale for the Y-Axis
Series	Changes the colors assigned to each series or hides series you don't want to see, such as a series that indicates a downward sales trend
Series labels	Adds value or percentage labels to each series
Plot	Returns the chart to its default position on the page
Note	Adds a note to the bottom of the chart
Table	Enables you to show the data table along with the selected chart

Many of the dialog box options include a check box labeled Show something. To display or hide a chart element, first select the element from the drop-down list and then check or uncheck the Show check box. If a Show something check box isn't visible, that feature can't be switched off or on in that way.

Adjusting Chart Text

Most charts offer several text elements, such as titles and legends. You can edit text elements on a chart by following this procedure:

1. **Click on the text you want to edit.**

   Love handles appear as proof that you selected the text.

2. **Wait a moment.**

   You don't need to wait long, just long enough for Approach 97 to catch its breath. Try counting to three.

3. **Double-click on the text.**

   An insertion point should appear. If the Properties dialog box appears instead, you didn't wait long enough. Dismiss the Properties dialog box by clicking on its Close button (the button with the X in the upper-right corner) and then try again.

4. **Edit the text.**

5. **Click outside the text after you're done.**

Part IV
Definitely
Database Grad
School Stuff

The 5th Wave   **By Rich Tennant**

" I SAID I WANTED A NEW MONITOR FOR MY BIRTHDAY! MONITOR! MONITOR!"

In this part ...

Turn to this part of the book when you really want to impress your friends by showing them how much more you know about Approach 97 than any normal person should need or want to know. Your friends will follow you around asking for your autograph when they find out that you know about setting up macros to automate routine chores, working with Approach 97 on a network and the Internet, getting the most out of the Approach 97 preferences, and converting data from other programs so Approach 97 can use it.

You may want to grab your pocket protector and propeller cap before proceeding. Don't worry — we explain everything in simple terms along the way.

Chapter 19

Creating and Using Macros

· ·

· ·

*W*hat the heck is a macro and why would you ever want to create
and use one? Good question! A *macro* is a sequence of commands that
Approach 97 records and makes available for you to play back whenever you want.

Huh? We'll put it another way: Macros let you create customized shortcuts for
things that you do over and over again. For example, you may need to search
your database for customers in California with outstanding bills and then
generate and print form letters to dun your naughty customers. And you have
to do this *every day*. A macro lets you combine these functions so that you
don't have to perform them separately each time. It's kind of like telling your
assistant to do something — the first time, you have to explain each and every
step. Thereafter, you just say to do the procedure, and it's as good as done.

In short, macros save you from spending major amounts of time to accomplish
mundane, repetitive tasks. Adding macros to your database takes some time up
front, but you'll thank yourself later.

This chapter is a brief introduction to macros. It explains how to create simple
macros, how to edit them if they don't do quite what you want them to do, and
how to run macros. Although macros are clearly an advanced Approach 97
subject, this chapter isn't so advanced that you require a pocket protector, so
go ahead and put it back in the drawer.

Creating Macros the Easy Way

The easy way of creating macros is technically called *transcripting,* just so you'll be confused and think that the task is difficult. *Transcripting* is the fancy way of saying that Approach 97 writes down all of the steps you follow. Because Approach 97 takes care of the labor of remembering what you did, this process is the easy way. To create a macro the easy way, follow these steps:

1. Open the database file in which you want to create a macro.

To open the file choose File⇨Open, press Ctrl+O, or click on the File Open SmartIcon to bring up the Open dialog box. Select the file you wish to open and then click on the OK button.

2. Choose Edit⇨Record Transcript.

The Record Transcript dialog box appears, as shown in Figure 19-1.

Figure 19-1:
The Record
Transcript
dialog box.

Record Transcript	
Record	
⊙ As macro: Macro	Record
○ As script:	Cancel
○ At script cursor	Help

Approach 97 uses this dialog box to record everything you do (but not everything you say) and turn your action into a macro. As Igor said in the movie *Young Frankenstein,* "Walk this way." Shuffle, thump. Shuffle, thump.

3. Click on the As macro radio button and type a descriptive name in the text box.

Macro isn't terribly descriptive, particularly after you create 25 of them, so choose something that will jog your brain when you see the name next year.

If you want to record over an existing macro (perhaps an earlier attempt that didn't cover everything you wanted it to), choose the macro name from the drop-down list beside As macro.

The As script and At script cursor options refer to LotusScript, which you probably don't want to get into when you are first finding out about macros. See the "LotusScript stuff you don't need to know" sidebar in this chapter for a little information about LotusScript.

4. Click on the Record button.

If the Approach 97 programmers had been really clever, you would have heard a beep like an answering machine. Unfortunately, you don't get any reminders. The recorder is on as soon as you click on the button.

LotusScript stuff you don't need to know

You can use macros to automate basic tasks in Approach 97. For more complex tasks, Lotus provides a programming language (also known as a *development environment*) called LotusScript to help you automate all kinds of simple and complex procedures in Approach 97 and the other members of the SmartSuite.

So when should you think about using LotusScript? Get ready for an answer you'll like to hear: almost never. You can use macros to handle almost every task you'll need to automate.

Why did we even mention LotusScript then? To tease you with the possibilities. LotusScript has more power than Tim "the Toolman" Taylor could ever fathom. For example, when you start Approach 97 and you see the Welcome to Lotus Approach dialog box, you can select the Create a New File Using A SmartMaster tab. The SmartMaster applications you find listed under this tab rely heavily on LotusScript to make them so flashy and easy to use.

Some of the prepackaged SmartMaster applications include a Video and Actor SmartMaster Application, a Meeting Room Scheduler, and a Contact Manager SmartMaster. Open and try some of these applications to get an idea of the capabilities of LotusScript. In particular, use the Contact Manager SmartMaster and start dreaming about how your particular problems could be automated.

In skilled and pocket-protected hands, LotusScript can accomplish almost any task that a person can perform. Even as you're reading this, Lotus programmers are working diligently on the LotusScript 2001 version that will make all users obsolete. (Author's Note: Lotus says that the preceding sentence is classified information, so delete it before printing the book.)

LotusScript is tremendously powerful, and also far more complex than you may be able to endure. If you need to automate a procedure in Approach 97 and you can't automate it with Approach 97 macros, you should probably seek out a starving propeller-head geek with a high tolerance for frustration and subcontract the scripting task to her.

If you feel that you've just got to discover more about LotusScript, check the Approach 97 Help (choose Help➪Help Topics) and read up on LotusScript or head to the grocery store, stock up on snack cakes, and prepare a geek trap in the front yard.

5. **Do the procedure you want to save as a macro.**

   Let your imagination run wild. Anything that you do daily or more frequently is a likely candidate for a macro. For example, you could run a find, switch to a report view, and then print the report.

6. **After you complete the procedure, choose Edit➪Stop Recording.**

   The Define Macro dialog box shows you the fruits of your labors. If you went through the procedure without problems, move to the next step. If you think you messed the operation up and you want to try again, click on the Delete button and return to Step 2.

   You can also use the Define Macro dialog box to edit the macro you just recorded. Look ahead into the "Creating Macros the Hard Way" section for the specifics.

7. Click on the OK button in the Define Macro dialog box.

You're done.

When you want to run the macro, just choose Edit⇨Run Macro and select the macro name from the list. Glance ahead to the "Running a Macro" section in this chapter for more information on running macros.

Creating Macros the Hard Way

If you're the kind of person who would rather scrub the floor with a toothbrush rather than a mop, you can create your macros the hard way, too. Using the easy way, you do the procedure and Approach 97 remembers what you did. Using the hard way, you precisely describe each step. We recommend the easy way, but, if you want, you can follow these steps to create a macro the hard way:

1. Try to talk yourself out of it.

If you just won't listen to yourself, then go to the next step.

2. Open the database file in which you want to create a macro.

 Choose File⇨Open, press Ctrl+O, or click on the File Open Smarticon to bring up the Open dialog box. Select the file you want to open and then click on the OK button.

3. Choose Edit⇨Macros.

You can also call up the Properties dialog box, click on the Macros tab, and then click on the Define Macro button. Either way, you are greeted by the Macros dialog box, which is shown in Figure 19-2. This dialog box is rather boring initially, but it gets more interesting after you create a few macros.

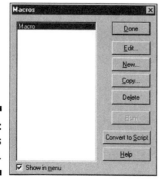

Figure 19-2:
The Macros
dialog box.

4. Click on the <u>N</u>ew button.

Yet another dialog box appears, this one called Define Macro. See Figure 19-3.

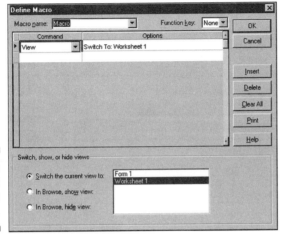

5. Type something more creative than *Macro* in the Macro <u>n</u>ame text box.

Think of a descriptive name for the macro to help you remember what it does.

6. Add the command that you want the macro to carry out.

The command area of the Define Macro dialog box is kind of like a spread-sheet. Each row contains a command to be carried out. The first column contains the name of the command, and the second column records any options that go along with the command, such as the name of the view that a View command should switch to or the search criteria for a Find command.

New macros are automatically set up to carry out a View command. You can, however, change the View command to some other command or to add additional commands. Just click on a cell in the Command column and then click on the cell again or click on the down arrow for the drop-down list. Either way, a menu appears that lists all the commands you can use in a macro. Pick the command you want to use and then click on it.

7. Set the options for the command that you picked in Step 5.

When you select a command, the bottom part of the Define Macro box changes to reflect the various options that are available for the command. Play with these options any way you want. For example, the Edit command offers options to Cu<u>t</u>, C<u>o</u>py, Pa<u>s</u>te, Select <u>A</u>ll or even Op<u>e</u>n the Paste Special dialog box and wait for input. Each different command provides different options. Get in there and explore.

8. **Repeat Steps 5 and 6 to add additional commands to the macro.**

9. **After you add all the commands that you want, click on the OK button.**

   The Macro dialog box reappears, and lo-and-behold, the name of the new macro is listed in the dialog box.

10. **Click on the Done button to dismiss the Macros dialog box.**

    You just created your first macro.

Table 19-1 lists the function carried out by each of the 27 macro commands. When you use the commands individually, they perform pretty simple functions, but in combination, they can do almost anything you want to do.

Table 19-1	What All Those Macro Commands Do
Command	*What It Does*
Browse	Switches to Browse mode
Close	Closes the database
Delete	Deletes the current record, found set, or file
Dial	Dials the phone number in the selected field (if you're hooked up to a modem)
Edit	Copies, cuts, or pastes data to or from the Clipboard. Selects everything in the view or opens the Paste Special dialog box and waits for user input
Enter	Accepts edits to the current record
Exit	Exits Approach 97
Export	Copies data from an Approach 97 database to a foreign file format or opens the Export Data dialog box and waits for input
Find	Finds database records (The macro can supply the search criteria, or you can have the user supply the criteria.)
Import	Copies data from a foreign file format into an Approach 97 database or opens the Import Data dialog box and waits for input
Mail	Electronically sends data to another computer user (An e-mail system has to be in place for this command to work.)
Menu Switch	Switches to a custom menu or the Short menu
Message	Displays a message on the screen
Open	Opens a file or opens the Open dialog box and waits for input
Page To	Goes to a specified page
Print	Prints the current view or opens the Print dialog box and waits for input

Command	What It Does
Print Preview	Switches to Preview mode
Records	Goes to a particular record, hides a record, or creates a new record
Replicate	Copies a Lotus Notes database or opens the Replicate dialog box and waits for input
Run	Runs another macro, depending on the results of the current macro being run
Save	Saves the Approach 97 file or opens the Save As dialog box and waits for input
Set	Sets the value of a field
Sort	Sorts database records or opens the Sort dialog box and waits for input
Spell Check	Runs the spelling checker
Tab	Tabs to position X of the current view's tab order
View	Switches to a different view
Zoom	Changes the zoom factor

Here are some key points to consider when you create macros manually:

- Macros are stored in the Approach file along with your views. Each macro that you create is available only when the Approach file that contains the macro is open.

- To delete a macro, choose Edit⇨Macros, select the macro you want to delete from the Define Macro dialog box, and click on the Delete button.

- To edit a macro, choose Edit⇨Macros, select the macro you want to edit from the Define Macro dialog box, and click on the Edit button.

- You can delete a command from a macro by calling up the Define Macro dialog box, clicking on the command that you want to delete, and then clicking on the Delete button.

- To insert a command in the middle of a macro, click on the command before which you want to insert the new command and then click on the Insert button.

- You can print the commands in a macro from the Define Macro dialog box by clicking on the Print button.

The many ways to include a Find in a macro

You can include several different kinds of Find commands in macros. (If you need a quick refresher on Finds, see Chapter 5.) To select the type of Find command that you want to use, just check one of the following options for the Find command in the Define Macro dialog box:

Perform stored find when macro is run: Stores the find criteria along with the macro and automatically runs the Find when the macro is run. After you click on the New Find button to set the criteria for the Find, you go to a variation of Find mode where you can type find criteria in each database field. After you enter the find criteria, click on the OK button to return to the Define Macro dialog box. After you set the criteria for a stored Find, you can change it by clicking on the Edit Find button.

Refresh the found set: Tells Approach 97 to redo the find to see if something has appeared or disappeared since the last find. The process is like checking for new mail in your e-mail program — often futile, but necessary at times, particularly in network settings in which another user may have added or deleted records since the Find was first run.

Go to Find and wait for input: Switches to Find mode when the macro is run and then waits for the user to enter the criteria for the query. After the user clicks on the OK button, the macro continues.

Find again and wait for input: Switches to Find mode and enables the user to repeat the preceding Find.

Go to Find Assistant and wait for input: Switches to the Find Assistant when the macro is run and then waits for the user to get with the program. After the user clicks on the OK button, the macro continues.

Find All records: Shows all records in the database and clears any previous finds.

When no records are found, run macro: Lets you select another macro to run if nothing is found by the Find macro.

Running a Macro

Creating a macro is just half of the battle. You also need to decide how you will run the macro in your database: You can run the macro from the Macros dialog box, you can choose Edit⇨Run Macro and the Macro name (or call up the Properties dialog box, switch to the Macros tab, and click on the Define Macro button), or you can *attach* the macro to a view (or to an object on a view), button, field, or function key so that the macro runs whenever the button or function key is pressed or whenever the user goes into or out of a field.

Running a macro from the Macros dialog box

You can run any macro from the Macros dialog box by following this procedure:

1. **Choose Edit⊃Macros.**

   You can also call up the Properties dialog box, switch to the Macros tab, and click on the Define Macro button. Either way, the Macros dialog box appears.

2. **Click on the macro you want to run from the Macros dialog box.**

3. **Click on the Run button.**

   The macro of your choice follows orders and runs.

Attaching a macro to a view

If you attach a macro to a view, the macro runs automatically whenever you switch to that view. You can use this feature to perform a Find or a Sort (or both) whenever you display a particular view.

You can also attach a macro that runs whenever you switch away from a view. Such a macro can, for example, use a Find command to show all database records.

To attach a macro to a view, follow these steps:

1. **Switch to the view to which you want to attach the macro.**

2. **Choose View⊃Design, press Ctrl+D, or click on the Design button to switch to Design mode.**

3. **Call up the view's Properties dialog box by clicking on the Properties dialog box SmartIcon or by pressing Alt+Enter.**

   The Properties dialog box appears.

4. **Click on the Macros tab to display the macro options.**

   Figure 19-4 shows the macro options on the Macros tab.

Figure 19-4:
The
Properties
dialog box
Macros tab
for a view.

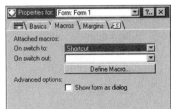

5. **Select the options you want to apply to your macro.**

If you want to run a macro whenever you switch to a view, select the macro name from the On switch to drop-down list.

If you want to run a macro whenever you switch away from a view, select the macro name from the On switch out drop-down list.

If you want the form to appear as a dialog box (and only as a dialog box), check the Show form as dialog check box. Only select this option if you include buttons on your form to enter the information. Otherwise, users will get to the dialog box and stall out because no way is available for them to enter the information.

6. **Click on the Properties dialog box's Close button (in the upper-right corner with the X on it) after you finish selecting your options.**

From then on, an On switch to macro is run when you switch to the view, and an On switch out macro is run when you switch from the view to any other view.

Creating a macro button

Another way to run a macro is to attach the macro to a button on a form or other view. Then Approach 97 runs the macro whenever you click on the button.

To create a macro button, follow these steps:

1. **Switch to the view on which you want the button to appear.**

2. **Choose View➪Design, press Ctrl+D, or click on the Design button to switch to Design mode.**

3. **If you don't see the Tools palette, call it to attention by pressing Ctrl+L or by choosing View➪Show Tools Palette.**

Figure 19-5 shows the Tools palette.

Figure 19-5:
The Tools
palette.

— Macro button

4. Click on the Macro button icon on the Tools palette.

The cursor changes to a crosshair, which looks like a big plus sign with an OK button beside it.

5. Draw the button on the form.

Point the crosshair cursor where you want one corner of the button to appear and then press and hold the left mouse button while dragging the mouse diagonally to where you want the opposite corner of the button to be. When you release the mouse, Approach 97 adds the button to the view, and the Properties dialog box shown in Figure 19-6 appears.

Figure 19-6:
The Properties dialog box options for a button.

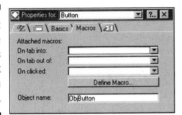

6. Assign the desired macro to the button by selecting the macro name in the On clicked list.

You can also specify a macro to run when the user tabs into or out of the button. This method is useful for fields that require unusual default values or fields that have complicated validation requirements that can't be handled by the program's normal default and validation options.

If you haven't yet created the macro, you can click on the Define Macro button to call up the Define Macro dialog box.

7. Click on the Basics tab in the Properties dialog box.

The Properties dialog box Basics tab appears, as shown in Figure 19-7.

Figure 19-7:
The Properties dialog box Basics tab for a button.

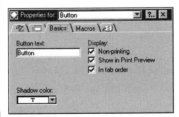

8. **Type a meaningful name for the button in the Button text box.**

   The text that you type here appears on the button.

9. **Choose any other options you want.**

   You can select boxes to make the button Non-printing, to Show in Print Preview, and to include it in the tab order of the fields on the screen.

10. **Click on the Properties dialog box's Close button (in the upper-right corner with the X on it) when you're finished.**

Some people like to create a separate form that acts as a menu of macro commands. To create a menu form, choose Create⇨Form to create a blank form. Then add a button for each macro that you want to be accessible from the form. A menu of macro commands allows users to run macros directly from a form, without having to bring up the Macro dialog box first.

Attaching a macro to a field

You can also attach a macro to any field on a view so that the macro is run whenever the user tabs into or out of the field or changes the contents of the field. You can use this feature to verify that correct data was entered into the field in cases where the program's data validation features aren't adequate. You can also use it to supply a default value for a field that you can't supply by specifying a default value in the Field Definition dialog box.

To attach a macro to a field, switch to Design mode, click on the field, and call up its Properties dialog box. Then click on the Macros tab and set the macro options.

Assigning a macro to a function key

You can assign a macro to any of the 12 function keys that live near the top of the keyboard. Then you can run the macro at any time by pressing the function key.

To assign a macro to a function key, follow these steps:

1. **Choose Edit⇨Macros.**

   You can also call up the Properties dialog box, click on the Macros tab, and click on the Define Macro button. Either way, the familiar Macros dialog box appears.

2. **Click on the macro that you want to assign to a function key from the Macros dialog box.**

3. **Click on the Edit button.**

   The Define Macro dialog box appears.

4. **Select the function key to which you want to assign the macro from the Function key list.**

5. **Click on the OK button.**

   You return to the Macros dialog box.

6. **Click on the Done button.**

   The Macros dialog box is whisked away.

Here are a few important caveats concerning function key assignments:

✔ Function key assignments are always available, no matter what view is displayed.

✔ If you assign macros to function keys, think about adding a text object to the database that lists the function keys to which you've assigned macros. Otherwise, innocent users won't have any clue about which function keys to press.

✔ Avoid assigning a macro to F1. Most Windows users expect F1 to call up the Help facility. If you assign a macro to F1, you can no longer use F1 to call up Help. Plus, you'll probably end up accidentally running the macro when you want to call up Help. Then you'll really need help!

A Real-World Example

To put the information in this chapter into perspective, Figure 19-8 shows an example of the type of macro that you can create to make a real-life Approach 97 application easier to use. This macro automates the steps that the user takes to display and print a report in a video rental store database. The report lists all customers who have videotapes checked out. The database lists customers in alphabetical order by name.

The macro has four commands:

View: The first macro command switches to the view named Daily Report, which contains the report to be printed. We created the report as a simple Columnar report by using the Report Assistant. See Chapter 10 for more about creating reports.

Find: The next macro command executes a find. This Find command runs a find that we defined and saved when we created the macro. The command selects only those records that have today's date in the last transaction field, indicating that the customer interacted with the company today. The effect of this command is to exclude from the report any customers who didn't interact with the company today.

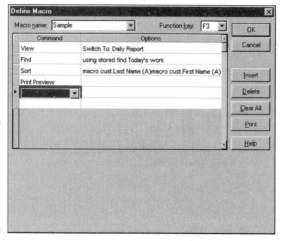

Figure 19-8:
A macro
that
prepares a
report for
printing.

Sort: The third macro command sorts the records into order by Last Name and then by First Name.

Preview: The last macro command switches to Preview mode so that the user can see what the report looks like. To actually print the report, the user clicks on the Print SmartIcon.

This macro can be attached to a button that appears on the main form or on the Status Report view itself so that it runs whenever the user switches to the view.

Chapter 20

Approaching a Network and the Internet

. . . .

. . . .

*J*ust a few years ago, computer networks were exotic beasts found only in large companies and science fiction movies. Nowadays, though, you see computer networks everywhere. Even companies that have only two computers have discovered that it's worth the $80 or so that it costs to network them together. Odds are your computer is connected to a network. Heck, even our four computers at home are networked!

This chapter is a brief introduction to what happens when you use Approach 97 on a computer that is connected to a network. We don't give detailed instructions for setting up a network or even for configuring Approach 97 to operate on a network. Those tasks are best handled by stiff-lipped professionals with pocket protectors, who are known as *network administrators.* Instead, this chapter assumes that Approach 97 is properly installed on a network; we just touch on the ways a network can complicate the way you use Approach 97.

If you have access to a network and other people also use the databases you use, you may find the information in this chapter useful. Networks are a great tool with which to share data, collaborate, and generally eliminate duplication of effort — why should you maintain a list of sales representatives if someone else keeps the same list on the network, right?

Of course, if you must know more about the technical aspects of getting a network up and running, you can always consult *Networking For Dummies,* 2nd Edition, by Doug Lowe, published by IDG Books Worldwide, Inc.

The last part of this chapter discusses how Approach 97 interacts and works with the Mother of All Networks — the Internet. Again, no details on the techie stuff. You get to read the bottom line and leave the details to those who thrive on that kind of stuff.

Remember that it is illegal to purchase a single copy of Approach 97 and put the copy on a network so that everyone on the network can use it. If you have a network, you need to purchase one Approach 97 license for each computer on which this program will be used.

What Is a Network?

A *network* is nothing more than two or more computers that are connected by a cable so that they can exchange information.

You can, of course, use other methods to exchange information between computers. Most of us have used what computer nerds call the *Sneakernet.* This method involves copying a file to a floppy disk and carrying the disk to some-one else's computer. (The term *Sneakernet* is typical of computer nerds' attempts at humor.)

With a computer network, you hook all the computers in your office together with cables, install a special *network adapter card* (an electronic circuit card that goes inside the computer) in each computer so you'll have a place to plug in the cable, set up and configure network software to make the network work, and voilà, you have a working network. Because Windows 95 has networking software built in, if you have two computers, you're only about $80 from having a network of your very own. That's all there is to it.

Here are a few important tidbits to remember about networks:

✔ If you use Approach 97 on a network, other people will probably have access to the same files you are using and could change information or views. If having other people change your database may be a problem, consider setting TeamSecurity and password options for your network database files. See Chapter 21 for the complete scoop.

✔ Networks are often called LANs. *LAN* is an acronym that stands for *Local Area Network.* Local Area Networks are networks in which all of the computers are within walking distance of one another, usually within the same building. These contrast with WANs (Wide Area Networks), which are LANs on a larger, often worldwide, scale.

✔ A network computer that contains disk drives, a printer, or other resources that are shared with other network computers is called a *server*. Server computers are usually the most powerful and expensive computers on the network. They often have huge disk drives and tons of memory.

✔ A network computer that isn't a *server* is called a *client*. Clients are the computers that people use to get work done. The computer that's sitting on your desk is a client.

✔ In some networks, the server computers can do nothing but be a server. In these networks, the servers are called *dedicated servers* in recognition of their dedication to a single task. In other networks, any computer can be a server, and a computer can be a server and a client at the same time. These networks are called *peer-to-peer networks*. Peer-to-peer networking software is built into Windows 95.

✔ The most popular type of dedicated server network is Netware from a company called Novell. Several types of peer-to-peer networks are in use, the most popular being Windows networking (Windows 95 or Windows for Workgroups) from Microsoft and LANTastic from Artisoft.

✔ To use a network, you have to *log in* by supplying a user ID and a password. Then you can access the disk drives and printers on the network servers. The ideal setup is for your computer to log on to the network automatically when you start the computer, and for the server disks and printers to be automatically accessed.

✔ Ask your network administrator about any procedures that you need to follow when you access the network. And pick up a copy of Doug Lowe's book, *Networking For Dummies,* 2nd Edition, brought to you by IDG Books Worldwide, Inc.

✔ For more information about network security, check out "Playing with Password Preferences" in Chapter 21.

Accessing a Network Database

When you use Approach 97 on a network, the most sensible thing to do is to store all of your databases on one of the network server's disk drives so that other network users can share the database. Then everyone can access the most current data.

You access network disk drives the same way you access local disk drives: by using a drive letter. Most computers have a local disk drive named drive C. Other drive letters are assigned to network drives. For example, if J is assigned to a disk drive on a network server, you access files on the server drive by using J for the drive letter. Your network administrator will tell you which drive letters to use for network drives.

To open a database that's stored on a network server, follow the same procedure that you use to open a database on a local disk drive: Choose File➪Open, click on the Open SmartIcon, or select Existing File from the Welcome to Lotus Approach dialog box. The only difference is that when you specify the location of the file in the Open dialog box, you specify a network disk rather than your local disk. Likewise, to save your work on a network disk drive, just specify the appropriate drive letter (as provided by your network administrator) and proceed as you would on your own machine.

If the database is password protected (network databases frequently are), you are asked to enter the password to access the database. Again, you must rely on your network guru for that information.

What happens if two people try to open the same database at the same time? Approach 97 lets both of them open it, but the program takes precautions to prevent both users from updating the same record simultaneously. Approach 97 displays a warning if a user tries to overwrite changes from another user. Generally, though, both users can freely access the data.

Accessing a Network Database in Single-User Mode

Although allowing several users to access a database simultaneously is great, on some occasions you may not want to permit simultaneous access. For example, if you want to change the design of a database by adding or removing fields, you shouldn't allow others to access the database while you work. Or if you want to print a critical report, you may need to lock out other users while the report prints.

If you turn on single-user mode when someone else is using the database, you won't be able to use the database until the other user finishes.

One way to prevent other users from accessing a database is to punch 99 on your telephone, or whatever number activates the officewide intercom, and say something such as, "Hey everybody! Don't touch the customer database for ten minutes, or I'll break your face!"

A more effective way is to follow this procedure:

1. Choose File➪Open or click on the Open SmartIcon.

The Open dialog box appears.

2. **Select dBASE or Paradox as the file type in the Files of _type field, depending on the type of database you want to modify.**

   Your database is probably in dBASE format if you used the Approach 97 defaults when you created it. If you aren't sure, just select your best guess — if you don't see the database you want to open in the text box, change the file type in the Files of _type field.

3. **Click on the Set_up button.**

   If you select the dBASE option, the dialog box in Figure 20-1 appears. For Paradox files, the dialog box in Figure 20-2 appears.

Figure 20-1:
The dBASE
Network
Connection
dialog box.

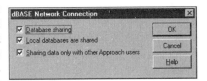

Figure 20-2:
The Paradox
Network
Connection
dialog box.

4. **Clear the appropriate data-sharing fields.**

   For dBASE files, uncheck the _Database sharing check box. For Paradox files, erase the contents of the _User name and _Network control file path fields.

   Be sure to write down the contents of these fields before you delete them; to restore shared access, you have to restore the contents of these fields.

5. **Click on the OK button.**

   You return to the Open dialog box.

6. **Select the file that you want to open from the Open dialog box (rummaging around on the disks if you need to) and click on the OK button.**

   Approach 97 opens the file for single-user access.

To enable other users to share the database, call up the Open dialog box and then click on the Setup button. Then click on the Connect button and check the Database sharing check box (dBASE files), or restore the User name and Network control file path text boxes to their previous contents (Paradox). If you're feeling particularly considerate, you may tell your coworkers that they can use the database again.

Setting Approach 97 Preferences for Network Sharing

Chapter 21 explains all about setting the Approach 97 preferences by using the File⇨User Setup⇨Approach Preferences command. Two of the preference options on the General tab affect the way Approach 97 works with a network:

- ✔ **Download data before Print Preview:** This option causes Approach 97 to copy all of a database to your hard disk whenever you enter Preview mode. The option shields you from database updates made by other users so you can be sure that the data you see is the data that prints.

- ✔ **Lock records using optimistic record locking:** This option enables several users to edit the same record at the same time. However, if both users try to save their changes, only the first user's changes are saved. The second user receives a warning that the changes will overwrite the first user's changes. This locking method is somewhat riskier than the more conservative method, which prevents users from editing the same records at the same time.

For more information about setting these preferences and other Approach 97 preferences, see Chapter 21.

Creating SQL Queries

Many companies are developing all kinds of enterprisewide database applications. Rather than use Approach 97, these companies create way-techie, programming-intensive, full-employment-for-nerds database software with the power and reliability to serve data to thousands of people.

The only reason that you may care about these databases is that you can use Approach 97 to haul data out of them for your own (obviously business-related) purposes. The big databases, at least the newer ones, understand a common language called *SQL,* or *Structured Query Language.* Approach 97 features a neat SQL Assistant that queries and retrieves the data you need. (*Query* is the fancy network database term for *find.*)

For example, if you work at a telephone company, you could use the SQL Assistant to set up a query to retrieve customer names, account numbers, and long-distance carrier preferences from the appropriate tables within the enormous company network database.

Assuming that you have access to these supersize databases, here's the procedure for setting up an SQL query to find and retrieve data and impress the boss.

1. **Choose File➪Open/Edit SQL.**

   The SQL Assistant appears, as you see in Figure 20-3.

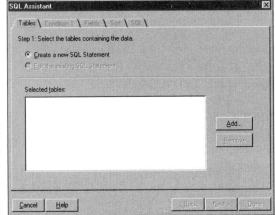

Figure 20-3:
The mighty
SQL
Assistant.

2. **Click on the Add button to add a database table.**

   Your query looks in each table you specify to find the data you're seeking.

3. **In the Open dialog box, select the appropriate file type under Files of type.**

   If you're selecting a table from Approach files you created, you're probably looking for a dBASE file. If you're looking for a table from the network somewhere, you have to defer to your server administrator's instructions.

   You may be required to log in to a server or to do some other bureaucratic and techie nonsense. Just do as they say. They've got you over a barrel.

4. **Root around until you find the database you want to build a query for, select it, and then click on the Open button.**

   You're now back at the SQL Assistant, with one table selected. You can select only one non-SQL database, such as Paradox, dBASE, or FoxPro, but you can select multiple SQL database tables.

5. Click on the Next button.

The Condition 1 tab appears (see Figure 20-4). This panel is very much like the Find Assistant dialog box, and the procedure you follow is very much like a Find.

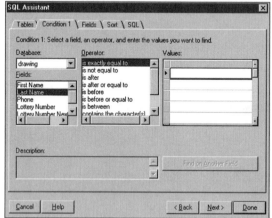

Figure 20-4:
The
Condition 1
tab of the
SQL
Assistant
dialog box.

6. Set the options available on the Condition 1 tab.

From the Fields list, select the field you wish to query in the database, select an Operator, and then enter the values you're searching for.

Note that after you select the Fields, Operator, and enter a value, Approach 97 provides a real English (mostly) Description so you can check your work.

The Operator specifies the relationship between the field you selected and the value or Values you entered.

7. Click on the Next button.

The Fields tab appears, asking you to add fields to the view.

8. Select each field you want to retrieve with your query and click on the Add button.

9. Click on the Next button.

The Sort tab appears. Skip this tab for now — just trust us.

10. Click on the Next button.

The SQL tab appears to show you how the plain English selections you just made were transformed into SQL gibberish. If you want to click in and edit this mess, you're welcome to. A better method is to go Back a couple of steps and let the Assistant do the editing for you. Figure 20-5 shows the results.

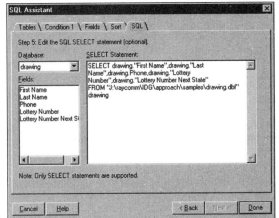

SQL Assistant

Tables \ Condition 1 \ Fields \ Sort \ SQL \

Step 5: Edit the SQL SELECT statement (optional).

Database:

drawing

Fields:

First Name
Last Name
Phone
Lottery Number
Lottery Number Next St

SELECT Statement:

SELECT drawing."First Name",drawing."Last
Name",drawing.Phone,drawing."Lottery
Number",drawing."Lottery Number Next State"
FROM "J:\raycomm\IDG\approach\samples\drawing.dbf"
drawing

Note: Only SELECT statements are supported.

Cancel   Help   < Back   Next >   Done

Figure 20-5:
The SQL
Assistant
presents
your query.

11. Click on the Done button.

You're done and your boss will be very impressed. Ya done gud! Now you have your selected set of records and fields to work with, just like a regular Approach 97 database. Cool!

Approaching the Internet

Approach 97 comes with all kinds of cool tools to let you use the Internet for collaboration or sharing data, just as you can use a regular, less-hyped, network for the same purpose. You can open files from the Internet, either from World Wide Web servers or from FTP (File Transfer Protocol) servers, and, if you have the requisite permissions from system administration types, you can save your files back to the Internet for someone else to use.

Using these techniques to share files over the Internet can help you work much more effectively by allowing you to open and save files halfway around the world almost as easily as you could on your own hard disk. Talk about a good tool for collaboration! Not only that, but the same techniques apply in Word Pro, 1-2-3, and Freelance Graphics.

If you want to Approach the Internet, but you're feeling less than savvy about your Internet skills, you can consult *Internet For Dummies,* 3rd Edition, by John R. Levine, Carol Baroudi, and Margaret Levine Young, published by IDG Books Worldwide, Inc.

By the way, pretty much everything about Approaching the Internet works just as well on your company intranet (*intranets* are like private little Internets that companies use to distribute data among their employees). The Internet and intranets have the same principles and procedures, but with slightly different names for certain things. If you have trouble working with your company's intranet, better call the closest computer guru you know.

Saving a database to the Internet

Saving a file to the Internet requires that you have *write access* to an FTP server on the Internet, that you remember the address and your ID and password, and that you want to. Nothing more. Write access means that you can add or change information on an FTP server.

Generally, you are only able to *write a file* to an FTP server if you have your own account on the server. Most FTP sites on the Internet allow you to log in as anonymous, but you can only read or copy files; you can't put anything out there.

The procedure is as follows:

1. **Open the database you want to save to the Internet by choosing File⇨Open or by clicking on the Open SmartIcon.**

2. **Select the database and then click on the OK button.**

   Root around on your disk, if necessary, to find the database you want to save on the Internet.

3. **Choose File⇨Internet⇨Save to Internet or choose File⇨Save Approach File and then click on the Internet button.**

   You see the Save to Internet dialog box shown in Figure 20-6.

Figure 20-6:
The preliminary Internet dialog box lets you save your file.

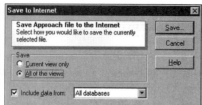

4. **Click on the All of the views radio button and select All databases in the drop-down list.**

   Selecting these options lets you save the whole database on the Internet. You could select the Current view only dialog box to save only the current view. Or, to save only a part of the database to the Internet, click on the down arrow beside All databases and select Found Set, Current Record, or All databases, depending on what you want to save.

5. **Click on the OK button to move on to the gonzo Save to Internet dialog box shown in Figure 20-7.**

Figure 20-7:
The Save to
Internet
dialog box.

6. **Click on the H̲osts button to set up the connection information.**

The FTP Hosts dialog box appears. (The host is the computer to which you're going to save your data.) See Figure 20-8.

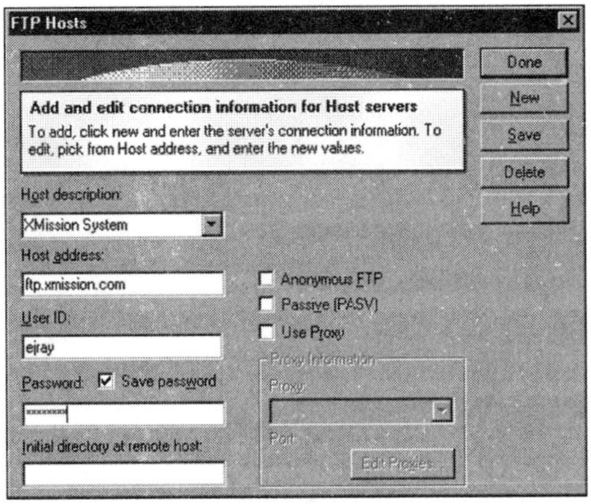

Figure 20-8:
The FTP
Hosts dialog
box.

7. **Enter the necessary information about your FTP connection in the appropriate text boxes.**

You should not have to guess here. If you have access to an FTP server to save files, the person who told you that you have access can also provide the information you need to fill out this dialog box.

Host description can be anything that is meaningful to you, and Host address is the address of your FTP server. The text box is probably case-sensitive, so type the information exactly as you get it from the person who gives you the address.

Either enter a User ID or click on the Anonymous FTP check box, depending on the type of connection. Again, if you don't know what type of connection you have, ask the host administrator.

Provide the Password, if required, and an Initial directory at remote host if you know what it should be. The Initial directory field will often be left blank.

Complete any additional fields that you were told to complete.

8. **Click on the Save button so that Approach 97 remembers the connection information.**

9. **Click on the Done button.**

   The Save to Internet dialog box reappears.

10. **Connect to the FTP server by clicking on the Connect button.**

    If you have a dial-up connection to the Internet, the Connect to dialog box appears so you can establish your Internet connection. If the dialog box doesn't appear, you may need to start your connection to the Internet before you attempt to connect to the FTP server.

    After a second of futzing around, text appears in the Save in text box and in the dialog box just below it. See Figure 20-9.

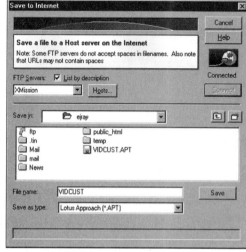

Figure 20-9:
The Save to Internet dialog box ready to save your database to the Internet.

11. Fill in a File <u>n</u>ame and click on the Save button to save your database to the Internet.

Avoid using spaces in your file names because the FTP server may require different file-naming conventions. If you enter a file name that the server does not accept, nothing happens when you click on the Save button.

The process may take a few seconds, but Approach 97 saves your file, breaks the FTP connection (but leaves you connected to the Internet), and makes the Save to Internet dialog box disappear.

You're in business!

 After you save a database to the Internet, you may want to close and restart Approach 97 before you work further on developing that database. Switching back and forth from saving on the Internet and saving locally can confuse Approach 97, and, as we now well know, a confused database is an unhappy database (and database user).

Publishing a database as a Web page

So, you think you want to publish your database as a Web page. For you, Mr. Rip Van Winkle, that means to save the Approach 97 file in a special format so that people on the Internet can use their Web browsers (such as Netscape Navigator or Internet Explorer) to check out the information.

Yes, Approach 97 does give you the option to publish as a Web page, but before you jump on the bandwagon, take a second to think about the following pros and cons:

Pros:

✔ Publishing as a Web page would let anyone with a Web browser and access to the Internet (or your corporate intranet) see the data. Your audience wouldn't need their own copy of Approach 97 to view your data.

Cons:

✔ Publishing as a Web page is not nearly as spiffy looking as leaving the information in Approach 97. The conversion to HTML (due to limitations in the HTML format) discards most of the form objects, formatting, and all that fancy drawing stuff that's so much fun (and impressive to the boss).

✔ Publishing as a Web page produces files that the readers can't change or easily navigate. For example, if your boss snags your new database off the Internet in the regular Approach 97 format, she can make changes and update information on the fly. If, however, that database is published as a Web page, she can't make any changes and will have to use a more unwieldy means of looking at the information. Bummer.

(Actually, presenting your audience with documents that they can't easily change could be a pro as well, but in our opinion, uneditable databases are pretty squarely on the con side.)

If, after careful consideration, you decide that you want nothing more in this world than to publish your database as a Web page, you'll be pleased to know that the process is very similar to saving to the Internet (see "Saving a database to the Internet" in this chapter for details).

(continued)

(continued)

Here's how:

1. **Choose File-⇨Internet⇨Publish as Web Pages.**

   You see the Save to Internet dialog box, just as you do when saving to the Internet. The only difference is that the Save as type and File name fields reflect a file type of HTML, rather than the APT file that Approach usually uses for saving to the Internet.

2. **Assuming you've already connected to the Internet, verify the FTP Server and then click Connect.**

3. **If necessary, choose a folder to Save in and check the File name.**

   Just as with Saving to the Internet, spaces in the file name are no-nos.

4. **Click on the Save button.**

   You see the HTML Preferences dialog box.

5. **Put a check beside each option you want to choose and then click on OK.**

   The default settings are probably as good as it gets, although you may want to choose Show table borders to make your data a bit more readable.

   The Creating an index page option produces a page with brief numeric links to the other pages. Don't bother with it.

You can choose to have navigation links at the top or the bottom of your pages. The longer the page, the more likely you'd want to have links at both ends.

If you want your readers to easily send you e-mail from your new Web pages, insert your complete e-mail address in the Send e-mail from HTML forms to this address field.

Click Save Default to save your settings for use the next time you publish your Approach data as a Web page.

6. **Wait for a little while.**

   Your screen will flicker as dialog boxes appear and disappear and then the Save to Internet dialog box will vanish.

Just use your Web browser to check out the pages from the Web server (your administrator may have to provide the address). You can't view the documents locally; you need to check them out from the server.

If you think that this process is conceptually pretty good, but you want to exercise some additional control over your Web pages (boy, you're just never satisfied, are you?), check out *Dummies 101: HTML* and *HTML For Dummies Quick Reference*, both by yours truly, published by IDG Books Worldwide, Inc.

Opening a database from the Internet

Sometimes colleagues at a different location save their database to the Internet and provide you with the address so you can retrieve the database and work on it. If you want to work on a database that's located on the Internet, you need to know how to open the database. Opening a file from the Internet is fundamentally the same as saving a file to the Internet. After you obtain the address of the file(s) on the Internet, follow this procedure:

1. **Choose File⇨Internet⇨Open from Internet or choose File⇨Open and click on the Internet button in the Open dialog box that appears.**

   You're presented with the Open from Internet dialog box, as shown in Figure 20-10.

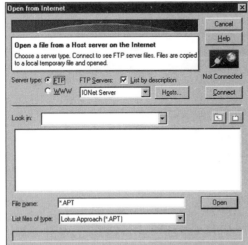

Figure 20-10:
The Open
from
Internet
dialog box.

2. **Connect to the site where the desired database file is located.**

   If you're opening a file from the World Wide Web, click on the WWW radio button.

   If you're opening a file from an FTP server, click on the FTP radio button and select the host from the drop-down list that appears.

   If the server to which you want to connect isn't a choice in the drop-down list under FTP Servers, click on the Hosts button to set up the connection information. The FTP Hosts dialog box appears. For details on filling out the necessary information in this dialog box, see the section "Saving a database to the Internet" in this chapter.

3. **Click on the Connect button to open the connection to the FTP server.**

4. **Select the name of the file you want to open.**

   After a brief pause, a list of files from the Internet FTP server appears in the dialog box, and you can click through folders to select the file you want to open.

Figure 20-11:
FTP server
dialog box
showing
folders
containing
files.

5. Click on the Open button.

That's it!

Some additional notes about saving files to and opening files from the Internet:

✔ If you want to open a file from a WWW (World Wide Web) server, click on the <u>W</u>WW radio button in the Open from Internet dialog box. The dialog box shown in Figure 20-12 appears. Enter the full file name in the File <u>n</u>ame text box; the file name should be a complete Uniform Resource Locator, or URL. The URL should look something like `http://www.raycomm.com/approach.tpt`. Then click on the Open button. After a moment, the database appears. That's it!

Figure 20-12:
Entering a
file name in
the Open
from
Internet
dialog box
with <u>W</u>WW
selected.

✔ If you're considering saving files to the Internet, keep security issues in mind. Although the Internet isn't the Wild West (as the media would have you believe), it also isn't nearly as safe and secure as your corporate network or the closet in your hall.

Avoid saving highly confidential or sensitive files to the Internet if at all possible. You can use the same procedure to save a file to a corporate intranet, though, and improve the security considerably.

✔ You can set up all your frequently used Internet connections at once by going to File⇨Internet⇨FTP Connection Setup, clicking on the Hosts button and filling in the blanks for each of your common connections, both read-only and write access. Be sure to click on the Save button after you finish so that Approach 97 remembers your settings for the next time.

✔ If you only open files from one FTP server or save files to one FTP server, although not necessarily the same one, you can set those connections to happen automatically. Choose File⇨Internet⇨FTP Connection Setup. Click on the Auto connect Open from Internet or Auto connect Save to Internet boxes, as appropriate, and select a server to connect to. Click on the OK button, and the specified connection occurs whenever you open to or save from the Internet.

✔ If your computer is protected by a *firewall,* an Internet security mechanism, you may have to set up a proxy server to help transfer your files (like sending your luggage through the X-ray machine at the airport). Choose File⇨Internet⇨FTP Connection Setup, or click on the Hosts button, click on the Use Proxy and Edit Proxies button, and then add the proxy information that your network or security administrator provides. Click on the Done button or on the OK button after you are finished.

Chapter 21

Playing with Preferences

· ·

In This Chapter

▶ Understanding Approach 97 preferences

▶ Setting display preferences

▶ Setting database order preferences

▶ Setting password preferences

▶ Setting the general preferences

▶ Customizing SmartIcons

· ·

*Y*ou can set dozens of preference options that affect the way Approach 97 works. Approach 97 preferences let you do fun stuff such as display a ruler, set the default sort order for your favorite databases, and customize your SmartIcon bar. After you get familiar with Approach 97 preferences, you'll begin to wish for real-life equivalents that let you spend your time having fun instead of toiling with your computer.

This chapter describes the most useful preferences, but, what's more important, it tells you which preferences you can safely ignore so that you can catch up on the things you really want to do.

What's with All the Options?

When you choose File⇨User Setup⇨Approach Preferences, you are presented with the killer Approach Preferences dialog box that has tabs out the wazoo (whatever a *wazoo* is). Each of the tabs has its own set of options controls. To switch from one tab to another, just click on the tab label at the top of the dialog box. Here's the lowdown on the seven tabs that appear on the Approach Preferences dialog box:

Display: Contains options that control the appearance of the Approach 97 window

Order: Sets the default sort order for databases

Password: Sets passwords for Approach files

Dialer: Configures the modem (that is, you copy settings out of your modem documentation) so that Approach 97 can instruct it to dial phone numbers

Database: Sets some techie-type options for databases

Index: Enables you to use dBASE, FoxPro, or Paradox indexes that have already been created by those programs (You only need this tab if you share your Approach 97 database with people who use these other database programs.)

General: Contains a hodgepodge of miscellaneous options that the Approach 97 programmers couldn't squeeze in anywhere else, including little stuff like using the Enter key to move from field to field in Browse mode, or automatically bringing up the Add field dialog box after you create a new field

To set preferences for Approach 97, follow these steps:

1. **Choose File⇨User Setup⇨Approach Preferences.**

   The Approach Preferences dialog box appears.

2. **Click on the tab that contains a preference you want to set.**

   If you're not sure which tab to click on, cycle through them all until you find what you need.

3. **Set the preferences however you want.**

   Most of the preferences are simple check boxes that you click on to check or uncheck. Some require that you select a choice from a drop-down list, and some have the audacity to require that you actually type something as proof of your keyboard proficiency.

4. **Repeat Steps 2 and 3 until you exhaust your options or you exhaust yourself.**

   You can set more than one preference with a single use of the File⇨User Setup⇨Approach Preferences command. Knock yourself out.

5. **Click on the OK button.**

   You're done! Approach 97 remembers your choices for everything except Order and Database. Order and Database are associated with the particular database you're using and only apply to the database you select.

Dealing with Display Preferences

You can use the options on the Display tab, shown in Figure 21-1, to customize the appearance of the program's humble display. You can see that the options are arranged into four groups: Show, Show in Design, Grid, and Named style.

Figure 21-1:
The
Approach
Preferences
dialog box
Display tab.

This list summarizes the functions of the Show preferences:

SmartIcons: This option displays or hides the SmartIcon bar. Uncheck it if you don't like the SmartIcons and you want to free up the screen real estate so you can see more of your database views. (But read up on customizing SmartIcons at the end of this chapter before you write them off for good.)

Status bar: This option displays or hides the status bar at the bottom of the screen. If you'd rather have the extra space to see more data and you don't use the status bar, uncheck this one too.

Action bar: This option displays or hides the Action bar at the top of your workspace. This bar is also disposable with a swift uncheck if you want more space on the screen, but if you get rid of it, you may have to work harder (slightly) to switch to Browse or Design mode, to create a new record, or to start a Find.

View tabs: This option displays or hides those tabs that enable you to switch quickly from one view to another. If you uncheck this option, you can see more of your data, but you have to use the View menu to switch among views.

Title bar help: Have you ever noticed that when you point to a menu command, a brief description of the command or icon appears in the title bar? If seeing that description bugs you, uncheck this option.

Welcome dialog: Uncheck this option to get rid of the Welcome to Lotus Approach dialog box. When this option is unchecked, you have to choose File⇨Open or click on the Open SmartIcon to open database files.

Report summaries: Uncheck this to eliminate automatic summaries in your reports if you find that the Approach 97 approach is cramping your style.

The Show in Design options apply only when you are working in Design mode:

Data: Mr. Data from *Star Trek: The Next Generation* appears on the screen. Okay, not really. Check this option if you want to see actual data in database fields rather than the field names.

Rulers: Displays a list of every U.S. President since George Washington. Okay, just kidding again. Check this option to display vertical and horizontal rulers to help align objects that you place on a form.

Add Field dialog: Check this option if you want the Add Field dialog box to automatically appear whenever you switch to Design mode.

Tools palette: Check this option if you want the floating Tools palette to appear automatically whenever you switch to Design mode.

The Custom Controls button takes you to a dialog box in which you can add controls to the Tools palette. This option is very cool if you find a tool that you would use frequently in Design mode.

The Named style box contains a single button that is labeled Default Style. If you click on this button, another dialog box (very similar to the Properties dialog box) appears that lets you set the formatting options that you want to apply to objects that you create in Design.

You use the Grid settings to control the grid, which helps align Design objects:

Show grid: Check this option if you want Approach 97 to display the grid automatically.

Snap to grid: Check this option if you want objects to stick to the grid.

Units: Use this option to change the unit of measure used for the next option (Inches or Centimeters).

Width: Use this option to change the spacing of the grid.

Ogling Order Preferences

You use the Order tab, shown in Figure 21-2, to establish a default sort order for a database. If you do not establish a default sort order, records are maintained in the order in which you enter them.

To set the sort order for a database, follow these steps:

   1. Open the database.

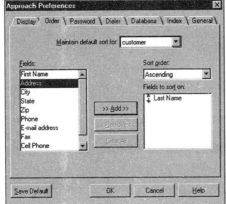

Figure 21-2:
The
Approach
Preferences
Order tab.

2. **Choose File⇨User Setup⇨Approach Preferences.**

3. **Click on the Order tab.**

4. **In the Maintain default sort for box, select the database with the sort order you want to set.**

5. **In the Fields list, click on the field on which you want the database sorted.**

6. **In the Sort order drop-down list, select Ascending or Descending to specify ascending or descending order for the field.**

7. **Click on the Add button.**

8. **Repeat Steps 5 through 7 if you want the database sorted on more than one field.**

9. **Click on the OK button.**

If you make a mistake, click on the Remove button to remove a sort field, or click on the Clear All button to remove all sort fields and start over.

Playing with Password Preferences

You use the Password tab, shown in Figure 21-3, to set a password for a database or an Approach file. A database can have two kinds of passwords: read/write and read-only. The *read/write password* enables you to update database records, whereas the *read-only password* enables you to read but not update database records. If you assign either type of password to a database, Approach 97 requires you to enter the password when you open the file.

This capability enables you to let some users access the database with full read/write privileges and others view, but not update, data in the database. Provide the read/write password only to those users who need to update the database and share the read-only password with all other users.

Because you can't assign a read-only password without first assigning a read/write password, the Read-only password field is grayed-out at first, as shown in Figure 21-3.

Figure 21-3:
The
Approach
Preferences
Password
tab.

To assign a password to a database, follow these steps:

1. **Open the database.**

2. **Choose File⇨User Setup⇨Approach Preferences.**

   The Approach Preferences dialog box appears.

3. **Click on the Password tab.**

4. **To assign a database password, select the database from the Database list and then type a password for the Read/write password box.**

5. **Approach 97 asks you to type the password again, so type it again.**

   Retyping the password is the Approach 97 way of making sure that you didn't type the password incorrectly. Notice that the password that you type doesn't display on the screen. Instead, any password that you type is displayed as asterisks. The asterisks keep the bad guys from reading your password when they peer over your shoulder. But if the bad guys can't see your password, neither can you. Typing the password again ensures that you didn't make a typo while you were entering the password. If you don't type the password exactly the same both times, Approach 97 makes you start over from the beginning.

When picking a password, don't use words or dates that identify you or things about you — such as your maiden name, birthdate, address, favorite place to shop, pets' names, or current significant other's name (names?). Remember that the purpose of a password is to keep people from being able to get into your files; your password should be a combination of letters or short words that only you know or could figure out.

6. **Write down the password and keep it somewhere safe!**

   If you forget it, you can't access the database.

7. **Repeat Step 4 to add a password in the Read-only password box or to password-protect other databases.**

8. **Click on the OK button.**

   When anyone tries to use the database, they have to enter the appropriate password before the database opens.

If you want to change the password later, open the database and type the password when prompted. Then repeat the preceding procedure, typing the new password in place of the old one. You can get rid of the password completely by setting the new password to nothing — just press Enter in the password field.

Approach 97 also lets you protect the Approach file itself. The TeamSecurity button at the bottom of the Password tab takes you to another dialog box with more password options for your Approach 97 files than you'd ever dreamed of. If you enable these security options, Approach 97 requires you to enter the password whenever you switch to Design mode. You can use these options to ensure that no one changes your views. If many people with different areas of responsibility work on the database, the TeamSecurity features can help ensure that people don't inadvertently change things they shouldn't.

To set TeamSecurity for your Approach 97 file, follow these steps:

1. **Open the database.**

2. **Choose File⇨User Setup⇨Approach Preferences.**

   The Approach Preferences dialog box appears.

3. **Click on the Password tab.**

4. **Select the database from the Database list.**

5. **Click on the TeamSecurity button.**

   You see the TeamSecurity dialog box, as shown in Figure 21-4, which lists four different levels of security, including Manager, Designer, Editor, and Reader. Each level provides different privileges for viewing or changing the Approach 97 file.

Figure 21-4:
The
TeamSecurity
dialog box.

6. **Select a team member and then click on the Edit button to add a password.**

The Edit TeamSecurity dialog box appears, as shown in Figure 21-5.

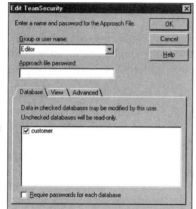

Figure 21-5:
The Edit
TeamSecurity
dialog box.

Enter the password and repeat it on command to make sure that you didn't accidentally make a typo.

You should also look through the Database, View, and Advanced tabs so you can check or uncheck different rights for the team member. Click on the OK button after you're finished.

7. **Click on the Done button in the TeamSecurity dialog box and then click on the OK button to dismiss the Approach Preferences dialog box.**

Consider these additional tidbits about TeamSecurity:

✔ If the four team members Approach 97 provides don't cover all the combinations of viewing and editing rights you need, you can add new members by clicking on the New button in the TeamSecurity dialog box.

✔ Don't get too carried away with setting different levels of security. You can easily construct such a maze that nobody knows what they can view or change.

Saluting the General Preferences

Back in the days of Approach 1.0, the preferences on the General tab were lowly Private Preferences. But they re-upped for Version 2 and eventually decided to make a career of it. Now, the options on the General tab are all the way to the rank of General. You'd better snap-to whenever you call up these preferences, which you see in Figure 21-6.

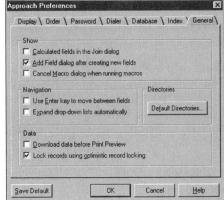

Figure 21-6:
The
Approach
Preferences
General tab.

This list enumerates what the Show preferences do:

Calculated fields in the Join dialog: Check this option if you want to join databases based on a calculated field.

Add Field dialog after creating new fields: With this preference checked, the Add Field dialog box is automatically displayed whenever you create a new database field.

Cancel Macro dialog when running macros: If you want to cancel a macro while it is running, check this preference.

The Navigation options on the General preferences tab let you do the following:

Use Enter key to move between fields: If you're entering data and want to move to the next field when you press Enter, check this option.

Expand drop-down lists automatically: Check this option if you want drop-down lists to open up as soon as your cursor moves into the field.

Under the Directories section of the tab is one lonely button that does the following:

Default Directories: Click on the Default Directories button to summon the Default Directories dialog box. Default working directory specifies the first directory you see when you choose File➪Open or click on the Open SmartIcon, while SmartMaster directory tells Approach 97 where to look for your SmartMasters. Changing the SmartMaster directory probably isn't advisable unless someone is collecting SmartMasters in a central location on the network. Otherwise, Approach 97 knows good and well where its SmartMasters are.

The Data options on the General preferences tab offer the following features:

Download data before Print Preview: If this option is checked, database data that lives on a network drive is copied to the local drive when you enter Preview mode. Then, when you print the data, the appearance matches Print Preview.

Lock records using optimistic record locking: This preference enables several users to edit a record simultaneously, but only the first user can save changes. Subsequent attempts to save changes to the record display a warning indicating that data may be lost. This method is faster, but not quite as reliable, as pessimistic record locking, which prohibits users from editing a record that is being edited by another user.

Making SmartIcon Bars Smarter

Smarter? SmartIcons? Well, actually, you won't be making them any smarter, but you can help ensure that you can work smarter, not harder. That's the idea, right?

Seriously, all those Approach 97 SmartIcons can easily be customized. For example, if you often interrupt your processes of entering data or browsing through your database to send someone an e-mail about the data, you could add a Send Mail SmartIcon to the default Browse SmartIcon bar. Or, if you often have to make envelopes, you could add a SmartIcon to add Create a new Envelope to your default bar. How to do all this? Read on! To customize your SmartIcons, use the following procedure:

1. **Choose File➪User Setup➪SmartIcons Setup.**

   Take a minute to survey the mongo SmartIcons Setup dialog box that appears. You see more icons and options than you'll use in a lifetime. (See Figure 21-7 for the hard copy version.)

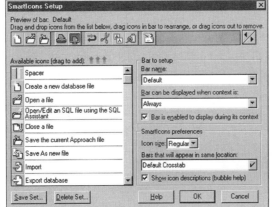

Figure 21-7:
The
SmartIcons
Setup dialog
box.

2. **Under Bar to setup, choose the Bar name that you want to customize.**

   Lots of choices, huh? Just take them one at a time, or until you get tired of customizing the SmartIcons and decide to just roll with the Approach 97 defaults on the rest.

3. **In the Bar can be displayed when context is drop-down list box, select when the bar should be displayed.**

   Select Always or the more limited context in which the bar should display.

   The Bar can be displayed when context is field allows you to make sure that the bar doesn't show up at inappropriate times. For example, having the Default Preview bar cluttering up your screen when you're designing a new form is pointless, so the Default Preview bar is set so it can only be displayed in the Print Preview context. Cool, huh?

   Checking Bar is enabled to display during its context forces the bar to display whenever it can.

4. **Drag SmartIcons from the Available icons (drag to add) list up to the bar at the top of the dialog box to add them to the bar.**

   You can control the order in which the SmartIcons appear on the screen by dragging the icons to the proper place in the bar.

5. **Drag unwanted SmartIcons off the bar and release them to get rid of them.**

6. **Repeat Steps 4 and 5 until the bar is just the way you want it.**

7. **Click on the Save Set button and then click on the Save As New button in the Save As New SmartIcons File dialog box to save your new SmartIcon bar under a new name.**

Enter a name for the bar and a SmartIcons file name, as shown in Figure 21-8. You may want to revert to the original settings at some point, so do not overwrite any of the default bars.

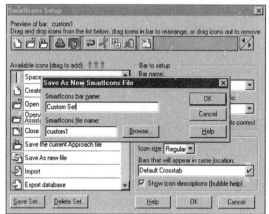

Figure 21-8:
The Save As New SmartIcons File dialog box.

8. **Click on the OK button.**

Some additional notes about customizing your SmartIcon bars:

✔ Your SmartIcons get much more usable if you change the Icon size to Large. The squint factor (at least for us), goes way down.

✔ Take the time to do it! As soon as you know which SmartIcons you use and when, which SmartIcons you'll never use, and which ones you can't use because you can't remember what they do, it's time to customize. You'll be amazed at how a custom set of SmartIcons can help your productivity. Customize your SmartIcons enough and nobody will ever borrow your computer to use Approach 97 more than once, either.

✔ Don't mess with the Bars that will appear in same location drop-down list box. We ended up wondering where our bars went because they were all stacked up on top of each other — bad move on our part.

✔ The Show icon descriptions (bubble help) option is great and should be checked if it isn't already. With this option checked, you can let your mouse hover over a SmartIcon and Approach 97 tells you what it does. You can't beat that for hand-holding help.

Chapter 22
Conversion Experiences

*I*t's a beautiful day in this neighborhood, a beautiful day for a neighbor. Would you be mine? Could you be mine? . . .Won't you be my neighbor?

Hello, boys and girls. This chapter explains how to exchange data with files created by neighboring programs. You don't live on Software Street all by yourself, you know. Other programs are here to stay, so you need to know how to get along with them.

Actually, Approach 97 is a bit peculiar when it comes to working with data created by other programs. Most programs have their own unique, proprietary file formats that they and they alone can use. Recognizing the need for cooperation in the computer world, most programs also can convert data that's stored in other, similar file formats. For example, most word-processing programs can open documents created by other word-processing programs and automatically convert the file format as they open the documents.

Not so with Approach 97. Approach 97 doesn't have its own database file format. Instead, it uses the database file formats used by several popular competing database programs — most notably dBASE (III+ and IV), Paradox, and FoxPro. Approach 97 can open these database files without the need for any conversion processes whatsoever. So if you turned to this chapter for information about converting dBASE, Paradox, FoxPro, or other database programs' data to Approach 97, you can stop right now. You already know how to convert them: Just open the file.

This chapter focuses on converting data into an Approach 97 database when the data isn't already in a format that Approach 97 can use. For example, perhaps you have a list of 100 names and addresses in a Lotus 1-2-3 spreadsheet, an old WordPerfect secondary mail-merge file, or a shareware database program called CheaperBase. This chapter explains how to deal with oddball neighbors such as these.

Opening a Foreign File

Approach 97 enables you to open files that are stored in various foreign formats. You can open Lotus 1-2-3 or Excel spreadsheet files to convert spreadsheet data to an Approach 97 database. Or you can open one of two types of DOS text files: delimited files or fixed-length files. These special text file formats are often used to convert files created by word processors or other programs to Approach 97.

When you open a file that has a foreign format, Approach 97 automatically converts the file to an Approach 97 database, normally using dBASE as the database file format (you can tell Approach 97 to use the Paradox or FoxPro formats instead of dBASE). Approach 97 also creates default form and worksheet views for the converted database.

Opening a spreadsheet file

Approach 97 enables you to open Lotus 1-2-3 or Microsoft Excel spreadsheet files, and it automatically converts them to database files. Each row is converted to a database record, and the spreadsheet columns represent database fields.

To convert a spreadsheet to a database, follow these steps:

1. **Call up the Open dialog box by choosing File⇨Open, clicking on the Open SmartIcon, or selecting Open an Existing File from the Welcome to Lotus Approach dialog box.**

   The Open dialog box appears.

2. **In the Files of type field, select the file type.**

   Select the appropriate file type. Excel (*.XLS) or Lotus 1-2-3 (*.WK*) are the most likely candidates for most purposes.

3. **Click on the name of the spreadsheet file that you want to open from the Open dialog box.**

   You may have to rummage about the hard disk to find the file.

4. Click on the Open button.

Depending on the file type you're opening, you see a dialog box appear. If you're opening an Excel spreadsheet, the Field Names dialog box appears, as shown in Figure 22-1. If you're opening a 1-2-3 file, the Select Range dialog box appears, as shown in Figure 22-2.

Figure 22-1:
The Field Names dialog box.

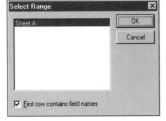

Figure 22-2:
The Select Range dialog box.

5. If the first row of the spreadsheet contains labels that can be used as field names, check the First row contains field names check box.

If the first row of the spreadsheet does not contain usable field names, uncheck this field. Approach 97 then uses the column headings for the field names (A, B, C, and so on). If you're opening a 1-2-3 file, click on the Range you want to import.

6. Click on the OK button.

The New dialog box appears, as shown in Figure 22-3.

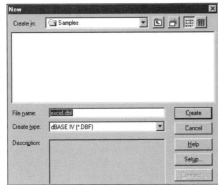

Figure 22-3:
The New dialog box, ready for you to enter the name and type of your new database file.

7. **Click on the Create button to accept the name and file format Approach 97 suggests for the new database.**

If you want to use a different name or file type, change the fields accordingly before you click on the Create button.

8. **You're done!**

Approach 97 converts the spreadsheet, and you even get a friendly-looking default form out of the deal, as if you created the database from scratch.

Opening a delimited text file

A *delimited text file* is a special type of DOS text file in which each database record appears on a separate line and database fields are separated from each other with a *delimiter,* which is usually nothing more than a computer geek term for a comma or something else that keeps the fields from bumping heads. (If you get good at this database stuff, you can find ways to work the terminology into your everyday life. "Honey, if you don't find a way to delimit those fighting cats, I'll. . .") By the way, in addition to being delimited, these fields are also usually contained within quotation marks.

Delimited text files are often used to convert data from another program, such as a word-processing program or a database program that Approach 97 doesn't recognize. Such programs don't routinely store their data in delimited text files, but they usually provide a command that you can use to convert their files to delimited text files. After you convert a file to a delimited text file, you can open the delimited file in Approach 97 and convert it to an Approach 97 database.

Here is an example of a delimited text file that contains two records:

```
"Johnson","Mary","234 Oakdale","Tohoma","CA","93844"
"Henry","Patrick","345 3rd Street","Orangedale","CA","93748"
```

If you open this type of delimited text file in Approach 97, the program assigns field names such as Field1, Field2, and so on, for each database field.

Some delimited text files contain field names in the first file record:

```
"Last Name","First Name","Address","City","State","Zip Code"
"Johnson","Mary","234 Oakdale","Tohoma","CA","93844"
"Henry","Patrick","345 3rd Street","Orangedale","CA","93748"
```

When you open this type of file, you can tell Approach 97 that the first record contains field names. Approach 97 then adopts the field names contained in the file.

To convert data to Approach 97 via a delimited text file, follow these steps:

1. **Create a delimited text file that you can import into Approach 97.**

   You have to check the foreign program's documentation to find out how to create a delimited text file. Usually, you just use an Export command, but sometimes you have to use a separate conversion program to create the delimited text file.

   Make sure that you use TXT for the file extension of the converted file. Otherwise, you won't be able to locate the file when you try to open it from Approach 97.

2. **In Approach 97, call up the Open dialog box by choosing File⇨Open, clicking the Open SmartIcon, or selecting Open an Existing File from the Welcome to Lotus Approach dialog box.**

   The Open dialog box appears.

3. **In the Files of type field, select Text – Delimited (*.TXT) for the file type.**

4. **Select the name of the text file that you want to open from the Open dialog box.**

   You may have to rummage about the hard disk to find the file.

5. **Click on the Open button.**

   The Text File Options dialog box, shown in Figure 22-4, appears.

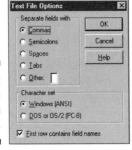

Figure 22-4:
The Text File
Options
dialog box.

6. **Change the settings on the Text File Options dialog box if you must.**

   Most delimited text files use Commas to separate the fields, but you can select Semicolons, Spaces, Tabs, or any Other character to use for the delimiter. Whatever you choose should correspond to the delimiter the other program used in creating the file. If you select the Other option, be sure to type the character that you want to use for the delimiter in the box provided.

You also can specify whether the file uses the standard Windows (ANSI) character set or the DOS or OS/2 character set. (This option usually doesn't matter, so you can safely just leave it set to Windows.)

Finally, you can tell Approach 97 that the database contains field names by checking the First row contains field names check box.

7. Click on the OK button.

When you click on the OK button, the New dialog box appears.

8. Click on the Create button to accept the name and file format for the new database.

If you want to use a different name or file type, change the fields accordingly before you click on the Create button. For more information about creating a new database, see Chapter 1.

You're done! Approach 97 converts the file. You can now open and use the database as if it had been created by Approach 97.

Opening a fixed-length text file

A *fixed-length text file* is a special type of text file in which each field occupies a fixed number of character positions. For example, the first 20 characters of each record in a customer file may contain the customer's Last Name. The next 20 characters may contain the First Name, and so on.

Some foreign programs store their data files in fixed-length format, so you can convert them directly to Approach 97. (The foreign program's documentation should tell you this.) Very few programs document the structure of their data files, though, so you have to examine the foreign files yourself and count the number of character positions allotted to each field. This work is definitely the kind of task that you should bribe a computer guru to do for you. Offer the guru a six pack of cola, a triple-cheese pizza, and a thick stack of napkins.

The procedure for opening a fixed-length text file is nearly the same as the procedure for opening delimited text files, with the following exceptions:

✔ When you call up the Open dialog box, specify Text – Fixed-Length (*.TXT) in the List files of type field.

✔ Instead of seeing the Text File Options dialog box, you see the Fixed Length Text File Setup dialog box shown in Figure 22-5. Use this dialog box to tell Approach 97 the name, starting position, data type (text or numeric), and width of each field in the database. (Approach 97 will try to guess, but it isn't always right.) Better yet, offer your pet guru a jelly donut to do this task for you.

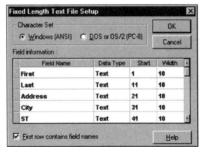

Figure 22-5:
The Fixed
Length Text
File Setup
dialog box.

Importing Foreign Data

When you *import* data into Approach 97, data is copied into an existing database. You can choose File➪Import Data to merge two Approach 97 databases or to add records from a foreign database to an Approach 97 database.

Here is the procedure:

1. **Open the database into which you want to import the data.**

   Choose File➪Open, click on the Open SmartIcon, or select Open an Existing File from the Welcome to Lotus Approach dialog box.

   For example, if you have an existing customer database and you want to add records from a delimited text file into it, open the customer database.

2. **Choose File➪Import Data.**

   The Import dialog box appears, which looks so much like the Open dialog box that we won't waste paper showing it to you here.

3. **In the Files of type list, select the type of file that you want to import and then click the file that you want to import.**

   You may have to search around on your hard disk to find the file.

4. **Click on the Import button.**

   Depending on the file type you select, you may see other dialog boxes. Refer to the preceding sections if you aren't sure what you should do.

5. **When the Import Setup dialog box appears, stare at it for a moment.**

   Figure 22-6 shows the Import Setup dialog box. It's a bit bewildering at first, until you figure out that it's asking you to match up fields in the file you're importing with fields in the Approach 97 database. In Figure 22-6, the Address and City fields were automatically matched up because the fields in the input file use the same names as the fields in the customer database.

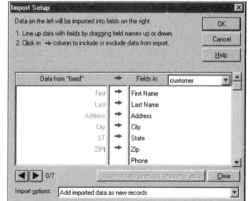

Figure 22-6:
The Import
Setup dialog
box.

6. Line up fields from the data file with fields in the database.

If the fields aren't lined up correctly, drag the database fields up and down in the Fields in text window until they line up with the corresponding fields in the Data from "fixed" text window. Then click in the column between the field names to add an arrow indicating that a field should be included when data is imported. To exclude a field, click the arrow to make it go away.

7. Select an option from the Import options drop-down list.

You can select from three options:

Add imported data as new records: Each record in the imported file is copied into the database as a new record.

Use imported data to update existing records: Uses data in the import file to update existing records in the database. Any records in the import file that don't have corresponding records in the database are ignored.

Use imported data to update & add to existing records: Uses data in the import file to update existing records in the database. Any records in the import file that don't have corresponding records in the database are added as new records.

If you pick the second or third option, an additional column appears in the Fields in portion of the Import Setup dialog box. In this column, click next to the fields that you want Approach 97 to use to determine whether a record in the import file matches a record in the database. For example, in a customer database, you may click the Customer Number field or the Last Name and First Name fields.

8. Click on the OK button.

Approach 97 imports the data. You're done!

Exporting Approach 97 Data

In Approach 97, you save database data in foreign formats by using the File⇨Export Data command. You may do this to share data with your database-disadvantaged coworker who is still using that old copy of PC-File that the boss picked up on the shareware remainder rack. Here's the procedure:

1. **Open the database from which you want to export the data.**

   Choose File⇨Open, click on the Open SmartIcon, or select Open an Existing File from the Welcome to Lotus Approach dialog box.

2. **Choose File⇨Export Data.**

   The Export Data dialog box appears, as shown in Figure 22-7.

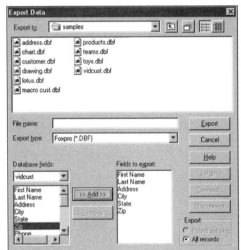

Figure 22-7:
The Export
Data dialog
box.

3. **Choose the file format in the Export type list.**

   Choose whatever file format your colleague claims to be able to import. If the colleague has several options, announce firmly that "Approach 97 can do anything — pick one!"

4. **Specify the database fields that you want to include in the export file by clicking on each field in the Database fields text window and then clicking on the Add button.**

5. **Select the All records option to export the entire database, or select the Found set only option to export only those records found by a Find command.**

6. Type a filename in the File name text box.

7. Click on the Export button.

8. If you selected a text file type, the Text File Options or Fixed Length Text File Setup dialog box appears. Fill out its options and then click on the OK button.

9. That's all.

Whew!

Part V
The Part of Tens

"OF COURSE IT'S PORTABLE SIR, LOOK, HERE'S THE HANDLE."

In this part ...

It wouldn't be a . . .*For Dummies* book without the Part of Tens. Each of these chapters consists of ten (more or less, but who's counting?) things that are worth knowing about various aspects of using Approach 97. Without further ado, here they are, direct from the home office in sunny Tulsa, Oklahoma. (And, yes, we do have running water here.)

Chapter 23

Ten Database Commandments

In This Chapter

▶ Thou shalt carefully planneth the layout of thy data

▶ Thou shalt avoideth redundancy, repetition, and reiteration

▶ Thou shalt frequently saveth thy design changes

▶ Thou shalt not hoggeth a network database

▶ Thou shalt backeth up thy hard disk religiously

▶ Thou shalt storeth each file in its proper directory

▶ Thou shalt not abuseth the Approach 97 design features

▶ Thou shalt not violateth thy Approach 97 license

▶ Thou shalt not fondleth thy `approach.ini` file or any other `ini` file

▶ Thou shalt remember thy computer gurus, to keep them happy

*F*ear not! For I bring you glad tidings of great joy.

For behold, a program shall conceive and bear a new version,

And the name of the program shall be Approach 97!

And it shall be a database unto you.

— Relationals 1:1

And so it came to pass that these Ten Database Commandments were handed down from generation to generation, to be worn as frontlets between the computer nerds' eyes (where their glasses are taped). Obey these commandments and all shall go well with you, with your children, and with your children's children.

I. Thou Shalt Carefully Planneth the Layout of Thy Data

The moment that you get the urge to fire up Approach 97 and begin defining the fields for a new database, stop yourself. Take a deep breath, count to ten, and then go have an ice cream. When you've wiped the last bit of ice cream from your chin, pull out a pad of paper and begin sketching out what fields the database should contain. Think about whether everything should go into a single database file or whether you should create several files that you can join. In short, plan ahead. Correcting a bad database design is much easier before you laboriously type 1,001 records into it.

II. Thou Shalt Avoideth Redundancy, Repetition, Reiteration, and Entering the Same Thing Over Again

We promised not to repeat this, so we can only say it once.

If you were a computer guru with no outside life, you'd probably study the technique of relational database design known as *normalization.* But you're not, so keep this basic principle of normalization in the back of your mind as you design databases: Try not to repeat yourself. For example, if you have two databases that require a customer's name and address, don't put the name and address fields in both databases. Instead, put the name and address fields in a separate database and join the other two databases to it. Then, if the customer moves, you have to update the address in only one place. Clever, huh?

III. Thou Shalt Frequently Saveth Thy Design Changes

Remember that although Approach 97 immediately saves database changes to the database files, design changes are stored in the Approach 97 file and are not saved until you save them. Whenever you work in Design mode, press Ctrl+S every few minutes or click on the Save SmartIcon to save your work. Saving files takes only a second, and you never know when the unthinkable may happen (except that it happens at the worst possible time). Hey, cat, get off that power strip!

IV. Thou Shalt Not Hoggeth a Network Database

Although it is possible to open a network database in single-user mode so that other network users are prevented from accessing the database, doing so is not a good way to make friends.

V. Thou Shalt Backeth Up Thy Hard Disk Religiously

Prayer is a wonderful thing, but when you lose an important database file, nothing beats a good backup disk or tape, or two. You can't have too many backups. Ever. Really. We've been there.

VI. Thou Shalt Storeth Each File in Its Proper Directory

Whenever you create a database or Approach 97 file, double-check the directory in which you're saving the file. Saving the file in the wrong directory is all too easy, and then you have to spend hours and hours searching for the file later.

VII. Thou Shalt Not Abuseth the Approach 97 Design Features

Yes, you can display every database field in a different font, use 92 colors on a single form, and fill every last pixel of empty space with pictures. If you want your forms to look like ransom notes, this is the way to do it. Otherwise, keep it simple.

VIII. Thou Shalt Not Violateth Thy Approach 97 License

How would you like it if Inspector Clouseau barged into your office, looked over your shoulder as you ran Approach 97 from a network server, and asked, "Do you have a liesaunce?"

"A *liesaunce?*" you reply, puzzled.

"Yes, of course, liesaunce. That is what I said. The law specifically prohibits the playing of a computer program on a network without a proper liesaunce."

You don't want Clouseau on your case, do you?

IX. Thou Shalt Not Fondleth Thy `approach.ini` File or Any Other `ini` File

These files are off limits. If you see files that end with `ini`, don't touch. If you break this commandment, you'd better keep the next one.

X. Remember Thy Computer Gurus and Keep Them Happy

Throw them an occasional donut. Treat them like human beings, no matter how ridiculous that idea seems. You want them to be your friends.

Chapter 24
Ten Approach 97 Shortcuts

. . . .

In This Chapter

▶ Keyboard shortcuts

▶ Places to click in Design mode

▶ Cut, Copy, and Paste shortcuts

▶ The Oops! key combination

▶ Design and browse shortcuts

▶ Other shortcuts

. . . .

*J*ust about anything that can be done in Approach 97 can be done via the menus or SmartIcons. But a few shortcuts are worth knowing about, and we tell you all about them in this chapter.

Keyboard Shortcuts to Change Modes

To change Approach 97 modes, remember the following keyboard shortcuts:

Mode	Keyboard Shortcut
Design	Ctrl+D
Browse	Ctrl+B
Preview	Ctrl+Shift+B
Find	Ctrl+F

Design Clicks

When you work in Design mode, keep the following mouse-click tricks in mind:

- ✔ Right-click on any object in Design mode to bring up a quick menu that lists things that you can do to the object.
- ✔ Double-click on any object in Design mode to bring up the Properties dialog box for the object.
- ✔ Hold down shift and click on or draw a selection rectangle around multiple objects to group select them.

Shortcuts to Cut, Copy, and Paste

Just about all Windows programs respond to these keyboard shortcuts:

Shortcut	Action
Ctrl+X	Cuts the selection to the Clipboard
Ctrl+C	Copies the selection to the Clipboard
Ctrl+V	Pastes the contents of the Clipboard

Before you use Ctrl+X or Ctrl+C, select the object that you want to cut or copy. Then use Ctrl+V to place the item wherever you want it to go.

Ctrl+Z, the Oops! Keyboard Shortcut

Oops! Did I do that? Press Ctrl+Z and maybe it will go away.

This trick works mainly in Design mode; you can't undo most changes that you make in Browse mode because they affect the data, not just the design.

Helpful Design Shortcuts

Here are some valuable keyboard shortcuts to use when you work in Design mode:

Shortcut	*Action*
Alt+Enter	Calls up the Properties dialog box
Ctrl+L	Reveals the floating Tools palette
Ctrl+M	Fast formats
Ctrl+J	Shows the ruler
Ctrl+Y	Snaps to the grid
Ctrl+G	Groups
Ctrl+U	Ungroups

Useful Browse Mode Shortcuts

These keyboard shortcuts apply when you work in Browse mode:

Shortcut	*Action*
Ctrl+Home	Goes to the first record
Ctrl+End	Goes to the last record
Ctrl+W	Goes to a specific record
Ctrl+N	Creates a new record
Ctrl+H	Hides the record
Ctrl+Delete	Deletes the entire record
Ctrl+P	Prints the current view

Shortcuts to Other Programs

These shortcuts aren't only Approach 97 shortcuts; you can use them with any Windows programs. To switch to another program, use one of these combinations:

Shortcut	*Action*
Alt+Tab	Displays the name of the next program of the ones you have open. While holding down the Alt key, keep pressing Tab until the icon of the program to which you want to switch is highlighted. Release both keys to switch to that program.
Ctrl+Esc	Brings up the Start menu.

F1, the Panic Button

Stuck? Press F1 to activate the Approach 97 Help. With luck, you can find enough information to get going again. The help is *context sensitive,* which means that it tries, generally successfully, to figure out what you were doing when you pressed F1 and gives you specific help for that task.

Chapter 25

Ten Things That Often Go Wrong

- -

In This Chapter

▶ You lose your file

▶ You run out of memory

▶ You run out of disk space

▶ You can't find Approach 97

▶ You can't find a record

▶ You accidentally delete a file

▶ You accidentally delete a record

▶ Your printer can't handle it

▶ Your car blows up

- -

*P*robably more like 10,000 things can go wrong, but this chapter describes some of the things that go wrong most often.

I Can't Find My File!

You spent hours polishing the most beautiful forms ever seen, and now you can't find the file. You know that you saved it, but it disappeared! We suspect one of two things: Either you saved the file in a directory other than the one you think you saved it in, or you used a different name to save it than you intended.

The solution? Start looking. Look in other directories besides the one you think you stored the file in. Look for file names similar to the one you intended to use.

If you're feeling bold and adventurous, pop up Windows Explorer by choosing Programs⇨Windows Explorer from the Start menu and try the Tools⇨Find⇨ Files or Folders command. It can help sniff out your missing files.

I Ran Out of Memory!

Many computers that have only 4MB of internal memory are running Windows these days. Although 4MB may be enough to load Windows and Approach 97, before long you may see messages about running short on memory, or you may find that Approach 97 is S-L-O-W. Instead of purchasing more computer memory (which isn't a bad idea if you have only 4MB), avoid running more than one Windows program at a time.

I Ran Out of Disk Space!

Nothing is more frustrating than running out of disk space when you are trying to save a file. What to do? First, minimize all programs you have open, find the Recycle Bin, and right-click on it. Choose Empty Recycle Bin to clear it out. Then, if that still doesn't free enough space, start Windows Explorer by choosing Programs⇨Windows Explorer from the Start menu and rummage through the hard disk, looking for files that you don't need. Delete enough files to free up a few megabytes. Then click on the Approach 97 button on the Taskbar or press Alt+Tab (a couple of times, if necessary) to move back to Approach 97 and try to save the file.

If the hard disk is full and you can't find more than a few files to delete, you may consider activating the Windows 95 disk-doubling program, DriveSpace. Check out *More Windows 95 For Dummies* by Andy Rathbone, published by IDG Books Worldwide, Inc., for information about using disk compression in Windows 95.

Approach 97 Vanished!

You're working at your computer, minding your own business, when all of a sudden — Whoosh! — Approach 97 disappears. What happened? Most likely, you clicked on some area outside the Approach 97 window, or you pressed Alt+Esc or Alt+Tab, which each whisk you away to another program. To get Approach 97 back, click on the Approach 97 icon in the Taskbar or press Alt+Tab until Approach 97 reappears.

Approach 97 can also vanish into thin air if you use a screen-saver program. Try jiggling the mouse to see whether Approach 97 reappears.

I Can't Find a Record!

Before you panic, try selecting All Records in the Named Find box in the Action bar. Just click on the down arrow and select All Records.

I Accidentally Deleted a File!

You just discovered how to delete files and couldn't stop yourself, eh? Relax. Accidentally deleting a file happens to the best of us. Odds are that you can get that deleted file back if you act quickly. Minimize all programs you have open so that you're back to the start screen. Double-click on the Recycle Bin and look for the file you just deleted. Select the file and then choose File➪Restore to save your bacon. Your accidentally deleted file will almost always show up in the Recycle Bin if you deleted it from your local drive, but you can't recover the deleted file if you were running the file off a network. If you were working from a network, cry briefly, and then call your system administrator and ask if he or she can restore the file from a backup. Promise anything if you have to. You may lose any changes you made since the backup, but at least you won't have to start completely from scratch.

I Accidentally Deleted a Record!

Funny thing, you can get a whole file back if you accidentally delete it, but if you accidentally delete a record, you're out of luck. It's very aggravating to accidentally delete a record and then call up the Edit menu only to notice that the Undo command is grayed out, unavailable for use. You can't undo a delete. The best you can do is retype the record's fields or fall back on a backup copy of the database.

If you accidentally delete a whole bunch of records, such as a found set or an entire database, the best thing to do is revert to a backup — reason number 10,001 to back up your files every day.

My Printer Won't Print!

What a bother. Your printer may not print for all sorts of reasons. Here are a few things to check:

- ✔ Make sure that the printer's power cord is plugged in and that the printer is turned on.

- ✔ The printer cable must be connected to both the printer and to the computer's printer port. If the cable is loose, turn off both the computer and the printer, reattach the cable, and then restart the computer and the printer. (You know better, of course, than to turn off the computer without first saving any work in progress, exiting from any programs, and shutting down Windows. So we won't say anything about it — not even a little parenthetical reminder at the end of this paragraph.)

- ✔ If your printer has a switch labeled On-line or Select, press it until the corresponding light comes on.

- ✔ Make sure that the printer contains plenty of paper.

- ✔ If you're using a dot-matrix printer, make sure that the ribbon is okay. For a laser printer, make sure that the toner cartridge has plenty of life left.

- ✔ Choose File⇨Print and make sure that you select the correct printer. If you aren't sure, you need to ask your computer guru for a positive ID.

- ✔ If you're printing on a network printer, holler at the network administrator until he or she fixes the problem.

My Car Blew Up!

Sorry, we can't help you with this one. You should have changed the oil more often and maybe checked the coolant level. We can say that having just the battery blow up is a somewhat traumatic experience, so we do sympathize.

Chapter 26

Ten Great Things about Approach 97

*A*ctually, narrowing the list down to only ten great things about Approach 97 isn't quite fair, but we took a stab at it. As the car dealers like to say, your mileage may vary. You will probably find some of these features more useful than others. Read the list and pick out your favorites.

Internet Integration

In the bad old days, saving a database to the Internet involved cryptic programs, arcane commands, frequent frustration, and occasional success. Approach 97 lets you just click on a button in the Save As dialog box, and, whiff!, your database is out there on the Internet. Click on a button in the Open File dialog box, and, wham!, here comes that database from the Internet. Choose Help⇨Lotus Internet Support and Home Page, Customer Support, or FTP Site and here comes the help. Dunno what those Internet technical support folks are going to do now, though. Maybe they'll have to have a party with the Maytag repairman.

LotusScript

Authors' Note: LotusScript made our top ten list of great things, but the program also nearly made the top ten list of things way too techie to put in this book. Don't say we didn't warn you.

LotusScript is a very technical, highly powerful, and extremely cool way of using all the good adjectives we had available for this whole chapter. If you have a data-management problem, from cataloging your CD collection to maintaining the donations and addresses database from a nonprofit organization, Approach 97 can do it. If you have a data-management problem, lots of donuts or some cash, and a need for a very flashy, easy-to-use, and powerful database application, call your favorite geek and tell him or her what you want. When the geek tells you it can't be, sigh and say that most good programmers can use LotusScript, and you know it can be done in LotusScript. Then stand back.

Transcripting

Suppose that you have some procedure that you do 15 times a day. Each time, the task takes the exact same 27 mind-numbingly boring steps. No sweat! Just check into transcripting.

On command (Edit➪Record Transcript, to be precise), Approach 97 starts recording everything you do (but not everything you say) and creating a macro. When you finish running through those 27 steps, you tell Approach 97 to stop recording by choosing Edit➪Stop Recording. Then, every time you want to do that procedure, just run the macro you created for it and go get a cup of coffee.

You can attach a macro to a view, to a button, or to a database field to make the macro even easier to run.

PowerClick Reporting

Forget about using complex commands or sitting with your calculator for hours to produce the reports your boss demands. PowerClick reporting gives you back your time and consigns your calculator to the grocery store shopping cart handle. When you're working in Design mode with your report, choose View➪Show Data and then click on the PowerClick SmartIcons to sort, sum, count, or average the values in columns.

Send SmartIcon

 Did you just stumble across the exact information that your coworker was desperately looking for? Are you not quite sure how to explain how you found it? No problem, just send the particular database record or view to you colleague. Click on the Send SmartIcon and use the TeamMail dialog box to attach the whole database, just the current view of the current record, or anything in between.

Properties Dialog Box

 The Properties dialog box is a single, consolidated control center for formatting design objects. By calling up the Properties dialog box for an object, you can set the object's text style, font, line width, color, background color, and border style. See Figure 26-1.

Figure 26-1:
The
Properties
dialog box
provides a
central point
from which
to control
any object
you're
designing.

Approach 97 Assistants

Approach 97 comes with several built-in Assistants, which are specially designed dialog boxes that take you through complex procedures quickly and easily. For example, Figure 26-2 shows the Report Assistant, which walks you through the steps necessary to create reports. The Assistants use a separate notebook tab for each step, so you can backtrack, if necessary. The Assistants include

- ✔ Chart
- ✔ Crosstab
- ✔ Envelope
- ✔ Find

✔ Form

✔ Form Letter

✔ Mailing Label

✔ Report

✔ SQL

✔ Worksheet

Don't hesitate to undertake what sounds like a complex procedure, because Approach 97 almost certainly provides an Assistant to help you. And you don't even have to pay them.

Figure 26-2:
The Approach 97 Assistants, including the Report Assistant shown here, walk you through all kinds of procedures.

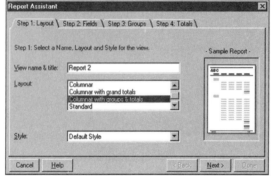

Structured Query Language Support

Structured Query Language (abbreviated SQL and pronounced *Ess-Que-Ell* or *sequel,* depending on your personal preference), was designed to be a friendly, plain English database query that allows nonprogrammers to retrieve information from a network database. As you can imagine, it quickly became a highly prized resume item because it's so darn complex. However, SQL does have the advantage of being able to scoop information out of the networked databases that permeate most medium and large companies.

Fortunately, Approach 97 provided an SQL Assistant, shown in Figure 26-3, so you can suck the information you need out of the big boy databases just as easily as you pull data out of a regular Approach 97 database. Thanks go out to all the Approach 97 programmers who worked on this feature.

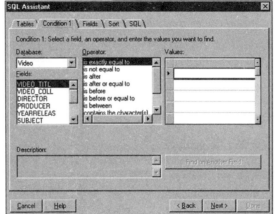

Figure 26-3:
The
Approach 97
SQL
Assistant
helps you
set up SQL
queries.

Consistency with Other SmartSuite Applications

If you already know how to do something in Lotus 1-2-3, WordPro, or Freelance Graphics, try the task in Approach 97. Chances are better than even that your previous SmartSuite knowledge works in Approach 97, too. Wherever possible, Approach 97 has borrowed the techniques used in the other SmartSuite programs.

Fast Format

The Fast Format command is one of our favorite features in Approach 97. This command enables you to spend all your effort getting one design object (a field, button, geometric shape, or whatever) to look precisely the way you want it to look. When you finally get the appearance just right, you can call up the Fast Format command to suck up the object's format and then spit it out on other objects to make them look the same instantly. Fast Format is a real time-saver, and it can help your database look neat and tidy.

Chapter 27

Ten Types of Form Fields

In This Chapter

- Adding field boxes
- Using drop-down list fields and field box and list fields
- Presenting fields as check boxes
- Showing fields as radio buttons

Here are ten (well, four actually, but who's counting?) different ways to display database fields on your forms. For more information about creating forms, see Chapter 9.

Adding Field Boxes

When you use the Form Assistant to create a form, database fields are added to the form as field boxes, such as the one shown in Figure 27-1.

Field boxes are the best way to display most types of database fields, such as name and address fields as well as numeric fields. Field boxes enable users to type any value they choose into the field. However, if you want to limit the values that the user can enter into a field, you should consider using one of the other methods of displaying form fields, such as check boxes or radio buttons (discussed later in this chapter).

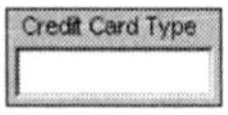

Figure 27-1: A field displayed as a field box.

Using Drop-Down List Fields and Field Box and List Fields

Approach 97 offers two types of view fields that enable the user to pick values from a predefined list of values: drop-down list fields and field box and list fields. If you use a drop-down list, the user can't type data into the field. Instead, the user picks one of several values from a list that drops down when the user clicks on the drop-down arrow that appears in the field. Figure 27-2 shows an example of a drop-down list field, both before and after the user clicks on the drop-down arrow.

Figure 27-2:
A field
displayed
as a drop-
down list.

A field box and list field is the same as a drop-down list field, except that the user can type a value into the field if none of the values in the list is appropriate.

To display a field as a drop-down list or as a field box and list field, follow this procedure:

1. **In Design mode, double-click on the field that you want to make a drop-down list.**

   The Properties dialog box for the field appears.

2. **Select Drop-down list or Field box and list for the Data entry type field under the Basics tab on the Properties dialog box.**

   A drop-down list forces the user to pick one of the values in the list, whereas a field box list enables the user to pick one of the list values or type a value in the field.

   Whichever you choose, the Define Drop-Down List dialog box pops up, as shown in Figure 27-3.

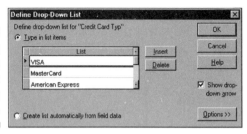

Figure 27-3:
The Define
Drop-Down
List dialog
box.

3. Type the allowable values in the List boxes.

In Figure 27-3, we typed three values: VISA, MasterCard, and American Express.

You can insert or remove items from the list by clicking on the Insert or Delete buttons.

4. Check the Show drop-down arrow check box to ensure that the drop-down arrow beside the list box is displayed on the form.

5. Click on the OK button.

You're done! Approach 97 displays the field as a drop-down list. Here are a couple of bonus points to consider:

✔ If you check the Create list automatically from field data radio button, Approach 97 scans the contents of the field in all records in the database and creates a list of all the unique values. For example, creating a list from credit card types would include VISA, MasterCard, and a few others from the existing records, without duplication and without having to type them in specifically as options for the drop-down list. This option is useful if the database already contains records.

✔ If you click on the Options button, you see a bunch of extra options for creating the list from field data. You can use these options to create the list from a different database field (or even a field in a different database) or to create a filter so that Approach 97 only uses certain records to create the list.

Adding Check Boxes

You can use check boxes to enable the user to select one of several preset values. Using check boxes is best if the user only has a small number of values to choose from (three or four at most).

Figure 27-4 shows an example of a database field presented in check box format. As you can see, each possible value is assigned a separate check box.

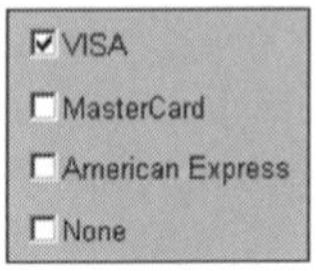

Figure 27-4:
A field
displayed in
check box
format.

To show a field in check box format, follow these steps:

1. **In Design mode, double-click on the field that you want to show as check boxes.**

   The Properties dialog box for the field appears.

2. **Select Check boxes for the Data entry type field on the Basics tab in the Properties dialog box.**

   The Define Check Box dialog box appears, as shown in Figure 27-5.

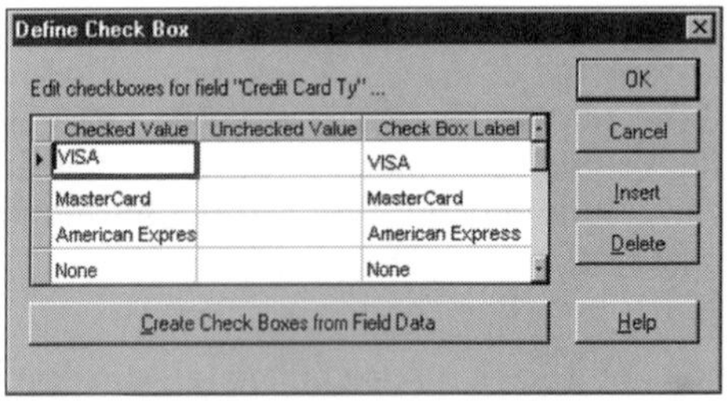

Figure 27-5:
The Define
Check Box
dialog box.

3. **Define the value you want for each of the check boxes for the field.**

   Type the value to be entered into the field if the user checks the box in the Checked Value column; type the value to be entered if the user unchecks the box in the Unchecked Value column; and type the label for the check box in the Check Box Label column.

   In Figure 27-5, we created three check boxes for VISA, MasterCard, and American Express. For each check box, we left the Unchecked Value cell blank: If the user unchecks a check box, the field is left blank.

   You can insert or remove items from the list of check boxes by clicking on the Insert or Delete buttons.

4. **Click on the OK button.**

That's all there is to it. Here are some points to keep in mind when playing with check boxes:

✔ A database field can have only one value at a time. As a result, only one of the check boxes for a field can be selected at a time. When the user clicks on a check box, any other selected check box is automatically unchecked.

✔ For a Boolean database field, use a single check box and set the Checked Value to Yes and the Unchecked Value to No.

✔ If you click on the Create Check Boxes from Field Data button, Approach 97 scans the contents of the field in all records in the database and creates check boxes for each unique value. For example, creating a list from credit card types would include VISA, MasterCard, and a few others from the existing records, without duplication and without having to type them in specifically as options.

Using Radio Buttons

Radio buttons are similar to check boxes except for an important difference: You can click on a check box to uncheck it, so that none of the check boxes is selected, but one of the radio buttons is always selected. You can't select more than one radio button, nor can you select no radio buttons at all.

Figure 27-6 shows an example of a database field displayed as radio buttons. Notice that we added an option for None — just in case the customer pays in cash or by check, as people still do on occasion.

Figure 27-6:
A field displayed as radio buttons.

To show a database field as radio buttons, follow these steps:

1. **In Design Mode, double-click on the field that you want to show as radio buttons.**

   The Properties dialog box for the field appears.

2. **Select Radio buttons for the Data entry type field on the Basics tab in the Properties dialog box.**

The Define Radio Buttons dialog box appears, as shown in Figure 27-7.

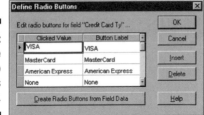

Figure 27-7:
The Define
Radio
Buttons
dialog box.

3. **Define the values you want for each radio button.**

   For each radio button that you want to display for the field, type the value in the Clicked Value column to be entered into the field if the user clicks on the button. Then type the label for the button in the Button Label column.

   In Figure 27-7, we created four radio buttons for VISA, MasterCard, American Express, and None.

   You can insert or remove items from the list of buttons by clicking on the Insert or Delete buttons.

4. **Click on the OK button.**

You're done. Keep these points in mind when tuning your radio buttons:

✔ For a Boolean database field, use two radio buttons, one that assigns the value Yes, the other that assigns the value No.

✔ Click on the Create Radio Buttons from Field Data button to cause Approach 97 to scan the contents of the field in all records in the database and create radio buttons for each unique value. Creating the list from credit card types would include VISA, MasterCard, and a few others from the existing records, without duplication and without having to type them in specifically as options.

Chapter 28

Ten Cool Approach 97 SmartMasters

● ●

In This Chapter

▶ Finding Web sites

▶ Scheduling a meeting

▶ Tracking customers, contacts, employees, and departments

▶ Tracking orders and invoices

▶ Finding tips and hints about Approach 97

▶ Browsing the Artist and Music Collection

▶ Tracking Videos and Actors

▶ Tempting Templates

● ●

*O*ne of the really great things about using Approach 97 is that you don't even necessarily have to develop your own databases. Why reinvent the wheel when you can just use one of the fabulous database applications or templates that comes with Approach 97, right? Approach 97 contains a number of prepackaged database applications and templates, called SmartMasters. The SmartMasters are very often just what you need, or close enough that all you need to do is make a couple of changes for them to be perfect for you.

To access the Approach 97 database applications and templates, in the Welcome to Lotus Approach dialog box, click on the Create a New File Using a SmartMaster tab. You see a list of SmartMaster applications. If you select Templates from the Smart Master types drop-down list, you see a list of the available templates. Click on the template or application of your choice and then click on the OK button. The database you selected appears, and you are ready to get started.

The following are some of the coolest SmartMaster Applications. You should use this chapter to get an idea about some of the applications that are available and to see what can be done with Approach 97. If you decide to use some of these applications, either as they were provided or with changes of your own design, spend some time working with them. Most of the applications offer some kind of online assistance or instructions, and that should help you get started.

By the way, even if you have no inclination at all to use the SmartMasters, you should take a look at them just to see what can be done. You are likely to be impressed with the power and ease of use of these templates.

Just for the record, we think that the Approach 97 SmartMasters are way-cool, but we still keep all our recipes on handwritten, grease-stained, misfiled, folded and spindled index cards (thanks, Mom!), and the recipes still work just fine. If you aren't really going to use the databases, don't spend the time keying data into them.

Discovering World Wide Web Sites

Approach 97 offers an Internet World Wide Web Sites database application for Web-hungry users. Not only do you start with a collection of over 500 Web sites in the database, you can also use — at the click of a button — the built-in Webster Web browser to surf your heart out from within Approach 97. Search the Web sites based on title, address, category, keywords, or date you viewed the site. If this application can't help you keep up with your favorite sites, nothing can. Adding new sites to the database is easy — just follow along with the on-screen instructions.

Using the Meeting Room Scheduler

Are you having trouble managing the office so that the meetings and meeting rooms work out evenly? Do you have one room with three concurrent meetings while the other ones go unused? Check out the Meeting Room Scheduler to end your scheduling pain forever.

Not only can you add and customize the room listings and descriptions, but you can also generate usage reports by room and by date. Most of all, you'll prevent . . . knock, knock. What? Oh, we'll be done in just a couple of minutes. Sorry.

Tracking Customer Calls

Suppose that you're trying to track the amount that your company spends on customer support, including being able to know just exactly who calls all the time and what exactly his or her problem (in terms of your product) is. You could either drop thousands of dollars on a high-end call-tracking software package, or you could use the built-in Customer Call Tracking SmartMaster in Approach 97, including forms to cull the information you need in virtually any way you can imagine.

Keeping Tabs on Employees and Departments

Human Resources departments are notoriously overworked and under-staffed — to the point that you sometimes wonder whether they'll ever find the time to let you know who they hired and how much they get paid. Heck, figuring out how much money you're spending on salaries in each department without having to add up all those pay stubs is just out of the question. Set your department to work, in its copious free time, on putting employees, depart-ments, salaries, and even personnel evaluations into the database, and watch the reports fly out. Try out the Employees and Departments application, but only if you want to reduce the workload in Human Resources.

Managing Your Contacts

Contact management has probably been a problem since the third phone was installed. Approach 97 has finally solved the problem, complete with a way to keep up with the who, what, when, and how of your discussions. Approach 97 even dials the phone at a click of a button. No problem! Just fire up this data-base and enter in all the name, address, contact, and personal information for your clients and then summon the information at will. The Contact Manager SmartMaster should fit the bill nicely, Mr., er, Ms., er . . . whatever.

Tracking Invoices and Orders

Does your level of detail on company orders and invoices consist of "Well, the trucks show up with deliveries most weeks, and we pay the bills when we get them"? The Invoice and Order Tracking SmartMaster can fix that. Not only can you keep up with contact information for your suppliers, you can also monitor the inventory you have on hand by product number or name and keep your product catalog up to date, all at once. Just get that information into the database the first time, and then report and query until you really know what's going on.

Using the Technote Database

This database gives you just tons of tips and technical notes about Approach 97, in almost any category you can imagine. You can either view or print the information. You can search for a specific topic or browse the database to find out more about Approach 97 than you ever thought possible. Of course, you can also add your own tips and categories about any number of other technical software packages.

Discovering the Artist and Music Collection

On a more personal and creative note, you can organize and categorize your CD collection six ways to Sunday with the Artist and Music Collection SmartMaster. Not only can you enter the artist and group name, but you can also keep up with music type, label name, and each individual CD or (!) LP in your collection. Never again must you wonder if you actually purchased that Gershwin CD or just thought about it. You can just check the database and find the information there just beside the Green Blind Monkeys CD that you got for Christmas.

Screening the Video and Actor Database

Is your video collection about to take over the living room? Do you remember that you have a movie by a particular director, but you can't remember the name to save your life? Would you like to be able to bring up the title, director, stars, subject, and play time of any movie in your collection? As soon as you can type in the data, the Approach 97 Video and Actor Database helps you answer these and other pressing questions.

Considering All Those Templates

Don't even get us started. Just look in the Welcome to Lotus Approach dialog box under the Create a New File Using a SmartMaster tab. In the SmartMaster Types drop-down list, select Templates to view the extensive list of Approach 97 templates. Dozens of them. Enough to get you off to a good start on any database from workout logs to art collections. Have fun!

Glossary

Access: A database program made by Microsoft. Similar in many ways to Approach 97, but a bit more complicated to use.

Action bar: A collection of buttons to access Browse and Design mode, create New Records, start a Find, and select the set of found records to use.

Approach 97: Only the best database program ever.

Approach 97 file: A file that contains the views, macros, and other Approach 97 goodies needed to play with a database. Everything except the actual database data is stored in the Approach 97 file; the data itself is stored in a separate *database file*.

arithmetic expression: An expression that produces a numeric result.

ascending sequence: A method of arranging information; for example, from A to Z or from 1 to 10.

Assistant: A special type of dialog box in Approach 97 that guides you through an otherwise tedious process, such as creating a report or form letter.

axis: Not the bad guys in WWII, but the horizontal and vertical lines against which chart data is plotted. See *x-axis* and *y-axis*.

back up: What you ought to do to your files *right now*. You can't have too many backups, no matter what.

boolean field: A database field that can have only one of two possible values: Yes or no, black or white, ying or yang, on or off, and so on.

Browse mode: One of four basic work modes offered by Approach 97. Browse mode enables you to examine and modify database records by using forms, reports, worksheets, and other views.

byte: A single character of information, such as a letter or numeral.

calculated field: A database field whose value is calculated based on a formula. The formula can refer to other fields. For example, a Sales Tax field may be calculated by multiplying the contents of a Subtotal field by a fixed tax rate.

cell: The intersection of a row and column in a table.

chart: A type of database view in which data is graphically represented as a line, bar, pie, or other type of graph.

Chart Assistant: An Assistant dialog box for creating new charts. See *Assistant.*

client: A computer that is on the network and has access to network data and devices.

Clipboard: A magic place where snippets of data can be temporarily stored, one at a time. To *copy* something to the Clipboard, select it and press Ctrl+C. To *cut* something to the Clipboard, select it and press Ctrl+X. To insert the contents of the Clipboard, place the cursor where you want Approach 97 to insert the Clipboard contents and press Ctrl+V.

columnar report: A report layout in which database fields are arranged in columns and each database record is printed on a separate line. Field labels are printed in the report heading at the top of each page.

columnar with grand total report: A report layout in which data is presented as in a columnar report, with the addition of a summary line at the end of the report.

columnar with groups and totals report : A report layout in which database records are grouped based on a database field and summary information is printed before and after each group of records.

comparison expression: An expression that produces a Yes or No result by comparing two values.

crosstab: An Approach 97 database view in which groups of records are summarized and presented in worksheet format.

Crosstab Assistant: An Assistant dialog box for creating new crosstabs. See *Assistant.*

database: A collection of information, such as an address book, shoe box full of tax records, and so on. A *computer database* is what you get when you store this kind of information on your computer.

database file: A file used to store database data, as compared to the Approach 97 file, which stores forms and views and stuff. Approach 97 doesn't have its own special type of database file. Instead, it uses and creates database files in dBASE, Paradox, or FoxPro format.

date field: A database field that holds a date.

DB2: A humongous database program that is used mostly on mainframe computers. Approach 97 can access data stored in a DB2 database but only when the appropriate voodoo incantations are spoken or the SQL Assistant is used. See *Structured Query Language.*

dBASE: The granddaddy of PC database programs. Many folks still use dBASE, even though better programs are available nowadays (like Approach 97).

descending sequence: A method of arranging information; for example, from Z to A or from 10 to 1.

dedicated server: A computer used exclusively as a network server. See *server.*

default value: A value supplied for a field if the user does not enter a value.

delimited text file: A file in which each database record appears on a separate line and database fields are separated from one another by a *delimiter character,* usually a comma.

delimiter: The special character used to separate fields in a delimited text file, usually a comma.

Design mode: One of four basic working modes offered by Approach 97. Design mode enables you to modify or create new forms, reports, worksheets, or other views.

design object: Something you add to a form or report, such as a database field, a bit of text, or a geometric object such as a circle or rectangle.

directory: A repository for files on a hard disk. If all of the files on a hard disk were stored in a single location, you'd never be able to organize and track them. Directories enable you to apply the concept of "divide and conquer" to your hard disk. Each directory has a name that can be up to 255 characters in length.

disk drive: A device that stores information magnetically on a disk. A *hard disk* is permanently sealed in your computer and has a capacity usually measured in hundreds of megabytes (also called *gigabytes*). A *floppy disk* can be removed from your computer and can have a capacity of 360K, 720K, 1.2MB, 1.44MB, or 2.88MB.

DriveSpace: A feature of MS-DOS 6.22 and Windows 95 that compresses data so that it requires less disk space. DriveSpace increases the effective capacity of the disk, often by a factor of 2:1 or more. DriveSpace was Microsoft's response to legal problems it encountered with DoubleSpace.

duplicate record: A record that is identical to another record in the same database. According to true relational database theory, having identical records is not allowed. However, Approach 97 allows duplicate records, turning up its nose at the relational zealots.

export: Saving data from an Approach 97 database in another format.

expression: A combination of operators and operands that yields a calculated result. See *formula.*

Fast Format: An Approach 97 feature that enables you to apply the format of one object to another object.

field: One snippet of information, such as a customer's name, address, phone number, or zip code.

field object: A design object that shows the contents of a database field.

file name: A name assigned to a file. The name can consist of up to 255 letters and numbers, plus an optional three-letter *extension* that identifies the file type. The extension is separated from the rest of the file name with a period, and it usually serves to identify the type of file (for example, to distinguish a word-processing file from a spreadsheet file).

Find mode: One of four basic working modes offered by Approach 97. Find mode enables you to set up search criteria to initiate a find. When Approach 97 finds records that match the search criteria, it flips back to Browse mode so you can examine and modify the *found set.*

find request: Search criteria that you put in a search field.

fixed-length text file: A file in which each database record appears on a separate line and each field occupies a fixed number of character positions.

flat-file database: A watered-down database program that is easier to use than a full-fledged database program, but too limited in function to be useful for anything more complicated than simple address lists.

foreign key: The term used by database zealots to refer to a field that corresponds to the primary key field of a different database. For example, the Customer Number field in an Invoice database is a foreign key, assuming that Customer Number is the primary key for the Customer Database.

form: A database view that presents database records in a manner that resembles a printed form, with just one database record shown on the screen at a time. Half the fun of using Approach 97 is creating good-looking forms.

Form Assistant: An Assistant dialog box for creating new forms. See *Assistant.*

form letter: Junk mail you can send to people whose names and addresses are stored in an Approach 97 database.

Form Letter Assistant: An Assistant dialog box for creating form letters. See *Assistant.*

formula: Determines the value for a calculated field. For example, the formula `SubTotal * 0.065` can be used to calculate the value for a Sales Tax field.

found set: A table that consists of all the records that match a search criteria.

FTP: File Transfer Protocol, or the process Approach 97 uses to save a file to the Internet.

FTP server: Where a file saved to the Internet ends up. You have to have an ID and password to save to most FTP servers.

function: An Approach 97 routine that you can include in formulas to perform complex calculations, such as calculating loan payments.

golden retriever: Definitely one of the less intelligent canine varieties, one of which just dug up a plant in our backyard.

graph: See *chart.*

grid: A pattern of evenly spaced dots that can be used to align objects while you are working in Design mode.

group: Design objects that have been combined so that they act as a single object.

guru: Anyone who knows more about computers than you do.

icon bar: A row of icon buttons, called S*martIcons,* that serve as special command shortcuts for Approach 97. The icon bar is just below the menu bar.

import: Merging data from another source into an existing Approach 97 database.

Internet: A humongous network of networks that spans the globe and gives you access to just about anything you could ever hope for, provided you can figure out how to work it. Approach 97 lets you save files to and open files from the Internet, thereby sparing you all kinds of hassles involved in using the Internet in most other ways.

join: A way of connecting two databases that have a common field, such as a customer number or inventory part number. For example, a Customer database may be joined to an Invoice database so that all of the invoices for a particular customer can be seen. See *one-to-one join, one-to-many join, many-to-one join,* and *many-to-many join.*

join field: The field used to relate two databases involved in a join.

LAN: *Local area network,* a network of computers that are relatively close to one another, generally in the same building. See *WAN.*

LANtastic: A popular peer-to-peer networking system. See *peer-to-peer network.*

layer: The position of a design object relative to other design objects, which is used to determine what happens when objects overlap. If two objects overlap, the object at the higher layer obscures the object at the lower layer.

lingua franca: A type of pasta consumed in mass quantities by relational database zealots.

local resource: A disk drive, printer, or other device that is attached to a computer rather than accessed via the network. See *network resource.*

log in: What you have to do to access a network. Logging in identifies you to the network and grants you access to network resources.

logical expression: An expression that produces a Yes or No result, usually by combining two or more comparison expressions.

Lotus 1-2-3: A spreadsheet program made by Lotus and included in SmartSuite.

Lotus Chart: The charting mechanism used in all programs in Lotus SmartSuite that do such things (1-2-3, WordPro, Approach 97, and Freelance Graphics).

Lotus Organizer: An address book and calendar program made by Lotus and included in SmartSuite.

LotusScript: A programming language, comparable to Approach 97 macros, but definitely on steroids and highly unfriendly. Handle with great caution.

love handles: Handles that appear on a field when you click on it. The handles allow you to move and resize the field.

macro: A sequence of Approach 97 operations that are carried out together. You can attach a macro to a macro button, to a view, or to a field.

macro button: A design object that looks like a dialog box button. The user can click the button to run a macro.

Mailing Label Assistant: An Assistant dialog box for creating mailing labels. See *Assistant.*

mainframe computer: A huge computer housed in a glass house on raised floors. Approach 97 has the capability to access data stored on a mainframe computer, but only after your friendly neighborhood mainframe computer programmers have authorized you to access it.

many-to-many join: A join in which records in one database can be related to many records in another database, and vice versa. In Approach 97, you can't create many-to-many joins directly, but you can create them by making an intermediate database that contains one record for each relationship between the two databases. For example, a Parts database that contains one record for each inventory item can have a many-to-many relationship with a Suppliers database that has one record for each supplier. In other words, each part may be supplied by more than one supplier, and each supplier can supply more than one part. An intermediate Part-Supplier database can be created that contains one record for each part-supplier combination.

many-to-one join: A join in which more than one record in one database can be related to a single record in another database. An example would be an Invoice database joined to a Customer database, where several invoice records can be related to a single customer record.

Media Player: The program needed to play video clips embedded in an Approach 97 database.

memo field: A database field that holds more text than a text field can accommodate.

menu bar: The row of menu choices that reclines atop most Windows application programs, including Approach 97.

mode: Approach 97 works in four distinct modes: Browse, Design, Find, and Preview. See *Browse mode, Design mode, Find mode,* and *Preview mode.*

NetWare: The chief priest of networks, the proud child of Novell, Inc. NetWare requires at least one computer on the network to be set aside as a dedicated server.

network: Two or more computers that are connected so that they can share information.

network adapter card: An electronic circuit card that goes inside the computer, often called an Ethernet card or a Token Ring card, depending on the network, and connects the computer to the network cable.

network administrator: A person who sets up, configures, operates, and takes the heat for problems with a network.

network resource: A disk drive, printer, or other device located on a server computer and accessed via the network, in contrast to a *local resource,* which is attached to a user's computer.

normalization: The process of eliminating unnecessarily duplicated database fields from a database design.

notetabs (tabs): Those tab divider things that appear at the top of many Approach 97 dialog boxes and enable you to switch between various sets of dialog box controls.

numeric field: A database field that holds numbers.

object-oriented database: The latest in database religions. Its proponents believe that relational database is the root of all evil.

OLE: *Object Linking and Embedding,* a fancy feature of Windows 3.1 and Windows 95 that lets you include data that was created by one program in a file created by another program. You use OLE to put sound bites and video clips in a database.

OLE object: A bit o' something that belongs to another program and is inserted into a database.

one-to-many join: A join in which each record in one database is related to one or more records in another database. An example is a Customer database joined to an Invoice database, where each customer record can be related to more than one invoice record.

one-to-one join: A join in which each record in one database can be related to only one record in the other database. An example is a Sales database that contains one record for each customer joined to a Credit database that also contains one record for each customer. In this example, each customer record in the Sales database is related to one customer record in the Credit database.

operand: A overly fancy word for a value that is used in an expression. An operand can be a number, a bit of text enclosed in quotes, or a database field, by which something else is multiplied, figured, or calculated.

operator: A symbol used in an expression to perform a mathematical operation, such as addition (+), subtraction (-), multiplication (*), or division (/).

optimistic record locking: A record locking technique that doesn't prevent multiple users from accessing records at the same time. However, Approach 97 issues a warning if a user attempts to modify a record and the program discovers that another user has sneaked in and modified the same record while the first user wasn't looking.

panel: A portion of a report that contains a particular type of information, such as the report heading, fields for individual records, summary fields, and so on.

password: A secret code that enables you to access something on the computer. Approach 97 enables you to protect databases by creating *read-write* or *read-only* passwords. Computer networks also use passwords so that only authorized users can access the network.

peer-to-peer network: A network in which any computer can be a server if it wants to be. Kind of like the network version of the Great American Dream. LANtastic and Windows for Workgroups or Windows 95 are popular peer-to-peer networking systems.

pessimistic record locking: A record-locking technique, originally developed by the donkey Eeyore, in which Approach 97 assumes that whenever one user wants to update a database record, another user will try to update the same record at the same time. Pessimistic record locking goes to great lengths to prevent other users from accessing a record that is being updated.

picture object: A design object that places a picture on a view. The picture can be any of several popular graphics file formats.

PicturePlus field: A database field that holds pictures or OLE objects.

polygamy: The practice of enabling one database to join with more than one other database.

Preview mode: One of four basic work modes offered by Approach 97. Preview mode shows how a form, report, or other view appears when printed.

primary key: A field that uniquely identifies each record in a database. Not every database requires a primary key, but a primary key is useful when you want to include the database in a join.

Primary sort field: The main field that is used to sort the database.

Properties dialog box: A multitab dialog box that enables you to control all formatting settings for a design object.

query: Approach 97 doesn't use this term much, but it refers to setting up the search criteria when you are working in Find mode or working with the SQL Assistant.

read-only password: A password that enables you to read the contents of an Approach 97 database but not to add new records or modify existing records.

read-write password: A password that enables you to read and modify the contents of an Approach 97 database.

record: All of the information gathered in a database for a particular thing such as a person, inventory item, and so on. For example, in a customer database, each customer has one record. Each record has one occurrence of each database *field.*

record locking: A technique Approach 97 uses to ensure that network users don't mangle a database record by modifying it at the same time. See *optimistic record locking.*

relational database: A religion whose followers believe that salvation will be awarded only to those who create databases that follow the relational database model. Approach 97 closely adheres to the relational database model.

relational database model: A style of database in which data is stored in tables that are made up of rows and columns and that can be manipulated only in strict adherence to the principles of mathematical set theory.

repeating panel: A portion of a database form or report that shows one or more records that are related to a database record via a join.

report: A database view in which database records are listed in various ways so that meaningful information can be shown. Reports usually end up being printed.

Report Assistant: An Assistant dialog box for creating new reports. See *Assistant*.

row: In relational database terminology, a *record*.

ruler: A representation of a ruler, above and to the right of the design area, that is used to align design objects. Pressing Ctrl+J summons the ruler.

secondary sort field: An additional sort field that is used to sort records with the same value for the primary sort field.

serial number: A special type of default value for a database field, in which each new record is assigned a number that is one greater than the previous record.

series: A collection of related numbers to be plotted in a chart. Lotus Chart can plot up to 23 series.

server: A computer that is on the network and shares resources with other network users. The server may be *dedicated,* which means its sole purpose in life is to provide service for network users, or it may be used as a client as well.

shape object: A design object that places an ellipse, circle, rectangle, square, or line on a view.

SmartIcon: The trademark name that Lotus uses for *icon*. SmartIcons are shortcuts for Approach 97 commands. You can also customize your sets of SmartIcons.

SmartMaster: A combination of format and layout options that guarantees that your database views will look mahvelous, dahlink.

SmartSuite: A big package that includes Lotus 1-2-3, WordPro, Approach, Organizer, Freelance Graphics, a 24-piece ratchet set, 6 Ginsu Knives, and a bird feeder all for one low, low price.

sneakernet: An inexpensive form of computer networking in which data is shared by copying the files to floppy disks and walking them between computers.

sort field: The database field or fields that are used to sort the database records. If you sort a database into alphabetical order by using a field called Last Name, Last Name is the sort field.

Sound Recorder: The program needed to play sounds embedded in an Approach database. Sound Recorder comes with Windows 95 and is buried in the Accessories group under Multimedia.

SQL: See *Structured Query Language*.

SQL Server: A database program made by Microsoft and Sybase that requires the use of Structured Query Language. SQL Server is used mostly on large networks.

standard report: A report layout in which each database record is shown in a separate panel, with field labels printed adjacent to each field.

status bar: A row of useful information displayed at the bottom of the Approach 97 screen. The status bar is filled with surprises — try clicking on various parts of it to see what happens.

Structured Query Language (SQL): A query language for relational databases that was invented by a couple of computer science PhDs and is best used by other computer science PhDs. Approach 97 uses its SQL Assistant to work with database programs that require SQL, but Approach 97 itself does not use or require SQL.

summary only report: A report layout similar to a trailing grouped summary report, except that individual records are not shown. Instead, only summary totals are shown.

table: In relational database terminology, a *database*.

template: A predefined database that you can use as a model for your own databases. Approach 97 comes with billions and billions of templates already set up for you.

text field: A database field that is made up of text characters, such as a name, address, product description, and so on. In Approach 97, text fields can be up to 254 characters in length.

text file: A file that can be edited with Windows Notepad. See *delimited text file* and *fixed-length text file.*

text object: A design object that places text on a view.

time field: A database field that holds time values.

TLA: Three Letter Acronym, such as *FAT* (File Allocation Table), *DUM* (Dirty Upper Memory), and *HPY* (hierarchical programmatic yodel).

Tools palette: A collection of design icons that floats freely so you can position it anywhere on the screen. You can summon the Tools palette by pressing Ctrl+L.

trailing grouped summary report: A report layout in which database records are grouped based on a database field and summary information is printed after each group of records.

validation: A way of keeping bad data out of a database. Approach 97 enables you to set the following validation options: Unique, which means that each record in a database must have a different value for the field; From/To, which means that any value entered into the field must fall within a specified range; Filled in, which means that the field cannot be left empty; One of, which means that the field's value must be one of a list of values supplied when you design the database; Formula is true, which supplies a formula that must be true for the field value to be accepted; In field, which enables you to look up the value in another database to validate it.

variable field: A field whose value can be changed (set) and examined by a macro.

view: A portal through which database data can be seen and manipulated. Approach 97 enables you to create several types of views: forms, reports, worksheets, crosstabs, form letters, mailing labels, and charts.

votive candles: Short stubby candles often used in religious services or when attempting troublesome computer feats.

WAN: *Wide Area Network,* which is a network that is spread all over the city, state, or continent, as opposed to a *Local Area Network,* which is usually contained in a single building.

Wave file: A file format (WAV) that allows you to use digitized recordings of real sounds.

Welcome to Lotus Approach dialog box: A dialog box that appears whenever you start Approach 97 or close an Approach 97 file. You use this dialog box to quickly open an existing file or create a new file.

Windows 95: An operating system that makes computers easier to use but whose main purpose appears to be to require users to purchase more memory and bigger hard disks.

Windows Explorer: A necessary but unpleasant part of Windows that enables you to copy, rename, and delete files as well as to create new directories and perform countless other boring file-management chores.

Windows for Workgroups: A special version of Windows designed to create peer-to-peer networks. Now superseded by Windows 95, which does everything except bake you a birthday cake. See *peer-to-peer network*.

WordPro: A word-processing program made by Lotus and included in SmartSuite.

worksheet: A database view in which Approach 97 data is shown as a spread-sheet, where each record is a row and each field is a column.

Worksheet Assistant: An Assistant dialog box for creating new worksheets. See *Assistant*.

x-axis: The line along the bottom of a chart that categorizes chart data.

y-axis: The line along the edge of a chart that scales chart values.

Index

• D •

• *G* •